LOST CIVILIZATIONS

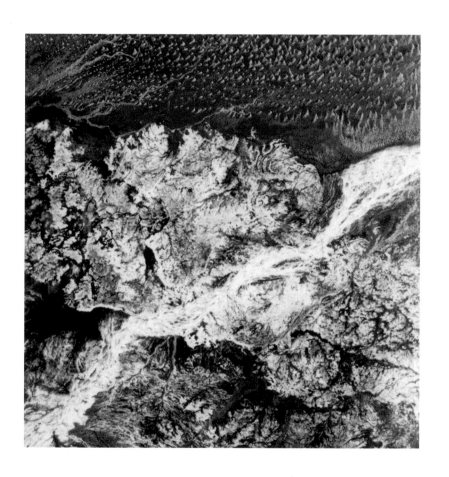

LOST CIVILIZATIONS

REDISCOVERING ANCIENT SITES THROUGH NEW TECHNOLOGY

AUSTEN ATKINSON

PAVILION

PICTURE CREDITS

The publishers would like to thank the following for permission to reproduce illustrations. Every possible effort has been made to acknowledge the copyright holders. However, should any photographs not be correctly attributed, the publisher will undertake any appropriate changes in future editions of the book.

1 NASA/Earth Observation Satellite Co/JPL.Caltech. 3 JdeG Archive. 5 Bridgeman Art Library/National Museum of India, New Delhi. 6 Ranulph Fiennes. 8 NASA. 9 American Foundation for the Study of Man. 10, Jacques Déscloitres/MODIS Land Rapid Response Team at NASA/GSFC11T NASA. 14–15, 31, 42, 43, 44. 45L, 45R, 48, 50, 51, 52, 53L, 53R, 54, 55, 56T, 56B, 57, 58 South American Pictures/Tony Morrison. 15BR Bridgeman Art Library/Museo de America, Madrid. 16, 23 Courtesy of Mesa Verde National Park.17 South American Pictures/Charlotte Lipson. 18 Kramer Gallery & Studio, Minneapolis, Minnesota. 19 National Geographic Society Image Collection/Ira Block. 22TL , 22TR NASA. 24, 25, 31 Christopher Talbot. 26 Bridgeman Art Library/British Museum. 30 National Geographic Society/Luis Fernando Luin. 33, 34, 36 South American Pictures/Robert Francis. 35, 40 Art Archive/Dagli Orti. 37T, 38 South American Pictures/Chris Sharp. 37B Robert Harding Picture Library/Robert Frerck. 39 AKG/Private Collection, Paris. 41 Sächsische Landesbibliothek – Staats-und Universitäts bibliothek Dresden. 46L, 46R, 49 Wright Water Engineers. 47 National Geographic Society Special Collections/Hiram Bingham Collection/Peabody Museum, Yale. 59 South American Pictures/IGM Bolivia. 60 NASA/GSFC/MITI/ERSDAC/JAROS and US/Japan ASTER Science Team. 61 *(inset)* BPK, Berlin/photo Reinhard Saczewski, Staatliche Museen zu Berlin – Preussischer Kulturbesitz, Munzkabinett. 62 Popperfoto/ © ReutersNew Media Inc/photo Tony Gentile. 63, 68 Art Archive /Dagli Orti. 64 NASA/GSFC/MITI/ERSDAC/JAROS and US/Japan ASTER Science Team. 65 AKG/National Archaeological Museum, Athens. 66 AKG /John Hios/ National Archaeological Museum, Athens. 69, 71 AKG. 70, 72, 73L, 73R British Museum. 76, 78, 80T, 80B The Helike Project. 77 Art Archive/ National Archaeological Museum,Athens/Dagli Orti. 79L, 79R, BPK, Berlin/photo Reinhard Saczewski, Staatliche Museen zu Berlin – Preussischer Kulturbesitz, Munzkabinett. 81B Radar Solutions International. 82 AKG/Erich Lessing. 83 Sonia Halliday/ Paul Whitton. 84 Ashmolean Museum, Oxford. 85 Pubbliaerfoto. 86–87 Bridgeman Art Library/Ashmolean Museum, Oxford. 88 AKG/ National Archaeological Museum, Athens/ Erich Lessing. 89 Art Archive/Dagli Orti. 90 Bridgeman Art Library. 91 Bridgeman Art Library/Bonhams. 92 Archivio Fotografico Foglia, Naples. 93 AKG/ Erich Lessing. 94–5 Pubbliaerfoto. 96 Bridgeman Art Library/Museo Archeologico Nazionale, Naples. 97 AKG/Erich Lessing/ Museo Archeologico Nazionale, Naples. 98 AKG. 99 Mary Evans Picture Library 100, 101, 107, 108 Troia Projekt. 102 Troia Projekt/J.C. Tucker (NASA). 102 Art Archive/Archaeological Museum, Istanbul/ Dagli Orti. 106 Troia Projekt. 107 Art Archive. 109T Bildarchiv Preussischer Kulturbesitz, Berlin/photo Klaus Goken. 109B JdeG Archive. 110–11 Art Archive/Dagli Orti. 111(inset) Ranulph Fiennes. 112 Network/Georg Gerster. 113 Art Archive/ Kunsthistorisches Museum, Vienna .115 AKG/Erich Lessing/Vorderasiatisches Museum Berlin. 118 AKG/Pergamon Museum, Vorderasiatisches Museum. 120 JdeG Archive. 121 AKG/Erich Lessing/Musée du Louvre, Paris. 122, 123, 125, 126, 127B American Foundation for Study of Man. 124 Bridgeman Art Library/Giraudon/Private Collection. 128, 130, 131, 132, 133 British Museum. 129 Bridgeman Art Library/Private Collection. 134 © Dr Joan Oates, Cambridge.135, 140, 142 Art Archive / Dagli Orti .136 Corbis/© Brian Vikandery. 137, 138 Bridgeman Art Library. 139 National Geographic Image Collection/James L. Stanfield. 141 Corbis/© Bettmann .143 Scala/ Museo Nazionale, Naples. 144 Ranulph Fiennes /© Kevin O'Brien. 145, 150B Ranulph Fiennes. 147 Royal Geographical Society. 150T, 152T Ranulph Fiennes/ © George Ollen 1992. 151L, 151R NASA/Earth Observation Satellite Co/JPL.Caltech. 152B, 153 Royal Geographical Society/Ranulph Fiennes . 154, 159 Network/Georg Gerster. 155, 156 British Museum. 158 Scala/ Iraq Museum Baghdad. 160 Art Archive /British Museum. 161T Art Archive/Dagli Orti. 161B Bridgeman Art Library/British Museum. 162–3, 164, 165, 166, 167 Michael Freeman.163, 179 Harappa Archaeologicl R (HARP). 168–9 Royal Geographical Society. 169T, 169R NASA.170 Robert Harding /Gavin Hillier. 171 AKG/Heming Bock. 172, 175, 176 Art Archive/Dagli Orti .173, 178 Robert Harding Picture Library. 174 Robert Harding/© Nigel Gomm 1991. 177 Robert Harding Picture Library/Rolf Richardson 306/2858. 181T © estate of Sir Mortimer Wheeler. 181BR, 184, 185L Art Archive/Dagli Orti/ National Museum of Pakistan, Karachi . 181BL, 185R National Museum of Pakistan, Karachi/Harappa Project. 187 Bridgeman Art Library/National Museum of India, New Delhi.

AUTHOR ACKNOWLEDGEMENTS

I want to thank all of the archaeologists, explorers and scientists who have contributed freely to my book, sharing their wisdom, skills and experiences – in particular Ron Blom for his energy and enthusiasm. My publisher, Vivien James, has remained doggedly behind this project and I could not have pulled the disparate elements together without my talented editor Nina Sharman. Our computer graphics experts, 4Site Visuals, picture researcher, Jenny de Gex, designer, David Fordham and researcher, Melvyn Broadbelt, have all contributed enormously to this book. Finally to my agent Simon Trewin at PFD, and my family and friends – thanks for tolerating the occasional heartache and the lost nights and weekends over the last few years. It was worth it.

First published in Great Britain in 2002 by
PAVILION BOOKS LIMITED

A member of **Chrysalis** Books plc

64 Brewery Road
London N7 9NT
www.chrysalisbooks.co.uk

Text © Austen Atkinson 2002
Design and layout © Pavilion Books Ltd.

Senior editor: Nina Sharman
Copy editor: Nicola Hodgson
Picture research: Jenny de Gex
Designed by David Fordham

Computer-generated images by Adam Howard at 4Site Visuals
Map on pages 12–13 by Julian Baker

A CIP catalogue record for this book is available from the British Library

ISBN 1 86205 522 X

Printed in Singapore by Imago

This book can be ordered direct from the publisher. Please contact the Marketing Department. But try your bookshop first.

CONTENTS

FOREWORD

BY DR RON BLOM

NASA Jet Propulsion Laboratory

EVERYONE IS FASCINATED BY ARCHAEOLOGY. BEYOND THE ATTRACTION OF F[...] and exotic ancient civilizations such as Egypt or the Inca, there is the simple [...] ant of how people actually lived their daily lives. But there are far more imp[...] we questions as well, which concern us all. Preparing for our future requires t[...] understand our past, and how we arrived at our present. Why did Rome fall? What, exactly, precipitated the Maya collapse? What really happened to each "lost civilization"? Indeed, why did humans not invent civilization at all until about 6,000 years ago even though anatomically modern humans have clearly been around for at least 40,000 years? While questions such as these will never be answered with the certainty scientists prefer, we must continue to refine old hypotheses, and propose and test new ones. This knowledge will help us to achieve the wisdom so that we will not become a lost civilization ourselves.

Fortunately, archaeology is rapidly embracing new technologies. This is important since our collective cultural heritage is being lost, stolen, or just paved over at a faster pa[...] than it is being discovered and documented. In order to discover secrets of the past before they are lost, we must increase the rate of discovery and documentation. Application of new technologies is the key indeed we are even discovering new things in old data through the power of technology.

In *Lost Civilizations* you will see that applications of new technology can lead directly to new discoveries in archaeology. Many of these key insights are provided by experts from other disciplines, such as scientists and geologists, working closely with archaeologists. In fact, archaeology is becoming a multidisciplinary endeavour, involving experts from many fields. The future of archaeology, and the insight it provides us for our own lives and future, is technology driven. Archaeology, therefore, has a very exciting future, and I hope you find the book an exciting overview.

ABOVE: Ron Blom in the Arabian Empty Quarter, at work as team navigator on the Lost City of Ubar expedition (1990–1997). Ron is lead scientist at the Terrestrial Sciences Research Element, Earth and Space Sciences division at the NASA Jet Propulsion Laboratory, California Institute of Technology (CALTECH). He is also adjunct professor of geology at San Diego State University. His work with CALTECH and NASA led to his involvement in the quest for Ubar, which has secured him a place in history as one of the site's co-discoverers.

INTRODUCTION

LOST CIVILIZATIONS IS A BOOK THAT WILL TAKE YOU ON A JOURNEY TO TWENTY fascinating places – rich in event and importance, beauty and conflict – all across the globe and throughout the history of humankind. It is a journey illustrated by wonderful photographs, cutting-edge computer graphics and scientific imagery. It is an attempt to bring some of these fragments of humanity-in-microcosm, lost to history, back to life. If this journey stirs thoughts about the human condition, our collective past and the fragile nature of our futures, then the book will have succeeded in some small way.

The word "lost" can have many meanings. In this book, it means the end of a settlement, a way of life or the complete destruction of a civilization. The people and societies featured in this book have often disappeared and been forgotten in the minds of the people who live on their lands today. These cultures have been unearthed through painstaking archaeology and, sometimes, through accidental discovery.

The modern discipline of archaeology grew from Renaissance Europe's fascination with Classical culture, evolving into a modern science in the 1860s. Careful excavation, the meticulous recording of the position of finds within strata, earthwork patterns and the mapping of man-made landscapes were the main archaeological methods of that era.

Today, archaeology involves more than digging and exploring; it is a field of study that depends upon cross-discipline analysis to form a complete and accurate picture of an ancient settlement. Different techniques, such as stratigraphy, anthropology, biochemistry, botany, dendrochronology, soil chemistry, hydrology and geology, can help archaeologists in the study of a site.

Stratigraphy – the analysis of different layers of earth at a site – helps archaeologists to determine the date of a human settlement. A site may have many layers of occupation, one lying on top of another, as successive generations developed and redeveloped a site. Catastrophe, the evolution of a building or city, or even abandonment due to climate change, can all be seen by observing the "layers" of a site. The position and context of finds, such as pottery, allow archaeologists to date a certain layer of habitation. This study of a horizontal layer of material can be interpreted as a slice through the history of a site, as each layer of habitation leaves its own traces. In some cases, however, the layers may have been disturbed – by more recent building work, for example – and the layers churned into one another, making stratigraphical analysis almost impossible.

ABOVE: Is this the Troy of legend or a computer-generated mirage? Homer, the ancient scribe, wrote of a titanic ten-year battle between the Trojans and the Greeks, sparked by a bid to rescue Helen, King Menelaus' abducted queen, at Troy. Using the latest archaeological data, leading computer graphics artists are able to reconstruct this fabulous historical gem within their computers, bringing the site and others like it back to life.

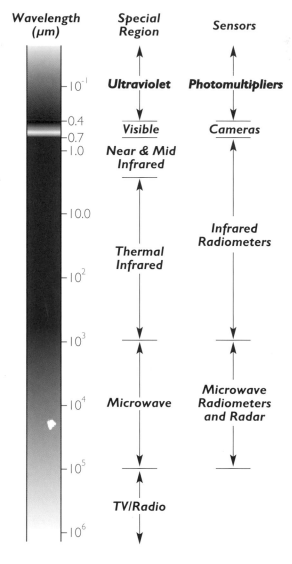

Wavelength (μm)	Special Region	Sensors
	Ultraviolet	Photomultipliers
10⁻¹		
0.4	Visible	Cameras
0.7		
1.0	Near & Mid Infrared	
10.0		Infrared Radiometers
	Thermal Infrared	
10²		
10³		
10⁴	Microwave	Microwave Radiometers and Radar
10⁵		
	TV/Radio	
10⁶		

What wavelengths say about the past.

Blue: Information on soil and plant types, forest types, buildings, roads, coasts, and water.

Green: Borders between types of vegetation and traces of buildings and roads.

Red: Chlorophyll absorption for plant identification and man-made features like buildings and roads.

Near-Infrared: The amount of biomass, vegetation types, water body identification, and degrees of soil moisture.

Mid-Infrared: The amount of moisture in vegetation and soils. Distinguishable differences among types of rocks.

Thermal Infrared: Vegetation stress differences, soil moisture and relative amounts of heat.

Microwave: Buried artefacts in arid regions (water absorbs microwaves). Man-made objects tend to reflect microwaves.

ABOVE: Remote-sensing technologies exploit the electromagnetic spectrum to probe the earth. From the blue end of the spectrum (ultraviolet) to the light we see (visible) to infrared and beyond, the use of electromagnetic energy has become an important part of modern archaeological fieldwork. Devices such as microwave radars probe the earth remotely — without d........ but by sending energy into the ground — hence the phrase remote sensing. As the illustration shows, different wavelengths of energy reveal different types of archaeological remains.

In the 1950s and 1960s, archaeologists began using chemical and physical analyses. Rad.. – exploiting the predictable decay of a radioactive isotope to date materials – has become of dating finds. This method emerged in 1949 when American chemist, Willard Libby (19... published his findings about carbon. Carbon takes three isotopic forms – 12C, 13C and 14C. Radiocarbon dating works on the principle that all radioactive isotopes have a set pattern of decay, radiating particles as they decay. Scientists refer to the half-life of an isotope – a point at which only half of the atoms remain. The half-life of Carbon-14 is 5,730 years. This means that after 5,730 years, half of the material's atoms have decayed and then after a further 5,730 years half the remaining amount has radiated and so on. Although after 50,000 years the amount becomes too small to measure, archaeologists exploit this constant rate of decay by counting the number of particles radiated by dead animals or materials made from vegetable matter, thereby obtaining a "carbon date" for an archaeological object.

The field of dendrochronology has become an important method for dating sites and for analyzing environmental flux. This discipline involves developing a map of tree growth over a period of decades or centuries in a specific geographical area, by counting the yearly ring-growth patterns within trees.

RIGHT: Archaeologists Dr William Glanzman and Dr Brian Moorman conduct a ground-penetrating radar (GPR) survey for the American Foundation for the Study of Man inside the "holy of holies" sanctuary, at the Mahram Bilqis, the Queen of Sheba's temple in Yemen, December 1999.

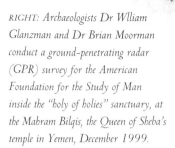

When there was an environmental downturn, such as a drought, recorded by poor growth within a tree, it suggests that humans may have also experienced hardship – when a tree suffered, crops would have suffered too. When studied alongside other evidence, it is possible to build up a picture of the environmental history of a region. Tree rings can be used to derive a precise calendar where the use of wood in a region can be pinned to a specific date. This sort of calendrical information can also be used to calibrate radiocarbon dates.

Aerial photography and reconnaissance are other valuable techniques. Archaeologists can gain a valuable overview of the geography and topography of a site by viewing it from the air. It is possible to spot disturbances such as plough furrows, earthworks and embanking, and even footpaths, that are of great age. Such techniques can also reveal subsurface structures. Where a landscape is stable and such traces have not been washed away by river water or shifting sands, these traces can lead the way to a site.

One of the most significant breakthroughs in archaeology in recent years is the use of terrestrial and space-based radar, optical and magnetic remote-sensing technologies. These are often referred to (not entirely accurately) as geophysics. What we term "visible light" gives us our impression of the world around us, but there are other wavelengths within the electromagnetic spectrum, including infrared, ultraviolet and x-rays that humans cannot perceive. By using electronic and analogue sensors, such as radar and infrared film, archaeologists can exploit these other electromagnetic wavelengths to penetrate layers of earth or reveal long-abandoned roads that lead them to previously undiscovered sites.

Remote sensing has become just as important as the process of excavating an archaeological site. Some ruins are considered sacred by local inhabitants, others are simply too difficult (or too costly) to excavate, and remote sensing offers an alternative means of garnering information about such sites. Remote-sensing data must be interpreted by skilled technicians to derive a picture of the structures buried at a site. Inevitably, in some cases, those interpretations are wrong. The only way to be absolutely certain of the facts is to excavate.

There are many remote-sensing ....ors and high-altitude sensors carried on satellites and manned spacecraft (such ....e Orbiter) and on board reconnaissance aircraft.

Synthetic aperture ....ar (SAR), often ....u aboard satellites designed for geological survey work, is one of the most accurate and useful of sensors for archaeological purposes. SAR operates by beaming a signal to earth and measuring the quality and nature of the energy that is reflected back. Materials such as water, earth, sand, stone, metal and vegetation absorb different wavelengths of energy and therefore emit or reflect that energy in distinctive ways. Once basic norms are established, it is relatively simple to measure the properties found by the SAR. When the data received by the satellite is processed back on earth, it can by interpreted, by computer software, to produce three-dimensional images of subsurface structures.

Other remote sensors are used extensively in archaeology. Microwave radar is employed in areas where man-made objects and structures are believed to be buried, as such objects reflect microwaves. Archaeologists also use magnetometers to detect buried structures. This form of remote sensing works on the principle that the earth's magnetic field is a known constant and other objects, such as iron-rich metals, generate anomalous magnetic fields of their own. These anomalies are detected and displayed on a magnetic map, plotted by taking a magnetic survey of the land in question. Excavation is needed to clarify results, where possible, but a magnetic map can produce good data, narrowing the focus for excavation teams.

Space-based remote sensors may reveal the location of human settlements that were submerged by rising sea levels as the planet left the last ice age and moved into the current interglacial period. Airborne oceanographic lidar (AOL), or its successor, a laser beam-based sensor that bounces laser light onto the surface of the earth 400 times per second, may one day penetrate the secrets of the oceans.

These and other emergent technologies will broaden the scope of archaeology. These new tools, and myriad others not mentioned here, have helped to locate and develop an understanding of many lost settlements and civilizations in recent years.

ABOVE: This satellite image taken over part of Europe shows the Aegean and the Mediterranean Sea — an area where many ancient sites are situated and where some, such as Helike, have only recently been discovered.

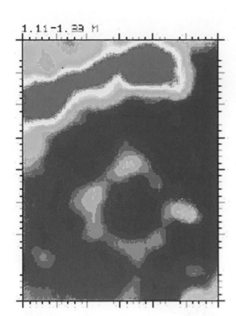

1.11-1.33 M

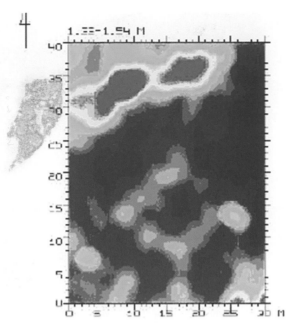

1.33-1.54 M

LEFT: A survey using ground-penetrating radar (GPR) was recently conducted at the ancient American Indian (Anasazi) site at the Great Bluff House, southeastern Utah, USA. The survey was carried out over a depression in the earth that was suspected to be the ruins of a buried kiva — a ceremonial meeting place in ancient Indian settlements. Data produced by the GPR revealed the partially collapsed wall of the kiva (left) and an as yet unknown square feature (right) within the kiva.

Some lost civilizations were rediscovered thanks to the determined historical detective work and physical archaeological efforts of explorers like Heinrich Schliemann (the discoverer of Troy). Despite the sometimes-heroic efforts of these archaeologists, the bigger picture of human antiquity always remained hidden. In the near future, our "eyes in the sky", such as space-based infrared cameras and charge-coupled device (CCD) cameras and telescopes, may allow us to detect traces of ancient human activity in the remotest corners of the earth. Perhaps then we will truly begin to understand our place in the world and the origins of the human condition.

This book revels in tales of determination and passion, be they the obsessions of the great "diggers" of the nineteenth century, such as Schliemann and explorers like Hiram Bingham, or those of the people who built and destroyed the civilizations. This book also explores the realities, or otherwise, behind some of the great myths of human history. Heroic stories of determination and discovery, and legendary adventures, sit alongside accounts of technological expertise and careful detective work.

RIGHT: Computer graphics artists transport us back through the vortex of time so that we can make "virtual visits" to many of the sites when they were thriving and teaming with life. Here we see the Hanging Gardens of Babylon, one of the Seven Wonders of the World.

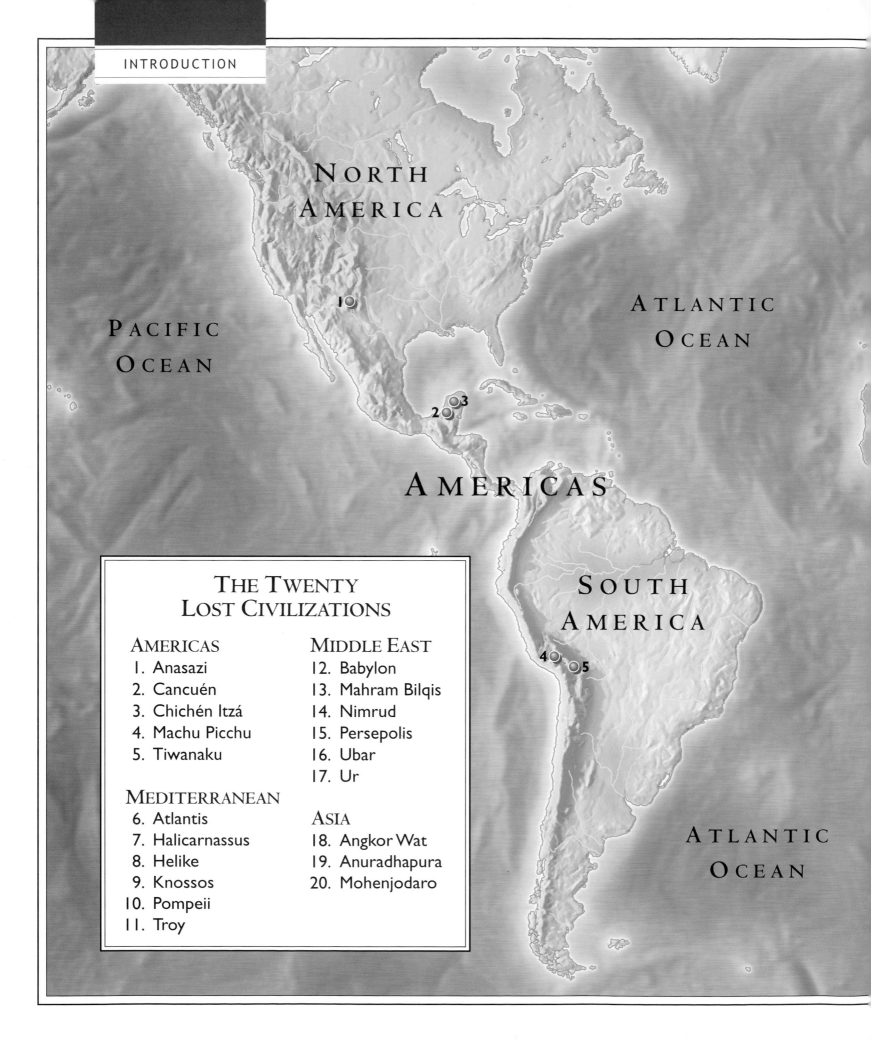

NORTH
AMERICA

PACIFIC
OCEAN

ATLANTIC
OCEAN

AMERICAS

SOUTH
AMERICA

ATLANTIC
OCEAN

THE TWENTY
LOST CIVILIZATIONS

AMERICAS
1. Anasazi
2. Cancuén
3. Chichén Itzá
4. Machu Picchu
5. Tiwanaku

MEDITERRANEAN
6. Atlantis
7. Halicarnassus
8. Helike
9. Knossos
10. Pompeii
11. Troy

MIDDLE EAST
12. Babylon
13. Mahram Bilqis
14. Nimrud
15. Persepolis
16. Ubar
17. Ur

ASIA
18. Angkor Wat
19. Anuradhapura
20. Mohenjodaro

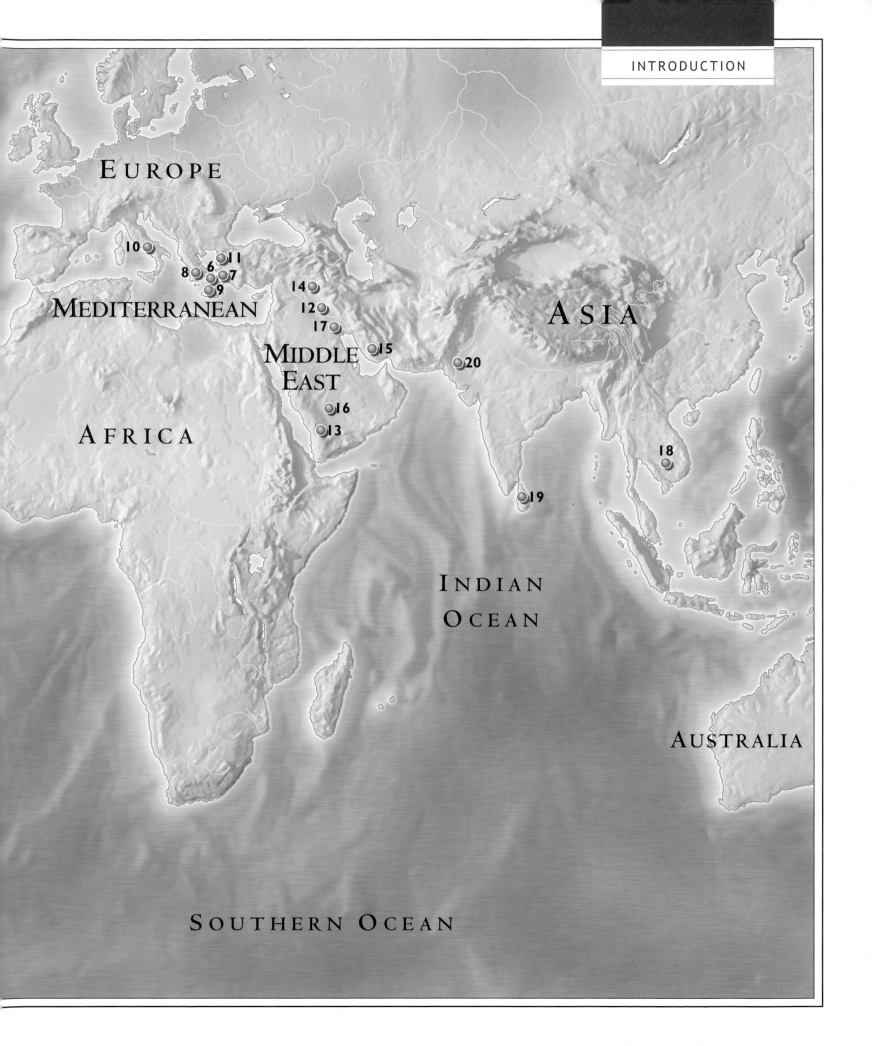

EUROPE

MEDITERRANEAN

AFRICA

MIDDLE
EAST

ASIA

INDIAN
OCEAN

AUSTRALIA

SOUTHERN OCEAN

10

11
6
8
7
9

14
12
17
15

20

16

13

18

19

AMERICAS

ANASAZI
THE LOST PUEBLO PEOPLE

T HE ANCIENT AMERICAN PEOPLE OF THE PUEBLO, a race known today as the Anasazi ("ancient people who are not us"), lived in a dry and barren land. The Four Corners region of the Colorado Plateau, which spreads 64,750 square kilometres (25,000 square miles) across the North American states of Arizona, New Mexico, Utah and Colorado, is typified by desert conditions. The area receives only 25–75 centimetres (10–30 inches) of rainfall per year. Yet the Anasazi found sustenance in this land of harsh beauty. The Anasazi descended from hunter-gatherers who migrated to the area, possibly from the south. The earliest Anasazi emerged in around AD 200. These people are known today as the "Basketmakers" because they used baskets as containers before discovering how to make pottery. Before c. AD 500, the Basketmakers lived in caves and rock shelters, although some groups lived in pithouses, dating back to c. AD 200. These houses were simple in construction – based around vertical poles and earth, built over holes in the ground.

By about AD 500–700, the Basketmakers adopted technology that enabled them to establish large settlements. Their primary breakthroughs were the acquisition of pottery-making techniques, in about AD 200, and the use of the bow and arrow in the sixth century AD. The making of sturdy pottery facilitated the long-term storage of food, and the use of the bow and arrow allowed for more effective hunting. Previously, the Anasazi had used the *atlatl* – a device for throwing spears featuring a sling-shot action – but the bow and arrow were much more accurate and allowed for a greater kill rate. These two developments coincided with the emergence ... means of producing food. These breakthrou... ...azi a chance to settle in one area and allowed t... ...o grow and their culture to develop.

By AD ... ...chitecture had emerged. These buildings were m... ...res with rock walls, which were often built around a ... rubble – a useful material for building that was widely available in the desert environment. The nature of the buildings allowed for a regulated temperature within them: they were mild in winter and cool in summer, thereby offering the Anasazi all-year shelter from the harsh desert climate.

ANASAZI

LEFT: *"Alone with the Past" is a well-known photograph which captured early nineteenth-century Navajo Indians looking at the Casa Blanca ruins built by the Anasazi Indians in Canyon de Chelley, New Mexico, USA.*

RIGHT: *An aerial view of the ruined sprawling Anasazi settlement, Pueblo Bonito. The site was built in Chaco Canyon, New Mexico, USA c. tenth century AD.*

One of the most important features of the pueblo buildings was a room known as a *kiva* – a form of elaborate pithouse that was sunk into the earth and accessible by ladder. The *kiva* was a centre for the community. It functioned as a forum for discussion, where the men smoked and talked, and where major decisions about the future of the community were reached. Ceremonies were conducted there, giving thanks for the harvest and offering prayers at planting time. Inside the *kiva*, benches were arranged around a *siapapu* – a hole in the ground through which, according to legend, spirits emerged from their subterranean world into the human world.

The Anasazi practiced an animistic form of belief, whereby animals and natural objects have souls as well as humans. They believed that humans should exist in harmony with nature, and that humans were not superior to any other form of life. The way through life was aided by spirit guides, supernatural beings known as *kachinas*, who acted as mentors for individuals.

It is possible that the religious practices of the Anasazi were similar to those of American Indians, such as the Hopi, who are believed to be descendants of the Anasazi. Their 500 divine ancestral spirits (*kachinas*) guide tribe members through life. *Kachinas* are believed to reside with the tribe for half a year. They will allow themselves to be seen by the community if the men properly perform a traditional ritual while wearing *kachina* masks. The "being" depicted on the mask – a spirit, a god or even a cloud – is thought to be actually present with the performer, temporarily transforming him in a form of spiritual possession.

The Anasazi probably used astronomy for religious and ceremonial purposes – tracking the movement of the stars and the sun in the heavens allowed the spiritual leaders of the tribes to know when to hold ceremonies during the year. The Hopi follow the lunar calendar and it is likely that the Anasazi did too. The lunar calendar, with its 28-day months, had strong links with female ceremonies – a woman's menstrual cycle being the same

The ancient buildings of the Anasazi were set in a wilderness of forested canyons and mesas; some were carved into the rock of the desert. The pueblos were oriented to the south, to benefit from the warming effects of the sun, following the freezing cold of the desert nights. The landscape was silent, save for the noise of tame dogs and domesticated turkeys creating a rumpus as they were scattered by children at play. The men went hunting, farmed maize on the vast mesas above the dwellings, and wove cotton cloth. Mothers, young women and children ground corn in sandstone troughs with flat, hand-held sandstone grinders. The sound of drums and rattles mixed with voices and floated over sparking, smoking fires. Artists carved ceremonial pictograms – known as petroglyphs (see Glossary) – into the rock walls.

The Anasazi civilization reached its height between AD 900 and AD 1200. By then, the early settlements had evolved into elaborate pueblo villages. Several of these are found in the Mesa Verde ('Green Table') area – named by the conquistadors (sixteenth-century colonial Spaniards) because of its abundance of plateau evergreens and juniper trees. Now a national park, this area contains some of the most impressive prehistoric Indian structures north of Mexico. These include Spruce Tree House, and Square Tower House and Cliff Palace, the largest pueblo settlement – a structure that encompassed 114 rooms, towers, houses and ceremonial centres. The Anasazi built this settlement in a vast pre-existing recess in a cliff wall, and it is a truly beautiful and spectacular sight.

Today these great settlements lie empty, sandstone and basalt mementoes of the past. Why did this thriving community disappear, when it was apparently capable of surviving in the harshest of climates? The main reason seems to have been changes in environmental conditions. As the population of this successful civilization increased, demand for food, water, clothing and other materials also escalated. Where, in some regions, rivers ran dry or the land became overfarmed, the puebloans had to move on. Frequent droughts and killing frosts caused crops to fail and forced people to move to more favourable areas. Even by AD 1300, the elaborate cliff towns of Mesa Verde had been abandoned. The Anasazi way of life was suited to lower-density populations, not because of a failure to develop adequate social

The great Anasazi site at Pueblo Bonito (left) was the heart of a network of settlements — a central point for a whole community that traded chacoan pottery, turquoise, cotton cloth and other wares. As the virtual bird's eye view (above) shows, the settlements were linked by linear roads that dealt with inclines by cutting steps into the landscape so that they never had to deviate from their straight path. At the bottom of the image Pueblo Arroyo was linked to Pueblo Bonito, with Casa Rinconada to the right and Chetro Keti at the top of the image. Pueblo Bonito was the largest site, which housed thousands of people.

21

CHACO CANYON

LOOKING SOUTHEAST

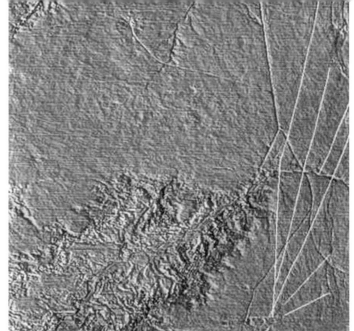

LEFT: Chaco Canyon's Anasazi roads seen from space rendered onto a three-dimensional realization of the landscape. This visualization shows how these linear roads ignore the topography of the land, going over difficult terrain rather than around it as a modern road (dc. . . or wheeled vehicles) would.

ABOVE: Linear Anasazi roads in Chaco Canyon, as seen from space, may have had a ceremonial function – possibly they were used as processional ways during religious festivals.

RIGHT: The Anasazi people of the so-called Classic Pueblo period, c. AD 1050–1300, produced pottery with black and white geometric patterns.

successful civilization increased, demand for food, water, clothing and other materials also escalated. Where, in some regions, rivers ran dry or the land became overfarmed, the puebloans had to move on. Frequent droughts and killing frosts caused crops to fail and forced people to move to more favourable areas. Even by AD 1300, the elaborate cliff towns of Mesa Verde had been abandoned. The Anasazi way of life was suited to lower-density populations, not because of a failure to develop adequate social and economic structures to support a large population, but simply because of the difficult environment. The puebloans moved south and east, and discovered that areas along the Rio Grande and the Upper Colorado River were able to support their needs. Traces of Anasazi culture have survived in enclaves of Hopi, Zuni and Navajo civilizations in Native American reservations in North America. However, the traces are faint and the civilization as it existed has long been lost.

Archaeological interest in Anasazi sites began in the 1890s, when amateur archaeologist Richard Wetherill explored the early Basketmaker settlements in the caves of the Grand Gulch, Utah. His finds included stone tools, basketry, woven mats and rope.

Although his an   limited to rudimentary excavation, Wetherill was the fi   son to distinguish between the early Basketmakers and   er puebloans. The dry nature of the desert environmen: .   nsured that many Anasazi artefacts have been preserved. Clotr   g, jewellery, a wealth of elaborate pottery and even corncobs   ave been found throughout the region. These finds, along w   i the architectural remains of the puebloans, have helped to give us some insight into this remarkable civilization.

The data discovered by traditional archaeological techniques has been complemented by recent technological developments. Commercial, military and scientific satellites and reconnaissance aircraft can take high-resolution images of sites – using stills cameras (including infrared stills), electronic sensors and radar. As we can see in the satellite images taken of Chaco Canyon, New Mexico, these have proved particularly valuable for archaeologists studying the Anasazi. The data from these sources allow archaeologists to study structures such as roads built by the Anasazi, and perform spatial analyses (comparisons between different structures and sites) across large areas, thereby deducing relationships between settlements. We now know, for example, that the Anasazi roads that cross Chaco Canyon, linked several settlements (see computer-generated image on page 21), with Pueblo Bonito acting as a central entrepot for trade.

Communications between settlements, including trails from Mesa Verde as far as the Californian coast and the Gulf of Mexico, had previously been suspected by archaeologists. Items such as sea shell bracelets and topaz stones found in Anasazi sites had clearly been imported into the desert region from the west coast. Surpluses of maize grown by the Anasazi were traded for bison hide and meat. Cotton grown and woven into cloth in Colorado is believed to have been traded for sandals woven out of fibre, fine pottery or banana yucca at Pueblo Bonito. The Anasazi also traded with Mesoamerica, exchanging local turquoise for macaws, macaw feathers and copper bells. The culture of commerce is far from a recent phenomenon in North America – the ancient people of the Four Corners had a thriving community long before the arrival of the Europeans.

ANCIENT ASTRONOMY AND THE ROADS FROM SPACE

MODERN IMAGING SYSTEMS have revealed long-abandoned Anasazi roads. They take the form of straight lines that cut across the landscape regardless of terrain, rather than following the contours of the land, as modern roads, built for the automobile, would.

"PEOPLE HAVE LONG ARGUED over why the Anasazi roads look the way they do. Some researchers have suggested that the roads follow a north-south path. To get a true north-south line the roads would have to be astronomically derived. Then the question arises: Is it a coincidence that all prehistoric roads follow a north-south path? If you look at the so-called "North Road" out of Chaco Canyon, segments of it are not quite due north. That said, if you follow it on a map, you couldn't spot the deviation from true north just by looking at it – that's how small the deviation is. It is possible that the roads are astronomically derived.

Alternatively, if you plotted the easiest route across the landscape you would get a wiggly line. In certain cases it can be more straightforward to go around rather than over an object on the landscape, but that is generally only true if you have a beast of burden or the wheel. The Anasazi did not have either. They travelled on foot. Yet, their roads went straight across the landscape over obstacles, whereas our roads, for example, meander to the topography of the landscape: it's a different mind-set.

I think, like so many things in our lives, the ancient roads had more than one use. People have tried to explain the Anasazi roads by claiming they had ceremonial uses and that certainly makes sense for some of the roads. There's always a measure of guesswork, but I think the sacred relationships between ancient humans and the landscape shows itself via these linearities. It's a way of imposing an order on the landscape that isn't there naturally.

I suspect that the Anasazi of Chaco Canyon attempted to lay out some of their roads astronomically in order to make them conform with their notions of cosmic/sacred order – where other factors allowed."

RAY WILLIAMSON PhD, ARCHAEO-ASTRONOMER,
GEORGE WASHINGTON UNIVERSITY,
MARYLAND, USA

CANCUEN
PLACE OF SERPENTS

I N JULY 2000, A TEAM OF ARCHAEOLOGISTS MADE a staggering discovery while exploring the banks of the Pasión River, in the southern region of the Peten province of Guatemala, Central America: the fabulous lost Mayan palace of Cancuén (the "place of the serpents"), hidden deep in the jungle. The palace, part of a settlement established in the fourth century BC, dates back to c. AD 700, a time at which the Mayan world was at its height. The Mayan empire stretched for more than 300,000 square kilometres (116,000 square miles) over areas of Guatemala, Mexico, the Yucatán peninsula, Belize, western Honduras and El Salvador. It encompassed ten million people, living in about forty cities.

Historians generally divide the Mayan epoch into three eras: the preclassic (c. 1000 BC–c. AD 250); classic, (c. AD 250–900); and postclassic periods (c. AD 900–1100).

By about 1000 BC, in the early preclassic era, the mountain regions of the Pacific were home to a growing population of proto-Mayans. By 300 BC, the organized cultivation of the land became prevalent and these people developed settlements large enough to be regarded as villages. The settlements grew and spread, and the people worked their way into the heart of the territory that would become known as Guatemala. The proto-Mayans generally lived well: the forestlands that they occupied provided a bountiful supply of food and they ate a diet of maize, beans, fish, and game such as birds and deer. Civilization grew apace in this region. By c. AD 250, the Maya entered a period of recognizable social organization: towns were established, skilled

OPPOSITE: Professor Arthur Demarest and Tomas Barrientes examine the ruins of the large Maya palace at Cancuén. Overgrown and once lost to the jungle, it is now the object of international archaeological fascination.

ABOVE: Among the recently discovered ruins at the Cancuén site, Professor Demarest and his team of experts discovered an altar and fallen stela.

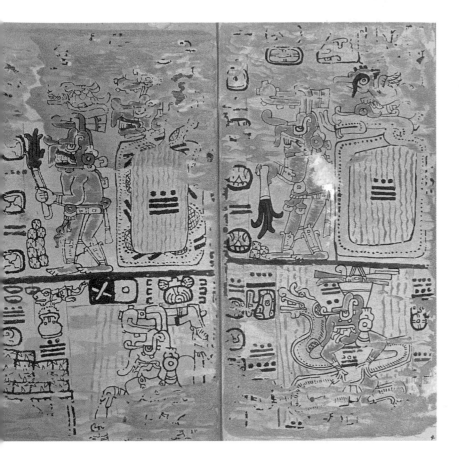

artisans such as potters and weavers emerged; and the concept of kingship and the need for a ruling élite had taken hold.

The Maya became a people of great invention, artistry and scientific knowledge. They excelled at manufacturing fine jewellery, and invented a system of hieroglyphic writing that many archaeologists consider to be the most complex written language developed in Mesoamerica. The Maya wrote on stone, wood, paper, ceramics and the plastered walls of their buildings. Their written language included 800 symbols known as glyphs, which represented syllables and words. These were written in columns that were read from top to bottom and left to right.

The Mayan people also excelled in stonework and architecture. Their skill is evident in the ceremonial stepped pyramids that are considered to be characteristic of their civilization (see pages 37–39). Ironically, it was the absence of such distinguishing features, in particular the absence of temples, which meant that the importance of Cancuén was overlooked for so long.

The site had been discovered and dismissed as unimportant by an archaeological team in 1905, and was surveyed by archaeologists from Harvard University in 1967. Guatemala's civil war, following the CIA-backed coup against the government of President Jacobo Arbenz Guzman in 1954, also meant that the area was a dangerous place in which to launch an archaeological expedition. In 1995 the conflict was, technically, brought to an end, but the area remains volatile.

In this uneasy atmosphere, a team of archaeologists, led by Professor Arthur Demarest, launched an expedition of the region (sponsored by the Guatemalan Institute of Anthropology and History, Vanderbilt University and the National Geographic Society) in 2000. Demarest mounted the expedition to pursue data found inscribed in hieroglyphics on artefacts excavated in Tikal, the Maya's biggest and most beautiful commercial trading settlement, 135 kilometres (85 miles) northeast of Cancuén. The data suggested that a remote site known as Cancuén was both a Mayan marketplace and the seat of a potent fourth-century BC Mayan king known as Tah Chan Wi ("Celestial Fire").

The remains of Cancuén were literally stumbled upon. Demarest was hiking across what he thought to be a jungle-covered hill when he fell into a vegetation-covered sunken courtyard. He realized that he had been walking over the roof of a building and had fallen, up to his armpits, into a place alive with vipers (Cancuén's name seems to have been appropriate).

The courtyard that Demarest had fallen into proved to be part of a three-storey structure. This building was only one small part of the palace at Cancuén, which has proved to be one of the largest Mayan palaces to have been found in the whole region. The palace, built of limestone, boasted about 170 rooms 6 metres (20 feet) high, built around eleven courtyards and spread over 20,900 square metres (25,000 square yards). Amazingly, the site

was virtually intact. Nothing comparable to this Mayan palace has been found since the early nineteenth century. The size and condition of the palace at Cancuén rival the buildings at the central acropolis in Tikal, previously considered one of the grandest seats of Mayan power.

Previous archaeologists had dismissed Cancuén because of its lack of temples. This apparent error was understandable, as a fundamental part of the Mayan religion consisted of the worshipping of their pantheon of gods in the pyramid-temples, such as those seen in majestic Tikal and Chichén Itzá (see pages 32–41). It was a key part of Mayan religion to be close to the heavens. This is why Mayas at other sites built temples that resemble mountain peaks. Instead of building such temples, Cancuén's population used the surrounding highlands and caves as sacred places of worship and as burial sites.

The Maya had many gods, but their principal deities were gods of nature, such as Chaac, a rain god, who dictated the success or failure of the harvest. Chaac was considered to be divided into four entities, each represented by the north, south, east, and west. Chaac was also associated with Kukulcán, the god of the wind, who is often represented on buildings and artefacts with the symbol of the plumed serpent (see pages 32–41).

Another four key gods who held up the sky at the four points of the compass were thought to be brothers. These brothers were believed to be the sons of the great creator and supreme being known as Itzamna. The four gods encompassed the world and preserved the sky and each was associated with a cardinal point on the compass. North was coloured white and symbolized joy and festivity. South was yellow and symbolized skin colour; flesh was the embodiment of life and priests often ritually tortured themselves in pursuit of piety and to honour the gods. East was red and symbolized blood; Mayan leaders would endure blood letting to honour the gods as they believed their blood fed the deities. Finally west was black, which symbolized d.

The Maya believed in offering blood as a gift to the carried out human sacrifices to keep the cosmo. pages 34–39). One of their most important religious sy was the sacred *ceiba* or "tree of life". The roots of the *ceiba* were thought to reach into the underworld and its branches to the heavens. The tree was embodied on Earth in the form of the Mayan rulers and the great temples and sacred areas dedicated to the ancestors.

The ceremonies of human sacrifice were overseen by four elders of the élite and dedicated to gods such as Kukulcán and the rain gods. There is some evidence that sacrifices of dogs and other small mammals were also made. Death, an ever-present element of Mayan culture, even played a part in the ball games that the Maya played for leisure.

The civilization at Cancuén seems to challenge many of the established theories about the nature of Mayan kingdoms. It was evidently successful and prosperous, yet, in a civilization with a strict belief-system, it had no temples. Academics had long considered warfare to be endemic in the Mayan world. A Mayan king was thought to derive his power partly from physical links with the gods (such as temples) and by proving his prowess in battle. However, the kings of Cancuén seem to have actively sought to avoid war. The discovery of these facts have sent ripples through the archaeological world in recent years, leading some – Demarest included – to re-evaluate their view of the Mayan world.

Demarest's team used hieroglyphic inscriptions to help decipher the puzzling dynasty that had thrived at Cancuén for hundreds of years. Scholars, including Mayan hieroglyphics expert Frederico Fahsen, revealed that the kings of Cancuén secured ability by forging alliances with other great cities. For example, it is recorded that in c. AD 735 Cancuén's king married his daughter, Ix Chac Kawail Ix Cancuén Ahau, to prince K'in K'awil of Dos Pilas (a Mayan settlement located 90 kilometres (55 miles) north-east of Cancuén in the nearby Petexbatun region), instead of engaging in war against him. In the eighth and ninth centuries AD, toward the end of the classic period of the Mayan world, Cancuén formed a joint kingdom with the dominions of Tres Islas and Machaquila, which meant that these combined kingdoms incorporated most of southern Peten. Whether the kings of the region were seeking powerful alliances in times of dire need is not clear. What is certain, however, is that the kings of Cancuén consistently chose political expediency over aggression when dealing with potential rivals – a remarkable and unusual policy in the Mayan world.

Cancuén further secured the status of its kingdom by taking advantage of a geographical quirk: it is located on the Pasión River, at the beginning of its navigable section, thereby enabling it to act as a channel for materials, goods and information between the Mayan lowlands and highlands. This ensured that its king governed the gateway to one of the primary trade routes of the Mayan world, thereby guaranteeing him status and his people considerable wealth.

The rulers of Cancuén were clearly opportunists, and their people talented craftsmen. Near the palace lie workshops for the working of jade, obsidian and other materials. Five cores of chert

LEFT: An area within the fabulous palace at Cancuén in Guatemala as seen here in a computer graphics artist's impression. It is one of the largest and grandest palaces ever built for a Mayan king. Built c. AD 700, the palace boasts approximately 170 rooms, built around eleven courtyards on three stories and was made of fine limestone masonry.

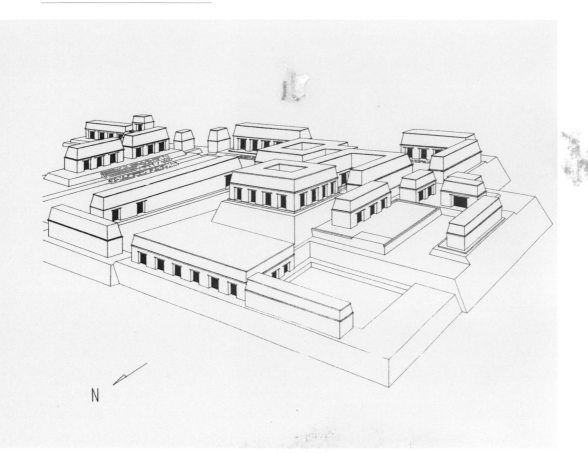

N

LEFT: An artist's impression of a section of a sprawling palace (see also pages 28–29) built 1,300 years ago by the Maya in the rain forest of Guatemala. The palace had been covered w___ ___rior to its d___ ___ is by Luis ___uin ___ ___as commissioned by ___ ___ National Geographic Society.

RIGHT: Classic period Maya polychrome pottery burial vase with geometric designs. The finest of these vases were placed in the tombs of honoured Maya dead.

(flint) were discovered at the site, along with limestone hammers and chert debris, evidence of the large-scale manufacture of sharpened stone tools and blades – obsidian was used to make the hardest and sharpest blades in the world at that time. Excavations at the site have unearthed raw materials, which include a 16-kilogram (35-pound) cut boulder of jade, tools of manufacture, and finished beads and other products. The team also discovered sheets of pyrite (often known as fool's gold), which was commonly fashioned into mirrors for use by wealthy Mayans. The kings of Cancuén controlled the most valuable resources in the Mayan world. They were imported into Cancuén, processed and worked into fine artefacts by artisans at the settlement, then were traded downriver with the Maya of the lowland regions.

The Maya did not use money, as we know it. Instead, wealth in the Mayan period was measured in terms of jade, obsidian, pyrite and other materials. On those terms, the entire population at Cancuén could be described as rich. Many bodies of people belonging to the common classes have been found to have had ten or more teeth inlaid with jade pieces.

Demarest believes that it will take ten years to excavate the site thoroughly. However, we already have a good idea of the city's structure. Set on the top of a hill was the central citadel, which was made up of staterooms and palaces. This is where the ruling priest-élite, including the king, who was also the high-priest, would have lived. Minor aristocrats, architects, builders and major craftsmen would have had quarters in the centre of the city. Within the ring of major buildings, there were public forums where festivals and spectacles such as sacrifices and games were staged. On other days, markets filled with people trading all manner of wares were held in these areas.

The surrounding terrain was very distinctive. It was a bare landscape, because much of the forest had been cut down to provide building materials and to form small drained fields, which were intensively farmed. Most of the population was scattered throughout the surrounding area, living in small cell-like units, akin to villages. These units were often gathered around their own ancestral shrines.

The people had a hard life, but a largely peaceful one. The social structure was based on kinship and blood ties and, although

DESTRUCTION OF A JUNGLE TREASURE

IT IS RARE TO FIND lost jungle sites in an intact state. However, damage to archaeological evidence, caused by the growth of new forest around the site and environmental perturbation, is usually minimal. It is human activity, not the effects of nature, which poses the greatest threat to such sites. In the Cancuén region, local people are being trained to fend off looters.

"THAT WHICH HAS BEEN COVERED by dense forest tends to be in the better state apart from root and plant damage, which can be rectified. However, a big problem in these areas is looting – tomb robbers digging up artefacts and selling them on the world antiquities market. It is an easy way for the local peasants to make a lot of money in a hurry and is done as part of the local economy, as is the growing and selling of drugs. The looters work in small bands but will work for weeks in the forest digging huge holes in order to find saleable items: pottery, figurines, jewellery and weapons, causing a great deal of damage, much of which cannot be rectified and disturbing the stratigraphy of the site in the process."

DR FRANCISCO ESTRADA-BELLI
ARCHAEOLOGIST, VANDERBILT UNIVERSITY, TENNESSEE, USA

basically hierarchical, offered some possibility of social mobility. People could move between classes by excelling as a warrior or by becoming a religious functionary, such as a shaman.

The classic Mayan period collapsed due to some unknown shock that tore through Maya society and ended its settlements in the Mayan heartland in c. AD 900. Although some settlements in the Yucatán peninsula (such as Chichén Itzá) were relatively unaffected, most settlements were abandoned. Such was the fate of Cancuén.

The settlement, one of the best preserved Mayan sites ever discovered, was found thanks to good detective work – particularly following the clues of the hieroglyphs at Tikal referring to Cancuén – modern science, and pure luck. An extensive study of this fabulous archaeological treasure may, one day, give us an understanding of the chain of events that led to its abandonment and thereby the dissolution of the whole Mayan civilization. If the discovery of Cancuén helps to resolve that mystery, Professor Demarest and his team will take their place alongside the great archaeologists and explorers of the nineteenth and twentieth centuries.

CHICHEN ITZA
CITY OF THE PLUMED SERPENT

THE WORD "MAYAN" CONJURES UP A WEALTH OF resonant images: human sacrifices, massive stone temples and the plumed serpents — symbols of the Mayan god of wind — adorning buildings. The word also conveys a sense of mystery and fascination, because the downfall of this remarkable civilization remains an enigma. The Mayan empire flourished between c. 1000 BC and c. AD 1100 (see page 25). However, by c. AD 900, most of the city-states in the Mayan heartland had collapsed. The populations plummeted, suggesting that the people had simply abandoned their cities. Only those settlements built in isolated areas like the Yucatán peninsula, including Chichén Itzá, survived the perturbations suffered in the heartland. The Maya recovered eventually, only to succumb finally to the destructive forces of the conquistadors in the sixteenth century (see pages 35–36).

Many Mayan sites were built on settlements developed by earlier peoples, such as the Olmecs. The Olmecs were the first organized social group to develop in the area of Chichén Itzá in the preclassic Mayan period c. 1200–100 BC. The Olmecs erected clay-brick buildings, developed pyramidal temples and showed great expertise in sculpting. The Olmec culture did not develop city structures as seen in the classic Mayan period (c. AD 250–900) — their settlements consisted of small towns.

The cities of the Maya were not under the control of one overall authority, as seen in the Inca empire (see pages 43–44). Instead, each Mayan settlement seems to have been run on a regional basis, with each city-state administering its own affairs. The evidence that remains (in the form of the hieroglyphs found

OPPOSITE: The ornate serpent columns of the Temple of the Warriors and the Chaacs Mool statues in the foreground reflect the importance given to religious imagery in postclassic Mayan culture. The reclining Chaacs Mool figures are thought to be connected with the cult of heart sacrifice and may have been idols representing Chaac, the rain god.

ABOVE: The main monuments of Chichén Itzá — the Mayan observatory known as the Caracol, meaning "the Snail" (foreground), and the 24 m (74 ft) high great pyramid known as the Castillo (above left). The Castillo's four sides are aligned with cardinal points of the compass. The number of stairs amounts to the total number of days in a solar year: 365 days.

in Maya temples, and the "codices", the Mayan books) suggests that there was no set pattern of government in Mayan city-states. Some were governed by kings (as was Cancuén), and others were ruled by councils. The councillors, or "elders", may have been the wealthy and the aristocratic, or perhaps those deemed as most fit to rule by the city's rich and powerful inhabitants.

The Mayan way of life was one of extremes. On the one hand, there was advanced learning and scientific achievement; on the

33

LEFT: *Two stone rings, one on each side, were located in the ball court at Chichén Itzá. In postclassic times (c. AD 900) players, protected by padding, used their elbows, knees, and hips to propel a solid rubber ball into their opponent's end of the ball court with the aim of putting the ball through one of the stone rings as shown here.*

RIGHT: *A Chaacs Mool figure found at the ruins of Chichén Itzá. Chaac, the rain god was divided into four entities (north, south, east and west). The Chaacs were thought to generate rain by carrying water in gourds and pouring it out across the lands when the whim took them. Their arrival was heralded by the croaking of frogs, who accompanied them. Thunderstorms occurred when the Chaacs threw their huge stone axes to the earth.*

other, violence and bloodthirstiness. For example, it was a practice of the priests and the ruling élite to cut slits in their tongues and pull knotted string through the hole to produce blood offerings to the gods and to open paths to the spirit world. Others cut their ears or their genitals to produce blood for sacrificial offerings to the gods in the hope that purity, enlightenment and success would follow, and as a ritual for personal spiritual betterment. Human sacrifices were made to mark special occasions, both dynastic and calendric. Often children were sacrificed, but why they were chosen is not clear – perhaps because children were considered pure and unsullied, and also, from the parent's point of view, the greatest sacrifice that could be made. Many Mayan works depict wars on neighbouring cities and the capture and sacrifice of nobles from those cities in honour of the gods. It was thought that chaos and ruin would ensue if sacrifices were not made. It is possible that children sacrificed in Chichén Itzá were captured in this way.

The Maya showed remarkable sophistication in marking time and developing calendars, and their priests were the great timekeepers of the ancient Mesoamerican world. They used two calendars simultaneously: the 260-day Tzolkin calendar and the 365-day solar-year calendar. This combination of calendars is referred to as a calendar round – a cycle that repeats itself after a period of fifty-two years. The calendar round was in existence in Olmec times, before 500 BC.

The Tzolkin calendar (also known as the ritual calendar) was used like an almanac, for divination and prophecy, and to mark key religious rituals. The solar-year calendar was used to mark and calculate solstice dates, religious festivals and planting and harvest times. It was devised by the astronomer-priests at the Copán observatory, located on the border between Belize and Honduras. The mathematical sophistication and brilliant observation of these priests made them some of the world's first great astronomers. They mapped the movements of the sun and the planets with such accuracy that they amazed the peasants (and no doubt their rulers) with their predictions of celestial events such as eclipses.

The astronomer-priests would consult both calendars when making judgements regarding important decisions such as planting times, times of war, or the choice of a new leader. The use of these calendars was swathed in a mass of codes and mystical

practices, which were impenetrable to ordinary people and the non-religious ruling élite. For everyday timekeeping, a system known as the "Long Count" was used. This was a method of keeping track of days elapsed from a specific base point, identified today as 13 August 3114 BC.

The Mayan agricultural system was also notably sophisticated. The Maya cleared forests, built raised terraces and irrigation canal networks, and planted cultivars of maize and other crops that could feed vast numbers of people. Although the Mayans probably used natural fertilizers, such as rotted dung, the land may eventually have been over-exploited and depleted during the classic period. It is possible that the decline of the land's fertility, and the subsequent difficulty in adequately feeding the people, contributed to the fall of the Mayan empire.

By c. AD 900, the Mayan civilization outside the Yucatán was in a dire state. Archaeological evidence suggests that the people were becoming malnourished, possibly due to a failure of their agricultural systems. Many of the people were forced to move away from the cities to try to cultivate virgin land. However, it seems that some social unrest had occurred before this mass

exodus. The Maya had a highly stratified society, with the leaders – kings, aristocracy, the rich and astronomer-priests – set far above the artisans and peasants. The lower members of society worked hard while their social superiors enjoyed the fruits of their labours. Only the priests could control the planting of the crops, and, consequently, the cycle of life. Only the priests and the leaders could design and build the great cities. Yet, as food grew scarce, and sickness grew more common, the ancient system of leadership was seen to be failing. An uprising of the common people was perhaps inevitable in these circumstances. It is possible that this combination of peasant revolt, sickness and hunger brought about the downfall of many classical Mayan cities.

The Mayan civilization did not vanish completely; it merely entered a new phase. In the postclassical period, many Maya lived in clusters of villages, attempting to return to normality after the decline of their city-states. The Mayan culture continued and evolved for another 400 years, until the arrival of the Spanish conquistadors in Central America in 1518. The Europeans were ruthless in their desire for conquest, but even more deadly than their ambition were the diseases they brought with them. The Maya

LEFT: The Cenote, a huge natural well, was created at Chichén Itzá when a limestone surface collapsed. Associated with the Chaacs (rain gods), the well was a sacred place and was presented with many offerings such as jade, gold and incense. Macabre though it may seem, human sacrifices were often made in the well — it was thought that anyone surviving potential drowning had been spared to bring a message about the year's crops from the Chaacs.

had no immunity against diseases such as smallpox and measles, which were previously unknown on the continent, and an estimated seventy-five per cent of the population died from sickness between the arrival of the Spaniards and the end of the seventeenth century. This onslaught finally terminated the Mayan civilization.

Chichén Itzá is an extraordinary example of Mayan design and was one of the largest cities in Mesoamerica: today the ruins of the city extend over 5 square kilometres (2 square miles). The city was constructed in c. AD 864, at the end of the classic period, and became the centre of the postclassic Mayan government. Its huge ball court and grand plazas, impressive temples and lime cement streets survive as a reminder of the sophistication of this culture. The city lies towards the northern end of the Yucatán peninsula. This great finger of land, pointing towards the island of Cuba, forms the southernmost point of the Gulf of Mexico. This is a fertile and beautiful region, offering an ideal place in which to build a city.

Chichén Itzá means "Mouth of The Well" or just "Mouth-Well". The site of the city was used several times in its history, the differing peoples within the civilization bringing new architectural styles to the city. The ruins that remain can be divided into two

eras. The older buildings were erected in the classic period between the seventh and tenth centuries AD. The architecture of this part of the city is typified by representations of the rain god Chaac (see page 27). The newer, postclassical, part of the city dates from c. AD 900 to c. AD 1200 and is characterized by simple monolithic architecture. The people of Chichén Itzá at this time were strongly influenced by the Toltec of central Mexico, with similar art and architecture appearing at both Tula (the Toltec capital) and Chichén Itzá. The Toltecs also influenced the religion of the Maya of Chichén Itzá, who adopted the Toltec wind god Quetzalcoatl, and gave him the name of Kukulcán. Many of the city's buildings of this period feature the symbol of Kukulcán, the feathered serpent, as a recurring motif.

Chichén Itzá features grand roadways and elaborate structures built around the great Castillo (Castle) step-pyramid – which may have been built at the very end of the classic period or in the early postclassic period, c. AD 900 onwards. The Castillo – a temple, covered in depictions of the feathered serpent – sits in the centre of the main plaza. Each of its four sides has a flight of steps leading to its summit, some 30 metres (100 feet) above ground level. The

ABOVE: *Excavations at the Castillo pyramid of Kukulcán produced evidence of an earlier construction that held a fabulous, jade-encrusted, red jaguar throne.*

RIGHT: *At the spring and summer equinoxes the setting sun throws a shadow down the staircase of the Castillo that creates the illusion of a great serpent slithering downwards, possibly inferring the movement of the god Kukulcán, the plumed serpent, from his monument atop the pyramid to the earth.*

steps on the Castillo symbolize each day of the year (according to the 365-day solar calendar): there were three flights with ninety-one steps, and one with ninety-two.

At the northern edge of the city lies the Cenote, a huge natural well that was used as a shrine of the utmost importance. In times of hardship or poor rains, pilgrims visited the well with precious offerings to the god of water. In times of truly dire need, such as drought, human sacrifices, sometimes of children, were made to the well. Carvings depict sacrifices made at times of war and periods of religious significance, but sacrifice was a relatively common event and therefore frustratingly little is known about specific instances of sacrifice in the Cenote. Visitors to the well also made offerings of semi-precious stones and metal and clay objects.

Most Mayan cities feature a ball court, but the one at Chichén Itzá, in the north of the city, is the largest one to have been discovered. The building's parallel walls, more than 30 metres (100 feet) apart, formed a court that may have been open at

either end. The court was 130 metres (430 feet) long, suggesting that the game was played along the wall as much as in the centre of the court. The aim of the game was to move a small solid rubber ball using only the hips, buttocks and possibly the arms – hands and feet were forbidden. The game was played by teams of varying sizes; it is not known how they scored. In the postclassic period, stone loops were added to either side of the court, suggesting that these were rival goal targets.

Games were played for extremely high stakes. Some people gambled their freedom or that of their children on the outcome of a game. It is thought that the participants may have become slaves or been sacrificed if they lost. It is believed that victors were hailed as heroes, while the captains of the losing teams were decapitated by the priests, using obsidian blades. However, it has been suggested that sacrifice was held in such high esteem that the winners of the game would have been offered as more worthy sacrifices to the gods than the losers. Mayan relief carvings often

depict ball courts with the focus on the ball, around which competitors face each other, knives drawn, with one figure holding the decapitated head of a loser.

On the eastern side of the city, opposite the ball court and east of the Castillo, lies the Temple of the Warriors. This is another magnificent stepped building, built in a rectangular shape with a vast staircase and great colonnaded halls. The Temple of Warriors, as its name suggests, was dedicated to the honour of the warrior gods and the warriors of the city – alive and dead – and features sculptures of warriors on its front and supporting pillars. The temple is a good example of the Toltec influence on Mayan architecture: the monument is very similar to one found in the Toltec capital, Tula.

In the south of the city, the buildings are much more restrained in their design, suggesting a different architectural style, possibly of an earlier occupation. The Caracol, the observatory, is in this district, and is evidence of the Mayans' interest in and knowledge of astronomy. The Caracol features an observation tower built on two rectangular platforms. Above the tower's doors are carvings of Chaac, to whom the building may have been dedicated.

The splendour of the city centre contrasted greatly with the surrounding districts. The majority of people lived in small stone-built houses with thatched roofs, close to the land they cultivated.

During the twelfth century, Chichén Itzá was abandoned and a new capital founded at Mayapan, although people still came to visit the *cenote*. However, the city itself was never completely lost. Even in the sixteenth century, scholars were studying its buildings and attempting to decipher its hieroglyphs to try to understand the ways of its people. We have now gleaned much information from the architecture of Chichén Itzá. However, our knowledge of the city's society and learning remains sketchy, because few written records have survived.

The people of Chichén Itzá covered the interior walls of their public buildings with colourful frescoes illustrating their history. These stories and images are also found decorating pottery. These stories seem to have been part of an oral culture. The stories were interactive, with the storyteller prompting responses from the audience. The oral transmission of these tales ensured that the people's history stayed alive. Some of the stories have echoes in other cultures. There is a story of a queen who deserts her king, to run away with a prince from another tribe, an action that starts a war. This tale resembles that of Helen of Troy's abandonment of her husband Menelaus for her lover Paris and the start of the Trojan war, as told by Homer (see pages 101–107) .

Englishman Sir John Eric Sydney Thompson (1898–1975) attempted but failed to decipher the hieroglyphic texts inscribed on the walls of the city buildings. Recently, it has been discovered that the Mayan texts recorded more than just religious rites, as had previously been thought; they were also historical records. Thompson also found that many Mayan customs survive in the beliefs of modern-day Mexicans, including the use of the 260-day Tzolkin calendar for the purpose of divination.

It is apparent from Chichén Itzá texts that each Mayan city in the Yucatán peninsula bore the responsibility for a period of twenty years to undertake religious rites and privileges and to keep a record of astrological, religious and cultural activities. The records kept at Chichén Itzá consist of inscriptions carved in stone using a special archaic style of writing. The way the astronomer-priests and their scribes used the language when it was their turn to keep the records was much more phonetic than the rest of the written Mayan hieroglyphic language, aiding scholars in deciphering the inscriptions.

The Mayans also used books (codices), made from fig-tree bark and folded concertina-like, to preserve the written word.

However, the conquistadors destroyed most of the books in c. AD 1562 as part of their mission to force Christian belief on the Mayan "savages". They burned the books, believing them to be filled with pagan rites. Ironically, the Spaniards were also destroying records of science and learning far in advance of many European cultures of the time. Only four Mayan books are known to have survived. One remains in Mexico, and three are in Europe. They were probably saved by one of the priests given the task of destroying the books, and were later presented to one of the Habsburg kings, the royal family that governed Austria and other parts of Europe from the medieval period until 1918. One of these four surviving books may have been written at Chichén Itzá and cared for by the astronomer-priests in the Caracol.

Today Chichén Itzá is a world-famous tourist site. Some areas were excavated and renovated by the Carnegie Institution of Washington, under the direction of Sylvanus Morley. This work was begun in 1924 and went on into the 1940s.

Work continues at the site today, and archaeologists are still trying to solve the puzzle of the collapse of the Mayan empire. Kevin P. Corbley and Terry Winemiller, researchers at Louisiana

State University, USA, are working with new digital mapping and remote-sensing technologies. Their research focuses on understanding the settlement of Mayan sites, with the aim of using this knowledge to find other lost Mayan cities, which may yet lie buried in the forests of Belize, Guatemala, Honduras and Mexico.

The migration of the Mayan people from the lowlands of what is now northern Guatemala southward, further into Central America and northward to the Yucatán, has long fascinated scientists. Digital mapping and remote sensing may help with our understanding of this migration. Data gathered via these methods can be used to build a model of Mayan lands. This study of spatial relationships between archaeological features and natural resources such as water and limestone (which was used for construction of Mayan cities) will help to give an insight into how the geography of the area influenced the Maya's decision as to where to establish their settlements. Such information may tun up clues as to where other lost sites lie.

Winemiller has used Chichén Itzá – a well-preserved, restored and excavated site – as a model. The layout of the temples, the plazas and ball court, as well as other features, will further refine the spatial analysis, which may be used to help locate other lost Mayan cities.

IN THE WORDS OF THEIR ANCESTORS

THE SPOKEN LANGUAGE of the Maya, so important in the maintenance of their oral history and culture, is now endangered.

"THE LANGUAGE OF THE MAYA, the builders of Chichén Itzá and other great cities in the Yucatán was, until relatively recently, still in use throughout a region that blankets three states of Mexico: not just in the rural areas, but in the cities as well. Some years ago I lived and studied in a small village with a population of about fifty people in which Spanish was rarely spoken and then only by the men. The women were less comfortable with Spanish and the children did not learn it until they went to school. But times have changed. Due to economic growth, a newly paved road has made travel to other towns easier, and most houses now have televisions that are immersing them in Spanish all day long, driving a change in the way the local people divide their time between Maya and Spanish. As a by-product of television, if the youth of the district begin to prefer Spanish over Maya, Maya could fail at some point to make the generational transition as a fully learned language and whither away. In an effort to reverse this trend, activists are working to promote the use of the Mayan language and we are beginning to see signs that it might be returning as a written living language, which is very encouraging."

DR JAMES A. FOX, ASSOCIATE PROFESSOR, DEPARTMENT OF
ANTHROPOLOGICAL SCIENCES, STANFORD UNIVERSITY,
CALIFORNIA, USA

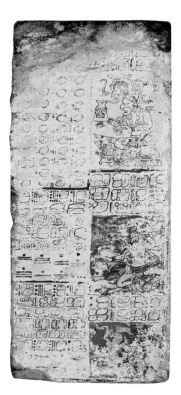

LEFT: The Dresden Codex is one of only four known Mayan books from the postclassic period (post AD 900) to have escaped the ravages of time and the fires of the invading Spanish priests.

MACHU PICCHU
THE SECRET OF THE INCAS

THE INCAS WERE A PEOPLE OF GREAT ACHIEVEMENT and advanced civilization – their expertise in building, agriculture, administration and art has left its mark on history. They first emerged in c. AD 1200, in the uplands of the Cuzco basin, Peru. The Incas developed, over the course of 200 years, from a small community into a thriving kingdom of between five and ten million people. The Incas were a wealthy people, thanks to a sophisticated exploitation of a lush and fertile domain, which supported them agriculturally, and to their prowess in manufacturing goods including cloth, art and tools. By the fifteenth century AD, the Incas were so wealthy that Cuzco, their capital city (founded by their ruler Manco Capac in c. AD 1200–1230), had buildings that were decorated in worked sheets of gold. The Incas described this city as the "Sacred City of the Sun", because of its great Temple of the Sun (also called Coricancha). Cuzco was divided into religious, military and residential areas, and featured fine temples and fortresses, all glittering in the sun because of their elaborate (and often golden) decoration.

The Incas developed an administrative system that, by the fifteenth century, held together one of the world's greatest empires, stretching from the region known today as Santiago, along the western coast of South America to Quito, in modern-day Ecuador. It was an empire that would today encompass Ecuador, Peru, Bolivia, Argentina and Chile, and brought together nearly one hundred nations and groups of peoples under its rule. In truth, the term "Inca" refers to the Inca royal family and the 40,000 direct descendents of the family who governed the empire. However, it is common practice to use the term "Inca" to refer to the Inca empire as a whole.

The Incas expanded their empire through military aggression. After conquering an area through war, the Incas established their rule by imposing their language, Quechua, and their worship of the

OPPOSITE: The stunning ruins of Machu Picchu with Mount Huayna Picchu in the background have come to epitomize ancient settlements and the pursuit of archaeological discovery.

ABOVE: Located near the Main Plaza at Machu Picchu is the Intihuatana – the "Hitching Post of the Sun". This ceremonial sunstone was carved from a single piece of rock and stands 1.8 m (6 ft) high.

LEFT: The Incas were extraordinarily sophisticated builders. Their mortarless walls, constructed from precisely carved stone blocks, are remarkable even by modern construction standards. This meticulous stonework was not restricted to temples but can also be seen in housing, such as in the Mortars area of Machu Picchu.

RIGHT: Inca construction techniques did not just depend upon finely hewn stone and rock. As seen in this reconstructed thatched house, they used a combination of materials to create spectacular and practical settlements .
FAR RIGHT: The Incas valued the flow of water, and their fountains, located all across Machu Picchu, are masterpieces of hydrological engineering, evidenced by the fact that they still work today.

sun god, Inti, on the local people. This initiative helped to secure a commonality and unity for all Inca peoples, which helped to strengthen the empire. The kings of the districts were allowed to retain power in each region, but only as puppet rulers; they had to bow to the will of the Inca emperor.

The emperor was considered to be a demi-god, the human incarnation of Inti, and his will was enforced, when necessary, with utter ruthlessness. Wars between rival Inca tribes were common, but they were rarely tolerated by the Inca rulers. Ringleaders were executed, and, on occasion, an entire community was eradicated.

Like the Romans before them, the Incas realized the advantage that a good communications network gave to an army. They built nearly 14,000 kilometres (8,700 miles) of roads, opening up the empire for commerce, communication, rapid military movement, and thereby efficient control of the domain. The roads facilitated good trade links between different parts of the empire, aiding the development of a unified Inca culture across the conquered tribes.

Of all the urbanized people of the Americas, the Incas were the most brilliant engineers, superior even to the Tiwanakans (see pages 51–59). The Inca built massive forts with stone slabs so

perfectly cut that they did not require mortar. These forts are so sturdy and well engineered that they remain to this day in a near-perfect state of preservation. The Inca built roads through the mountains from Ecuador to Chile with tunnels and bridges. They also built aqueducts to their cities – such as that seen in Machu Picchu (see page 49). The Incas were also capable surgeons, performing amputations and minor surgery.

The Incas held unquestionable power within their own domain, but their empire collapsed when faced with the invasion of the Europeans in the sixteenth century. In 1531, an expedition of Spanish adventurers or conquistadors, led by Francisco Pizarro (c. 1478–1541) a soldier of fortune, set out from Panama with an invasion force that would threaten the Inca empire. The group, which included 200 horsemen and foot soldiers, landed at Tumbes in April 1532. The Spaniards were mercenary and ambitious, bent on seeking gold, territory and a subservient labour force. They penetrated the Inca defences and convinced the Inca emperor, Atahualpa, to come to a conference at the city of Cajamarca. When Atahualpa arrived, Pizarro took him prisoner and killed many members of his entourage and family. Pizarro first

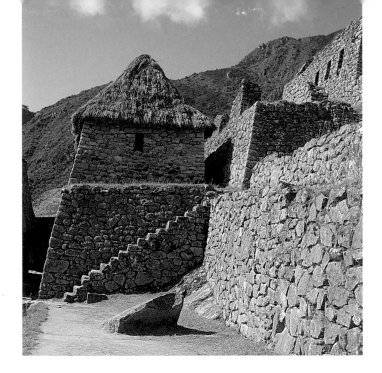

tried to employ him as a puppet ruler, but this failed. Pizzarro then staged a show trial which found Atahualpa guilty of polygamy and fratricide. Pizzarro had Atahualpa killed in 1533. The demi-god ruler of the Incas was strangled and then burned – an indication of the conquistadors' contempt for the Incas.

By the end of 1532, the Spanish adventurers had conquered the Inca empire and looted the fabulous Inca gold. They ruthlessly crushed any displays of resistance, even releasing hunting dogs on the people to tear them apart. The Inca empire depended on centralized control and the absolute authority of the Inca emperor, who was considered to be a living god. The murder of Atahualpa, their leader, threw the population into a state of shock, leaving them defeated and utterly demoralized, and consequently the empire collapsed.

For the Incas, the Europeans spelled the end of the world. Their ancient legends told of the creator-god Viracocha's Caucasian nature, and that of his powerful warriors. When the Incas suffered at the hands of the Caucasian invaders, it must have seemed that, just as the Inca world had been created by a Caucasian, so was it destroyed by another – Pizzarro. Perhaps the people thought that they had brought this destruction upon themselves; we shall never know for certain, however, as the Incas had no form of writing with which to preserve their fears for prosperity.

Some Inca people led a resistance movement, but their task was an impossible one. Over the next forty years, the Spanish struggled with insurrection in the region, but by c. 1575 the conquistadors had destroyed all remaining resistance to their rule. The Inca civilization was at an end, its people butchered or cowed.

In 1911, American Hiram Bingham (1875–1956), Assistant Professor of Latin History at Yale University, began a mission to explore the territories of South America. He set out for the Incas' capital city, Cuzco, travelling overland from Lima on a donkey. He sought the last great settlement of the Inca empire, Vilcabamba. This city had been a refuge for the leaders of the Inca resistance movement in c. 1572, Inca Manco – the brother of Atahualpa –

MACHU PICCHU

and his sons. Their rebellion was suppressed by the Spaniards, but Inca Manco managed to escape from Pizzarro and his troops.

Bingham's claim to fame was his discovery of the lost hill city of the Incas: Machu Picchu, which he incorrectly identified as Vilcabamba. Ironically, Bingham was the first modern explorer to reach Espiritu Pampa, located about 110 kilometres (60 miles) east of Machu Picchu on the Amazon – a site now recognized by most experts as the actual remains of Vilcabamba. Bingham did not recognize this, though, preferring Machu Picchu as his choice for the lost city of Vilcabamba. Bingham had little evidence to guide him on his quest. One source of information was the writings of a seventeenth-century Catholic missionary to the area, Father Antonio de Clancha. De Clancha believed that another refuge of the Inca resistance, Vitcos, was located near an overhanging white rock at the site of a temple of the sun. Under difficult conditions and with little information, other than what he could gain from local people, Bingham found the overhanging rock. It was located on the banks of the Urubamba river in Peru. There he also found the ruins of what were obviously ancient buildings, which matched de Clancha's description. Bingham had

ABOVE: The Incas constructed drainage channels and water outlets that crossed agricultural terraces. While some scholars have hypothesized that the abandonment of Machu Picchu occurred because there was not enough available water, hydrological engineer Kenneth R. Wright determined that there was no need for irrigation as there was plenty of rainfall. The Inca canal delivered water to the emperor's residence and provided the remainder of the royal estate with a domestic water supply. (See page 49 and for Wright's account see: Machu Picchu–A Civil Engineering Marvel *and* The Machu Picchu Guidebook.*)*

46

found Vitcos. Bingham was not satisfied, however. He still wanted to find the city of Vilcabamba – Manco's refuge – and so he continued his exploration.

Bingham endured extreme hardship on his mission. He climbed glaciers and struggled through the mountainous terrain, suffering severe cold and, beside the Amazon, terrible heat. Along his journey he spoke to local people to glean knowledge from them. To Bingham's surprise, they had no apparent interest in the legends. They regarded Machu Picchu simply as a ruined settlement that was no longer needed or useful, but they were happy to assist Bingham in what they saw as a foolish adventure.

Bingham endured further physical hardship in the exhausting climate. With the help of his local guide, he crossed the Urubamba river on a makeshift log bridge, and then climbed up between two mountainous peaks. There, 80 kilometres (50 miles) northwest of Cuzco, Peru, on 23 July 1911, Bingham found Machu Picchu. He wrote, "We rounded a knoll and suddenly faced tier upon tier of Inca terraces rising like giant stairs. Each one, hundreds of feet long, was banked with massive stone walls up to ten feet high. What settlement of Incas had needed a hundred such terraces in this lofty wilderness? Enough food could be grown here to feed a city!" ("Great Adventures", *National Geographic*).

Bingham had found two sites, Huayna Picchu ("Old Mountain"), covered in ruins, and, on the opposite peak, Machu Picchu. The site of Huayna Picchu included temples and terraces. It is still possible to visit the Temple of the Moon, thought to be the only intact Inca temple, but earthquake tremors have demolished most of the other temples and key structures at Huayna Picchu. The lost city of Machu Picchu lies in a depressed ridge between two mountainous peaks, wreathed in mist, with the backdrop of a snow-capped mountain 5,550 metres (18,000 feet) high. Far below can be seen the glittering curve of the Urabamba river. This is a magical place, which generates feelings of wonder.

Bingham's discovery shed new light on the tremendous organizational abilities of the Incas. Machu Picchu was constructed, probably at the orders of Inca Emperor Pachacuti (AD 1438–1471), using similar techniques to those employed by the ancient Tiwanakans. However, the carving and workmanship discovered at Machu Picchu was much more sophisticated.

Machu Picchu was not an ordinary city, although its function is not fully understood. It may have been a place of worship and a place where the Incas could connect with their gods – a place of spiritual retreat. Since it was unknown to the Spanish invaders (their documents do not mention it), it may have acted as a refuge for Inca Manco. The architecture of the city suggests a strong

ABOVE: Hiram Bingham's colleague Sergeant Carrasco was photographed standing by the Intihuatana sundial *with the farmer's son who guided Bingham and Carrasco into the ruins of Machu Picchu in 1913.*

emphasis on religion as opposed to war and its location on the eastern border of the empire may have meant that it was a frontier outpost – a bastion of Inca culture.

Machu Picchu may also have been a royal estate that was only used at certain times of the year, and may have been visited by the Inca ruler himself for religious ceremonies. If it was a royal residence, the population of the city most of the year would have numbered about 300, mostly consisting of servants, stonemasons and other tradesmen. The population would rise significantly to approximately 1,200 people when the emperor and his retinue were in residence. We may never know why this city was built in such a remote location, in 70 kilometres (43 miles) of mountain terrain at a height of 2,440 metres (8,000 feet), and, moreover, how the Inca managed the feats of engineering and transportation needed to construct it.

The site stretches over about 13 square kilometres (5 square miles). Its great terraces were built around a central plaza. The city's buildings are made of granite. Originally gleaming white, they are now grey from pollution. The interiors were covered in plaster, and each had a thatched roof. The beauty of Machu Picchu lies in its detail: the precise carving of the lintels and posts of the

RIGHT: The temple district of Machu Picchu is located in the western part of the settlement. Standing near the southwestern corner of the main plaza is the Temple of the Three Windows. This great hall, measuring 10.6 m (35 ft) in length and 4.2 m (14 ft) wide, is set apart from other temples by its three great stone windows, all inset along one wall. These windows are the largest yet discovered in Inca architecture and offer a stunning view of the mountains beyond.

FAR RIGHT: In 1998 Kenneth Wright's team discovered a previously unknown series of fountains downhill from Machu Picchu. Adjacent to some of these fountains, Wright's team discovered an important Inca trail — one of a series of roads once used by the Inca to traverse their empire — which connected Machu Picchu to the Urubamba river in the valley below.

doors and windows and the stories of the workmen whose tools were left inside walls.

During his excavations at Machu Picchu, Bingham found 555 vessels, nearly 200 artefacts of bronze, copper and silver, as well as objects of stone and other materials. The ceramics show graceful forms of Inca art, and the bracelets, decorative pins, earrings, knives and axes also reveal sophisticated craftsmanship. Even though Bingham failed to find items made of gold (these may have been looted previously), his findings were sufficient to prove that Machu Picchu was a site of great significance, a fact that the city's architectural style indicated. After initial publication of his find, Bingham returned to the site in 1912, 1914 and 1915, accompanied by various scientists, in order to draw up maps and explore the site and its surroundings in detail. His activities, and those of his colleagues, made the site world-famous.

There have been numerous theories as to why the site was abandoned. It is possible that after the invasion of the conquistadors and the rapid collapse of the Inca empire, the

inhabitants of Machu Picchu simply put down their tools and returned to their home villages. They had no reason to stay. They were, themselves, visitors to the area, possibly forced into working there as a means of paying off a debt to the emperor.

Whatever the reason, Machu Picchu fell into decline. Just as the formidable empire of the Incas was lost, so too was this hidden realm. Was it the last refuge of the Inca resistance, or merely a summer palace and sacred place for the emperor? In time, we may learn the truth of this secret site.

Machu Picchu was listed as a world heritage site by UNESCO in 1983 and much work has continued on the site since Bingham left it. In 2001, Japan's Disaster Prevention Research Institute (DPRI), based at Kyoto University, issued warnings regarding the safety and stability of Machu Picchu, stating that the ancient city was under threat from mudslides. Using a sensing device known as an extensometer, the DPRI detected the rapid movement of earth on the western slope of the site. The earth slides were found to be moving at the rate of one centimetre per month. If the DPRI's warning is correct, Machu Picchu might be ruined in two disastrous events. First, the already dangerous western slope could give way in a massive rockslide. The eastern slope would soon follow, probably destroying the city in the process. If action is taken, Machu Picchu can possibly be saved from ruin.

The story of the site's rediscovery, in 1911, must rate as one of the most famous archaeological adventures of all time. Hiram Bingham is an inspirational archaeological figure and his exploits have influenced fictional heroes too – Hollywood's remarkable archaeologist Indiana Jones bears some comparison to Bingham. Machu Picchu was his, and the lost Incas', gift to the world.

UNCOVERING THE SECRETS OF THE INCAS

IN 1994, AN AMERICAN civil engineer, Kenneth R. Wright, received a long-sought permit to define the ancient water handling and water use at Machu Picchu. What he found has been enlightening.

"MY INTEREST AND WORK at Machu Picchu stems from a question my wife, Ruth, asked in 1974 upon returning from the site: "How could the Inca engineers develop a water supply so high up on a mountain?" As a water engineer in Colorado, I decided to find out the answer to her question; however, it took twenty years before the *Instituto Nacional de Cultura* in Lima finally granted me a permit for the field research. Eventually, I was able to assemble enough technical data on Machu Picchu to define the underground water supply originating in the faulted and fractured bedrock granite and a spring that still flows reliably. The route of the Inca canal was then surveyed and measured and its capacity was computed at 300 litres per minute. Ruth pitched in as a field partner and analyzed the city planning and original roof types used five centuries ago. Our engineering team then went on to study the prehistoric agriculture, urban drainage system, unfinished Machu Picchu construction and landslide problems experienced by the Inca. In 1999 we explored the forest adjacent to Machu Picchu. There, on the east flank of Machu Picchu, we found the impressive extension of the Inca Trail that went all the way down to the Urubamba river. Ceremonial fountains and great terraces were discovered. Once cleared and excavated, the fountains immediately sprang to action and began flowing as before, after centuries of being buried! We determined that a limited water supply was not the reason for abandonment of Machu Picchu and that the Inca residents did not need to irrigate the terraces because there was plenty of rainfall to grow crops without irrigation. The Inca canal delivered water first to the emperor's residence, and an additional fifteen fountains provided the remainder of the royal estate with a domestic water supply. The Inca kept drainage and runoff water separate from the water supply, illustrating their knowledge of the elements of modern hygiene long before the people of London even recognized the Thames as a polluted drinking water source. I proved that Hiram Bingham was correct when he said the Inca were good engineers. More important, however, is the fact that our studies demonstrate that Machu Picchu is a masterpiece of prehistoric construction."

KENNETH R. WRIGHT, HYDROLOGICAL ENGINEER,
WRIGHT WATER ENGINEERS, DENVER, COLORADO, USA

TIWANAKU
PEOPLE OF THE SKY GOD

THE ANDES MOUNTAIN RANGE STRETCHES FOR 8,000 kilometres (5,000 miles) along the Pacific coast of South America. Lying between the eastern and western Andean ranges, in Bolivia, is the Titicaca basin. Here lies Lake Titicaca, the largest navigable lake in South America and, at 3,850 metres (12,600 feet) above sea level, the highest in the world. Fifteen kilometres (nine miles) south of the lake, in a harsh and barren landscape, stand the remains of a remarkable ancient city – Tiwanaku.

The Tiwanaku civilization arose in c. AD 500. It evolved out of settlements that had depended on farming and fishing for their survival. Tiwanaku came to dominate the Titicaca basin and its culture radiated out from the Altiplano (the high plain) around Lake Titicaca across Bolivia, Chile and Peru. From c. AD 600 to AD 900, Tiwanaku was the dominant cultural and religious centre in South America.

There is much discussion about the nature and extent of Tiwanaku's influence. Some antiquarians argue that the city-state was the centre of a great empire. Their evidence includes the discovery of pottery and other Tiwanakan artefacts as far afield as the lowland eastern slopes of the Andes and the coastal valleys of Chile and Peru. These states may have fallen to Tiwanaku expansionism as they went in search of materials that their homeland could not offer them. Others argue that this is not evidence of an empire: there may simply have been well-established cultural and trade links between Tiwanaku and its neighbours. Another argument suggests that the religious and ritualistic elements of Tiwanakan culture were carried far and wide from their

OPPOSITE AND ABOVE: The monolithic Tiwanakan Gateway or Portal of the Sun was carved from one piece of andesite rock and built on the Kalasasaya mound, a low platform with alternating walls of tall megaliths or masonry with a sunken court, its axis facing the equinoctial sunrise. The worship of the Staff God often (but perhaps erroneously) referred to as Viracocha, was of great importance to the people of Tiwanaku. It was carved in relief on arguably the most important monument at the site. Sunburst rays emanate from his head, terminating in heads and circles. This iconography had precedents on the Peruvian coast and is pan-Andean.

LEFT: Gateway of the Sun, shown here as found and photographed in the 1880s, partially collapsed before restoration to its original position as it can be seen today. The entire upper panel has a repeating pattern of images, carved "Winged Figures" arranged around the central image of the Staff God/Gateway God.

source, and this diffusion had nothing to do with imperialism. The Tiwanakan "empire" may have been more like a confederacy of tribes who shared a common cultural and religious background, with each hailing the city of Tiwanaku as their major cultural centre. Whatever the truth, Tiwanaku's cultural, religious and political influence was widespread in the region in c. AD 500–900.

The Tiwanakans were an extremely advanced society, most notable for their sophisticated irrigation and terraced farming systems and monumental architecture that is impressive both artistically and as a feat of engineering. Tiwanaku was the capital of a theocratic state governed, like many states in the Americas, by priest-kings, with the help of courtiers and other administrators. Most of the population was made up of the common classes – artisans and farmers who cultivated crops, herded llamas and fished in Lake Titicaca.

Trade, using animal caravans as a means of transport, took place throughout the region of Tiwanakan influence. Pottery, textiles, metal objects such as tools and jewellery, precious stones, tobacco and hallucinogenic drugs were traded to areas such as the Brazilian Amazon, coastal Peru and Chile.

The city of Tiwanaku extended over four square kilometres (one and a half square miles). It was laid out on a grid system, aligned to the points of the compass. The city was ringed by a

moat, which may not have had a military purpose. Alan Kolata (Professor of Anthropology and Social Sciences at the USA's University of Chicago) suggested in 1993 that the moat functioned as a ceremonial aid: it creates the effect of an island, simulating a mythological island of creation. Crossing the moat while under the influence of hallucinogenic drugs, would have given a pilgrim to the cultural religious centre of Tiwandakan society a spiritually moving experience. The moat also acted as a means of distributing rain around the city, into canals that drained excess rainwater into the Tiwanaku river, thereby avoiding flooding.

The layout of the city consisted of a central core of ceremonial buildings, which was surrounded by a vast network of residential dwellings for the 30–40,000-strong population. The domestic zones may, as in other Tiwanakan sites found across the coastal desert and to the slopes of the Andes, have been divided into areas with members of different artisan groups, such as potters and metalworkers, living and working in their own districts. However, the majority of the population lived in the centre of terraced fields either on the valley sides or at lower altitudes in small village groups. Their houses were constructed out of stone with thatched roofs made of reeds and grasses and were often built on artificial, raised earthwork platforms to guard against the intermittent flooding to which the area was prone.

LEFT: Renderings of the human form, large and small, were important to the Tiwanakans. A doll found at Tiwanaku may have symbolized fertility in religious ceremonies, or within a family setting.

RIGHT: On the Kalasasaya mound, near the Gateway of the Sun, stand large anthropomorphic figures (often referred to as the Ponce Monoliths). These figures resemble pillars covered in relief carvings and some carry beakers.

The grand monolithic structures found in Tiwanaku's ceremonial centre are particularly remarkable. The city's pyramids and subterranean temples are the work of extremely skilled architects and builders. They even developed a system of sound amplification in the walls of their buildings, presumably to give an ethereal and spiritual quality to song and worship by adding resonance to the human voice and music.

The main god of the Tiwanakans was the so-called Staff God (also known as the Gateway God). It is not known by what name the Tiwanakans called this deity, as no written records have been preserved. In time, worship of the Staff God spread across the Andes: the Tiwanakan state religion was embraced by other tribes and settlements, bringing them under the influence of Tiwanaku. It is most likely that the Staff God was a sky or weather deity, and he was certainly linked to the summer solstice. Surviving images of the deity show a striking figure with a fierce face that is framed by a crown of the sun. Tears, representing rain, fall from his eyes. He carries two staffs, one in each hand, held high, perhaps representing lightning. His dress is ornate and highly patterned.

One of the most notable structures in Tiwanaku is the Gateway of the Sun, which was dedicated to the Staff God, and stands on top of the Kalasasaya mound (see below). The gateway is a monolithic structure nearly four metres (thirteen feet) high.

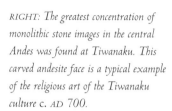

RIGHT: The greatest concentration of monolithic stone images in the central Andes was found at Tiwanaku. This carved andesite face is a typical example of the religious art of the Tiwanaku culture c. AD 700.

On top of the gateway is set a statue of the Staff God, surrounded by three lines of winged men and mythological condor men. Mask-like heads and fretwork form a foundation or step at the bottom of the structure. The simplicity of the gateway's design ensures that it has a powerful effect on observers, particularly on the occasion of the summer solstice, when the sun rose through the gateway. This suggests that the Gateway of the Sun may have been used as an astronomical calendar. However, because the Tiwanaku did not develop a written language, we may never know the true import of this figure and his gateway. What does seem apparent is that Tiwanaku became a centre for the worship of this god, visited by pilgrims from across the Tiwanakan region.

Other notable buildings of Tiwanaku include Akapana, Puma Punku, and Kalasasaya. Akapana was a huge step pyramid, believed to have been dedicated to the Staff God. Magnificent in its day, much of the temple's stone was plundered by sixteenth-century Spanish settlers for use in their own buildings.

The pyramid's base was constructed of perfectly cut and joined stone facing blocks. The building itself consisted of seven terraces, six of which were T-shaped with vertical stone pillars. The terrace walls are also constructed in typical Tiwanakan style, with mortarless, precision-joined masonry. The floors were made of hard-packed earth, perhaps the waste material produced when the moats surrounding each structure were dug. There were buildings and a sunken courtyard on top of the pyramid, thought to have been for the use of rulers and high priests as a place of worship and communion with the gods. Excavations of the courtyard have revealed a ceramic vessel in the form of a puma,

an animal that had sacred significance for the Tiwanakans. Also found at the site were silver, copper and ceramic artefacts used as ritual offerings.

Near to Akapana lies a partially subterranean temple. This rectangular building features forty-nine pillars decorated with stone heads, fused into the walls. These may represent revered ancestors of the Tiwanakans, or may depict the different ethnic groups that were part of the Tiwanakan empire.

The ceremonial centre features a second massive pyramid, architecturally similar to the Akapana, known as the Puma Punku. Some archaeologists have suggested that this structure was a counterpart of Akapana and that they were used in unison with one another during ceremonies. Both edifices have doorways that face the rising sun, indicative of the importance of sun worship for the Tiwanaku.

A low platform mound with a sunken central court, called the Kalasasaya, is located next to the Akapana. This structure measures 130 by 120 metres (425 by 395 feet). In the Kalasasaya forecourt lies another sunken court. The axis of this complex faces the equinoctial sunrise, again reinforcing the centrality of sun worship in the religion of Tiwanaku. This structure is believed to have had an administrative, political and religious function. Professor Kolata theorizes that the Kalasasaya was the seat of Tiwanaku's rulers. Worked gold, obsidian and lapis lazuli have been found in the sewer beneath the Kalasasaya, and metalsmiths' and stone-masons' tools in the palace itself, indicating the breadth of artisanry in the city.

The masonry work seen at Tiwanaku is extremely skilled. The assembly of the Tiwanakan structures required pinpoint accuracy, a difficult task, even using modern technology, while suspending

RIGHT: Although the origins of the Tiwanakan civilization are still unknown to historians, the civilization influenced a great deal of South America c. AD 250–750. The use of stone art spread throughout its sphere of influence. Religious symbolism and clean, angular lines typified Tiwakanan art, such as seen in this basalt monolithic figure, possibly representing a god, c. AD 700.

tremendous weight. The stones are carefully balanced and positioned, held in place by bars that slotted into carefully cut grooves in the stones. The sheer weight of the blocks, in excess of one hundred tons, and the precision demonstrated in the preparation of the stone, is remarkable, bearing in mind the relatively simple stone hammers, wooden wedges and abrasive sand that the Tiwanakan builders used as tools. The transportation of the massive blocks of stone was an impressive feat in itself, though archaeologists have yet to answer the question of how this was achieved.

One of the reasons why Tiwanaku thrived and was able to support a large population was the civilization's ingenious farming methods, which ensured an abundant supply of food. Tiwanaku was located at a great height, which meant that the land and its crops froze at night. The Tiwanakans devised a thermal system, providing sufficient warmth during the night to stave off frost and protect the crops: they cultivated fields that were raised on elevated platforms of earth and surrounded by moat-like irrigation ditches and canals. The design of raised fields allowed heat generated by the sun during the day to be stored in the walls of the platform and radiated back into the fields, thereby protecting crops during the night and early morning. Pond life, which lived in the ditches, produced organic material that could be used to fertilize the crops.

The crops that the farmers grew were the result of careful breeding from wild plants. Their main cereal crops included a hybrid of a corn plant that normally cannot thrive at that height, and potatoes that were specially bred and altered. They even developed a method of preserving vegetables, particularly potatoes, by dehydration. The method depended upon exposure to the blistering sun and the freezing cold of Tiwanakan nights, over a two-week period. This process reduced the vegetables to a dried, preserved state, which allowed them to be stored for later consumption.

It has been calculated that building and maintaining the earthworks and terraced fields required many more people, with a greater range of skills, than was needed to build the grandiose structures of the city centre. The major buildings may not have been constructed by groups of state engineers, as once believed. It is possible that farmers built the buildings in the city, undertaking the work as a form of public duty.

The textiles and clothing of the Tiwanakans were made from cotton, grown in irrigated fields in the lowland coastal strip, and wool from the domesticated alpaca. This animal produces fine wool that was woven into blankets and warm garments, which were necessary given the high altitudes. Another animal fundamental to the Tiwanaku civilization was the llama. This was a beast of burden, whose droppings were used as fertilizer on the terraced fields.

Despite the extraordinary technological accomplishments of the Tiwanakans, it is the small things that remind one of the people who built the society – the fragments of plaster and painted frescoes depicting daily events or religious ceremonies, found on the interior walls of the central buildings; the fingerprints of the

potter on a fragment of an earthenware pot; or the tools found buried within the walls, lost during a day's work centuries before.

Tiwanaku was a busy, productive and successful community. It thrived, at its peak, for approximately 200 years, until c. AD 900, when the balance of power began to shift away from Tiwanaku towards Pachacamac, a coastal Peruvian settlement close to modern-day Lima. The great highland states, including Tiwanaku, seemed to gradually lose their strength and spirit until the late fifteenth century AD, when perhaps the most powerful of all Andean civilizations blossomed – the Incas (see page 43). The Incas became a unifying force, through military might, their civilization developing from the remains of previous great

ABOVE: Carved tenon heads decorate the walls of a semi-subterranean temple, which is located in the Kalasasaya forecourt. To modern Western society, this symbolism may seem macabre, but the heads may have symbolized the benevolent presence of the gods/ancestors in a place which played host to religious, administraive and political functions and may, therefore, have helped to secure, in the eyes of the Tiwanakans, the smooth running of their society.

societies, including Tiwanaku, many of which they conquered and absorbed. To some extent, Tiwanaku lived on in the architecture, technology and culture of the Incas, but even these traces were lost when the Inca empire fell to the conquistadors in the sixteenth century (see Machu Picchu pages 42–49).

A thousand years ago, the landscape in the region was very different; the entire floodplain was covered with rows of lush raised gardens intersected with canals. The raised fields system was so successful that it could produce enough crops to sustain a sizeable populace. Yet the Tiwanakan settlement collapsed, for an as yet unknown reason. It is possible that there was a shift of power around a rival ideology, or an environmental disaster, such as a severe drought. Whatever the cause, the city began to decline in influence in c. AD 900 and was abandoned by its people in c. AD 1200.

Although it was abandoned, the city was never completely lost. The sixteenth-century Spanish settlers took stone from the city to build their homes and churches in nearby villages. Nineteenth-century visitors to the area paid tribute to the beauty of the ruins of the city. However, it was not until twentieth-century excavations that the history of the city began to be fully investigated. The site was declared a national monument in 1945. Bolivian archaeologist Carlos Ponce carried out intensive exploration of the site between 1952 and 1982. In the 1990s, Bolivian archaeologist Oswaldo Rivera and Alan Kolata teamed up to investigate the remnants of the raised field system in the plains around Tiwanaku. Excavation of the site continues today – the pyramid of Puma Punku, for example, is a recent discovery – and the site was named a World Heritage Site in 2000.

Today, thanks to centuries of subjugation by the Spanish-descended ruling élite, a harsh climate, lack of education and resources, and ignorance of their ancestors' farming methods, the people of the Tiwanaku district, the Aymara, are some of the poorest people on earth. However, despite their poverty, they are fighting to reclaim their lost glory. They have begun a process of re-education, learning to use their own resources and skills rather than using western methods. Although the city is long dead, its surrounding lands still feed the descendents of the once-great people of Tiwanaku.

ANCIENT WISDOM MAY SAVE THE PEOPLE

T HE PEOPLE OF TIWANAKU were responsible for huge advances in agricultural technology. They solved difficult problems of farming in a high-altitude, cold and risky mountain environment, producing a highly efficient system that used raised fields, terraces and sunken gardens to allow Tiwanaku farmers to feed thousands in a metropolitan community. On the basis of this success an empire was formed. The great leaders that drove that expansion have long since turned to dust, but their agricultural brainchild has been born anew, thanks to modern research.

"T HE HIGH CIVILIZATION of Tiwanaku is long dead but some of its agricultural knowledge and much of the engineered landscape has survived to the present. Archaeologists and agronomists have recovered this indigenous knowledge through the study of ancient crops, technologies, irrigation canals, raised fields and terraces. Modern farming techniques such as heavy tractors, fertilizers and pesticides introduced from the West have had limited success in alleviating poverty. By reintroducing some of the time-tested techniques of their forefathers, farmers may be able to raise crops more efficiently and sustainably."

DR CLARK ERICKSON, DEPARTMENT OF ANTHROPOLOGY,
UNIVERSITY OF PENNSYLVANIA, PHILADELPHIA, USA

LEFT: The largest structure at Tiwanaku, the Akapana step pyramid, consists of seven terraces rising to 17 m and 200 m (56 ft and 656 ft) per side with a sunken court, 50 m (164 ft) a side, set into the top. A row of tall worked stones running roughly east/west stand at the Akapan summit.

LEFT: The Akapana dominates the centre of this aerial photograph. When first recorded, this pyramid was largely covered with earth but after several decades of excavation, some walls have been uncovered. It was built originally to open towards the east. The dark line across the lower part of the photograph is the railway line to La Paz, the Bolivian captial. The rectangular outline above the Akapana is the Kalasasaya enclosure.

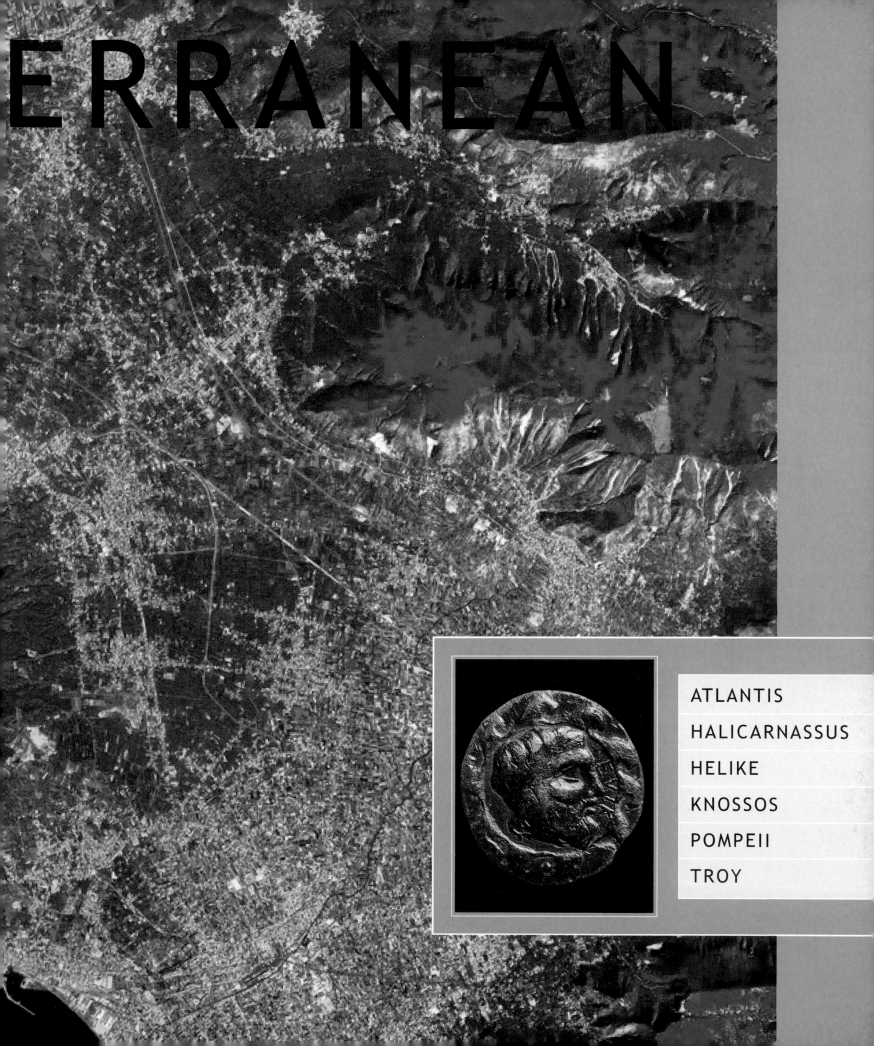

ERRANEAN

ATLANTIS

HALICARNASSUS

HELIKE

KNOSSOS

POMPEII

TROY

ATLANTIS
PLATO'S PUZZLE

"ON THIS ISLAND OF ATLANTIS had arisen a powerful and remarkable dynasty of kings, who ruled the whole island ... This dynasty ... attempted to enslave, at a single stroke, your country and ours and all the territory within the strait ... There were earthquakes and floods of extraordinary violence, and in a single dreadful day and night ... the island of Atlantis was ... swallowed up by the sea and vanished."

TIMAEUS 25, TIMAEUS AND CRITIAS, PLATO, TRANSLATED BY SIR DESMOND LEE

THE GREAT ATHENIAN ARISTOCRAT PHILOSOPHER AND scholar, Plato (c. 428–347 BC), was the first person to record the story of Atlantis. But is Atlantis just a story, an elaborate fiction devised to espouse the philosopher's ideology, or does it have basis in fact? This question has vexed academics for centuries. The tale of Atlantis is one of a powerful civilization, highly advanced and capable of both exquisite artistry and fierce war, but which faced catastrophe in retribution for its misdeeds, in particular its attempted invasion of Greece.

This apparently mythical civilization causes widespread fascination in popular culture. Scores of books on the subject were published in the twentieth century alone. It is perhaps the similarity between our own civilization and the Bronze Age Atlanteans, particularly their instability due to war and environmental flux, which strikes a chord with us. Our world is constantly wracked with war and unrest, much like the world Plato describes in his story of Atlantis. Our world is in the grip of climate change resulting in violent storms, flooding and extremes of weather that in some parts of the world threaten our way of life on a seasonal basis. The Atlantean world, according to Plato, also suffered at the hands of nature. Perhaps this resonance allows us to read a warning from history in the Atlantis story.

If there is some factual element to this myth, where do we begin to search for evidence? First, by examining Plato's text in his two works, the *Timaeus* and the *Critias*.

Plato's account of Atlantis is related as deriving from the notable Athenian political figure Solon (c. sixth century BC). Solon, whose work is thought to have greatly influenced Plato, reportedly heard stories of Atlantis from Egyptian priests while on a visit to Egypt. The priests described Atlantis as a powerful island empire that had sought to dominate the Mediterranean world in c. 9500 BC.

The story portrayed the Atlanteans as heavy handed and often brutal. To Solon, a social and economic reformer, the Atlanteans must have sounded like oppressors – they had made an aggressive stance across Europe, culminating in their challenge of Athenian supremacy. He reported that the Atlanteans' attempts to expand their empire were terminated when Athens repulsed their army. Soon after the defeat of Atlantis' forces, the city and all its inhabitants were destroyed by an earthquake and flood that submerged the city. The Athenian army also drowned in the flood.

Plato characterizes the civilization as being a centre of advanced learning and great knowledge, and governed by an ideal political system that eventually corrupted and began to act as an instrument of destruction and war. The civilization's downfall came about when the rich and learned Atlanteans became greedy

OPPOSITE: Did a great volcanic eruption destroy an advanced civilization 9,000 years ago? Is the Atlantis story a political allegory or perhaps a retelling of the destruction of Thera?

ABOVE: The origin of the Atlantis story is unclear but it certainly begins in written form with Plato. This painting of early Greek philosophers of the fourth century BC shows Plato and Aristotle, and is taken from Raphael's sixteenth-century AD fresco "The School of Athens" painted for Pope Julius II.

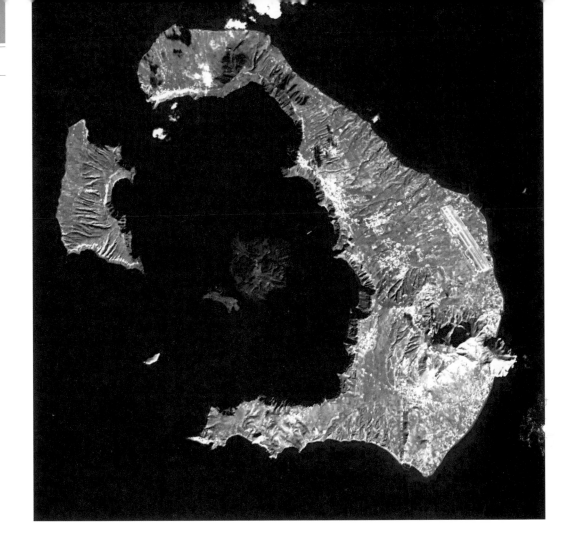

RIGHT: *A bird's eye view from space, made by the ASTER (Advanced Spaceborne Thermal Emission and Reflection Radiometer) spacecraft, of Thera/Santorini. The data was obtained on 21 November 2000 and clearly shows the underwater crater that marks the point of origin of the great eruption c. 1628 BC.*

for more lands, power and wealth. Their greed led them to their ultimate destruction at the hands of Poseidon, the god of the sea. Plato's account of Atlantis is a moral tale warning of the follies of war and the pursuit of wealth.

Noting some similarities between the history of Athens and that of Atlantis, some historians have suggested that Plato used the story of Atlantis as an allegorical device to discuss contentious issues of his day. Shortly after Plato was born in c. 428 BC, Athens went to war with Sparta – a state with which Athens had long had a love/hate relationship. Athens' supremacy came from its naval fleet, Sparta's from its land army. This war, the Peloponnesian War, ensued for twenty _____ ntil Plato was thirty years old, when Sparta finally defea___ __ns.

This long and ultimately unsu___ ssful war may have informed Plato's line of thought when relaying his story of Atlantis. Plato was a teacher and philosopher who believed in the power of democracy – his was a society ruled by a democracy, but a democracy in the hands of a ruling élite. The poorer people were disenfranchised and had no say in the running of the state. Historically, it is usually the ruling elite who start wars, not the

common people. Did Plato simply manip___late Solon's account of Atlantis to convey his own political opinions ___ ___ way in which a seemingly perfect society might have in___ _ failings?

The description of Atlantis, in particular of the capital city, may owe much to Plato's fascination with mathematical perfection and what he saw as the ideal division of resources. He was given to rationalizing the world around him in mathematical terms. Consequently, his description of Atlantis may have been more a concept of the ideal city-state as he imagined it, than a state that actually existed.

In Plato's account, Atlantis was a large, mountainous island in the Atlantic Ocean, west of the Pillars of Hercules. The location of these "pillars" is something of a mystery, further frustrating attempts to understand Plato's text. It is possible that the pillars were in fact the Straits of Gibraltar. The island was long and narrow, with the two longer coastlines facing north and south. It possessed bountiful mineral resources, lush woodland and plentiful animal stocks. On its southern face was a vast, fertile plain, stretching over an area 603 by 402 kilometres (375 by 275 miles). This plain was populated by prosperous, contented people;

RIGHT: A thirteenth-century BC
*fisherman from Thera, as depicted in
Minoan-style Theran art.*

surrounded by mountains; and criss-crossed by a series of canals, probably laid out in a perfect grid pattern – further enforcing the notion of Plato's mathematically perfect city-state. The canals were used to transport timber and minerals across the island.

The capital city seems a fantastical place. It was built in a series of three concentric rings; a transport and irrigation canal separated each ring, and each ring formed an island in itself. Again, the ring-structure of the city suggests the mind of a mathematician in its design. Four bridges linked the ring-islands, the fourth bridge joining the islands to the outer city. The city was built immediately south of the grid of canals that traversed the southern plain. The city had access to the sea via another canal, at its southernmost point, which cut through the outer city. The greater city area stretched for ten kilometres (six miles) in all directions, enclosed by a boundary wall.

A visitor travelling into Atlantis from the sea, via the southern canal, would c   to a harbour. Travelling over land, across the first of the bridges,   ould enter the largest ring-island. This was the city's leisure area, which contained parkland and lavish gardens, complete with gymnasiums, stadiums and equitation centres. Its size and dominance, encircling the rest of the inner city, indicates the importance of leisure in the city. Continuing his journey, the visitor would cross to the smaller ring-island, where he would find residences, towers and gates. Finally, the last bridge would take him to the very heart of the city – the citadel.

Towers and gates flanked the entrance from the bridge. Immediately opposite the bridge lay the great shrine to the god Poseidon. Poseidon was, in legend, said to have been the creator of Atlantis, building the city in order to protect his love, Cleito. The citadel contained a vast temple to Poseidon, and its pinnacled roof was said to be so high that its spires touched the clouds. The temple housed a gold sculpture of Poseidon at the reins of a chariot drawn by dolphins and sea nymphs.

Lush gardens lay to the east of the shrine, irrigated by freshwater springs. Sparkling fountains were set in the grounds of fabulous places of learning.   utheastern extremity of the citadel lay the palace of the gr   uynasty of Atlantean kings – each born of Poseidon's love, Cleito. It was a remarkable domain – a place of wealth, great learning, art and achievement. It is little surprise that this image of a utopian state has been preserved for centuries and still resonates today.

Could Atlantis have existed anywhere but in Plato's mind? It is, of course, possible that a great nation built such a place. It is more

likely, however, that Plato's portrayal of Atlantis owed more to his vision of the perfect state and the ideal city, marred by a dangerous desire for imperialist expansion. But if such a place did exist, where could it have been located?

Many hypotheses have been put forward as to the exact location of the lost island. Some people believe that Atlantis was located in the area now occupied by Lake Poopo, in the Bolivian altiplano region of Oruro, near the border with Chile. Others suggest that the city was on an island that split apart to become Antarctica and the British Isles. The main clue to the island's possible location is the time of its purported annihilation. Some historians believe that Plato's story contains mathematical errors, and that the destruction of Atlantis' took place in the seventeenth century BC. If this is the case, it is more feasible that Plato recorded an actual historical event. A huge volcanic eruption occurred in c. 1628 BC, in ancient Thera (known today as Santorini), the southernmost of the Cyclades islands in the Aegean Sea. This eruption made the 1883 explosion of Krakatoa in Indonesia look feeble by comparison. The Krakatoa eruption, one of the most devastating ever to be recorded, saw ash ejected from the maw of the volcano to a height of 80

kilometres (50 miles). The explosion was heard 3,200 kilometres (1,990 miles) away in Australia. The eruption gave birth to a new island, more than 800 metres (2,600 feet) high and created a sea basin 280 metres (920 feet) deep. The violence of the eruption triggered huge tsunamis (tidal waves) that flooded the coastal regions of nearby Sumatra and Java, destroying everything in their path and killing 40,000 people. Massive islands of pumice stone floated on the ocean for many years after.

Yet the eruption at Thera was four times as powerful as that of Krakatoa. The air turned black for miles around as the volcano tore the landscape apart, destroying the centre of the island and leaving only an outer ring of land behind. The vast soot cloud would have blocked out the sun for months, possibly years, making it impossible to grow crops. Lava flows, ash bursts and mega-tsunamis would have devastated the land and its people.

In the 1930s, Greek archaeologist Spyridon Nikolaou Marinatos (1901–1974) – who had earned great respect following his discovery of the site of the Battle of Thermopylae (480 BC) and the burial ground linked to the Battle of Marathon (490 BC) – put forward the idea that Minoan Crete (see Knossos, pages 83–89) and Atlantis were one and the same. Working from a hypothesis first postulated in a paper published by K.T. Frost in 1913, titled *The Critias and Minoan Crete*, Marinatos sought to prove that the Theran volcano had destroyed Plato's near-mythical island power base.

Thera was occupied before 2000 BC and was known at this time as Calliste (most beautiful). In 1967, Marinatos found a wonderfully preserved city close to Akrotiri in southern Thera. Its style of architecture, with three-storey houses, typically built on many levels, sumptuous furnishings and fine pottery, was evidence of an advanced Bronze Age culture (*c.* 2500–1000 BC). The city was so advanced that its inhabitants enjoyed the benefits of running water in their houses. The style of art, with beautiful frescoes featuring splendid detail and decoration, seemed to indicate that Thera had been influenced by Minoan civilization, even if it had not been part of it politically. It is possible that a folk memory of the splendour of Bronze Age Thera, and the catastrophe that destroyed it in *c.* 1628 BC, survived to Plato's time, and inspired him to write his works on Atlantis.

During his excavations at Thera, Marinatos realized that the Therans had returned after the first volcanic eruption in an attempt to reclaim their houses and restore their civilization. However, the great volcano erupted twice more, finally covering the city in a layer of ash nearly 25 metres (80 feet) deep. Marinatos believed the final blow for Minoan Crete and Thera came when the mouth of the volcano crumbled, triggering huge disturbances of the land and consequential inundation of the settlements by the sea. There are, however, difficulties with this rationale. The eruption of Thera occurred at least 100, and possibly 200, years before the cataclysm that devastated the superb palaces of Crete.

The study of Atlantis means working on conjecture and hypothesis, with few solid facts. Research continues, and may do so for many decades. Whenever new finds of submerged settlements occur, such as the recent discovery of Helike (see page 80) in the Gulf of Corinth or finds in the Black Sea, both of which occurred in 2000, there is excited speculation that Atlantis has been found at last.

We may never know whether Plato's story was an elaboration of a real catastrophe, or a brilliant fantasy. However, the story of Atlantis still has an extraordinary resonance. It may be read as a warning from Plato, urging us to curb our excesses and war-like activities, to be humane to our neighbours and the environment, or face the consequences.

SEEKING TRUTH IN MYTH AND LEGEND

UNRAVELLING TRUTH from metaphor is never easy, particularly when the material in question is more than two thousand years old and written by a man renowned for his visionary stories. Nonetheless, it is possible that Plato's story of Atlantis is grounded in truth. However, there are problems with his facts.

"I HAD THE PRIVILEGE of knowing Spyridon Marinatos, the Director General of Greek Antiquities. He was totally convinced that Atlantis once existed and that it was in fact Minoan Crete. However, the problem is that the number of people, the size of the island and the age of the civilization as given to us by Plato, are far too great. Plato suggested that the civilization was destroyed something like 11,500 years ago. At that time, Europe was coming out of an ice age, but Plato described a very advanced Bronze Age civilization. The two just do not tally. Professor Galanopoulos, the vulcanologist, suggested that an additional zero had been added in translation to all large numbers. Consequently, the date would be more like 900 years before Solon's visit to Egypt. If so, and we apply the same logic to population and island size, we produce a more acceptable description more in accordance with Minoan Crete and its destruction by the explosive eruption of Thera."

PROFESSOR ARCHIBALD ROY, SENIOR RESEARCH FELLOW, DEPARTMENT OF PHYSICS AND ASTRONOMY, GLASGOW UNIVERSITY, SCOTLAND

HALICARNASSUS
THE MARK OF MAUSOLUS

H ALICARNASSUS, FOUNDED BY THE GREEKS IN c. 900 BC, was home to the tomb of Mausolus, one of the Seven Wonders of the World. It was located in Caria, in the arc of Anatolia, on the Gulf of Kos, Turkey. Today it is the modern city of Bodrum. Culturally, Halicarnassus was part of the Greek world, although it was held under Persian rule for long periods of time. The settlement reached the zenith of its prosperity in the fourth century BC under the reign of Mausolus, the satrap (district governor) appointed by the Persian regime. He reigned from 377 to 353 BC, with his sister-wife Artemisia at his side (it was customary for satraps in the region of Caria to marry their sisters).

Mausolus was clever, cunning and something of a visionary. He was steeped in Greek philosophy and its approach to life. He spoke and read Greek and entreated his communities to engage in a political system based on the Athenian model of democracy. Despite these tendencies, Mausolus remained aligned to Persia; he took part in a revolt of the satraps in c. 360 BC, but managed to recover his position with the Persian authorities when the revolt failed. Mausolus was a canny politician and a true survivor.

The satrap was, in theory, a ruler controlled by the Persian hierarchy, but in practice it was a self-governing autocratic role. Mausolus was an acquisitive man, determined to play a larger role in the politics of the region; he extended the reach of his power to include the islands of Rhodes and Kos, among others. When Mausolus became satrap, he decided to shift the capital of his territory from Mylasa (known today as Milas) to Halicarnassus. Although little information is available on the population and size of the settlement at that time, we do know that Halicarnassus was referred to as a "town" when Mausolus ordered its expansion. Mausolus saw its potential as a strategic base: the natural coastline offered an ideal environment for fortification, and the town's location would allow it to thrive as a centre for trade and naval activity.

Mausolus uprooted many of his subjects, notably from eight settlements on the Halicarnassus peninsula, and forced them to resettle in Halicarnassus and other cities that were developing. Many of the people of Halicarnassus were Carians from nearby towns and villages.

OPPOSITE: Where once one of the Seven Wonders of the ancient world stood — the former Mausoleum of King Mausolus from Halicarnassus (now known as Bodrum, in Turkey) — today there is nothing but ruins.

ABOVE: The fabulous stepped pyramid roof of the Mausoleum, surmounted by a statue of a four-horse chariot, was given new life in this artist's reconstruction in a hand-coloured woodcut c. AD 1890 by Oskar Mothes (1828–1903).

Under Mausolus' rule, Halicarnassus developed into a large and splendid city, which was, in essence, Mausolus' homage to the Grecian city-states he so admired. Among the city's notable features were three large citadels, ringed by a huge fortified wall. The wall had guard towers along its perimeter, and the three citadels themselves were heavily reinforced and fortified. The buildings of the expanded city were modelled on Greek settlements, with a vast encompassing wall, marketplaces, Greek temples and a hero's tomb. There were also two harbours by the marketplace, from which warships would set sail for battles and fishermen carried out their work. The settlement was protected with a fortress and a palace was built on land opposite the bay. Little is known about the size of the enlarged settlement, because of historical destruction and looting at the site.

Mausolus' reign was marked by the rapid adoption of the city-state mentality espoused by Greece. His people paid dearly for his plans, facing heavy taxes and enjoying little self-determination; his decision to abolish settlements and remake others in Greece's image is a case in point. In some ways, these measures were at odds with his apparent desire to emulate the Athenian democratic mentality. However, while his actions cannot have been entirely popular, his long reign appears to have been successful, and Mausolus and his sister-wife were largely responsible for the spread of the Hellenistic way of life throughout their domain – something that Mausolus believed passionately in.

Athenian democratic principles, embraced by Mausolus, functioned via Sortition, a process that appointed government officials via election by lot. Candidates offered themselves for election, much as political candidates do today in Western democracies. The government had a council of 500 individuals. In the judiciary, judges and magistrates were appointed by lot and this process ensured that new individuals were appointed regularly when a functionary failed in his role or chose to move on. This system had relevance only to the top tier of society – approximately ten per cent of the population, but did at least make for a reasonably fair and stable form of government and a certain amount of education and learning was needed to fulfill these roles within government, ensuring education for the people. The Athenian way of life that Mausolus so admired was based around regal sports such as equestrian pursuits and athletics. For the lucky few, it was a life of privilege. The working classes did not fare as well, the regal sports were beyond their reach and they toiled to ensure the lifestyle of the rich. Nonetheless, Athenian culture strove to offer the best for all and this adoption of the Athenian way must have been a remarkable and positive change for the people of the region around Halicarnassus.

As influential as Mausolus was in life, it was his death in 353 BC that sparked a series of events that ensured his place in history. The temple erected in his honour after his death, the "Mausoleum" (the origin of the word now used to refer to a grand tomb), was an astonishingly beautiful building, and it was agreed at the time to be one of the Seven Wonders of the ancient world.

The building of the tomb is believed to have been commissioned by Artemisia. It is unlikely that Mausolus died without making provision for a tomb, but the grandiose nature of the memorial was apparently conceived by his grieving wife. Artemisia was distraught by her brother-husband's death, even, reportedly, swallowing his ashes. She organized a great athletic games to be held in his honour, at which Theopompus, a traveller and well-regarded author of the fourth century BC, is said to have been declared champion. Such games were an integral part of the religious rites of the Greeks and Greek-influenced cultures, such as Halicarnassus. Champions of the games were held up as gods on earth. Artemisia's games were successful, but she also wanted a permanent memorial for her husband. Although we do not know the true cost of the Mausoleum, it is evident, from the grandeur of its design, that Artemisia spent a good deal of her state's wealth on building the Mausoleum. Artemisia died in 350 BC before she could see the tomb's completion, and was laid to rest alongside her beloved husband.

Artemisia had turned to Mausolus' Greece for the tomb's craftsmen. Chief among them was the renowned sculptor Scopas (pronounced "Skops"). He created elaborate friezes, some disturbing in nature, depicting battles and death scenes, at many of the Hellenistic world's most important temples, including Athena Alea, at Tegea, Greece, and the renovated temple of Ephesus on the west coast of Asia Minor (Greece). Four other distinguished sculptors – Bryaxis, Leochares, Praxiteles and Timotheos – worked alongside Scopas. The fact that Scopas, who was credited as the sole architect of the temple at Tegea, needed four equally skilled men working with him at Halicarnassus indicates the huge scale of the enterprise.

The Mausoleum was built on a site that stretched over 20,000 square metres (24,000 square yards). It was a huge and impressive edifice, set on a hill, positioned to overlook the city, ensuring that

ABOVE: *The Temple erected in honour of Mausolus, which became known as the "Mausoleum", had many levels and ornate sculptures as seen in this hand-coloured woodcut after a drawing by Ferdinand Knab (1834–1902). It was a truly magnificent building worthy of its status as a "Wonder of the World".*

ABOVE: *The beauty and power of the horse was captured with breathtaking skill in the sculptures of the chariot horses, as can be seen in this surviving sculptural fragment from the top of the Mausoleum.*

it was a monument never far from view or from the minds of the people. The site must have been breathtaking. It was accessed from the east, through a giant gate that led into the zone of the Mausoleum itself. Its foundations were carefully designed around a drainage system to protect it from flooding and dampness.

The structure of the Mausoleum was relatively simple: it was rectangular in shape, and took the form of a large stepped podium supporting a colonnade. The structure was topped by an elaborate twenty-four-stepped pyramid roof, on top of which there was a statue depicting a four-horse chariot with Mausolus at the reins.

The distinguished Roman admiral and author Gaius Plinius Secundus (born AD 23), often referred to as Pliny the Elder, who died attempting a naval rescue at Pompeii in AD 79 (see Pompeii, pages 90–99), left a description of the tomb's structure. In all, including the chariot sculpture, the edifice stood 45 metres (150 feet) high, 38 metres (125 feet) long and 32 metres (105 feet) wide. Pliny estimated that the colonnade around the building stretched 15 metres (50 feet) in height. The podium was about 15–18 metres (50–60 feet) high; the pyramid nearly 8 metres (26 feet), and the chariot sculpture 5–8 metres (16–26 feet) high.

Two friezes ran around the podium, which was formed of three tiers. Two of the tiers were adorned with friezes. One depicted the legendary battle between the Greeks and the Amazons, the race of warrior women – a favourite choice of subject for Greek artists at that time. The other frieze depicted another mythological scene, that of the battle between the Centaurs (creatures who were half-man, half-horse), and the Lapiths, people of Thessalay.

Statues that were approximately life-sized ringed the third tier of the podium. There were at least fifteen statues on each side of the tomb. The artistry of the statues was supreme. The figures were beautifully rendered: their draped clothing, every fold, and every detail, faithfully represented in stone. Among the statues were figures of Mausolus and Artemisia. The statue of Mausolus shows a benign, neatly bearded man, with shoulder-length hair swept back from a noble brow.

The colonnaded tier of the tomb was encircled by approximately thirty-six columns, between each of which was set life-sized statues thought to be depictions of the ruling classes. Around the top of the colonnade were statues of stalking lions, posed as if guarding the twenty-four steps that led to the chariot statue on top of the pyramid.

The building was faced with brilliant white marble and limestone, and must have shone in the fierce Anatolian sun. The

inner structure of the tomb was lined with local volcanic stone that shone emerald green, throwing the white of the marble and limestone into sharp relief.

Alexander the Great conquered Halicarnassus in 334 BC. He paid his respects to the site rather than destroying it. Alexander was also greatly influenced by the Greeks and built cities modelled on Greek ones, as Mausolus did. Alexander also adopted the concept of the mausoleum. The old city of Halicarnassus fell into disrepair after countless attacks, even by pirates in the first century BC, but the Mausoleum stood intact for many centuries until it suffered heavy damage in a terrible earthquake that ravaged the city in AD 1304.

ABOVE: The great man, Mausolus, was immortalized in stone by the remarkable sculptors of the Mausoleum (above left), as was his loving wife Artemisia (above right). Their love has transcended time in our culture (even now we regularly use the word "mausoleum") and in history thanks to Artemisia's determination to build a wondrous tribute to her husband.

ABOVE: *The battle of the Greeks and the Amazons was captured in a marble frieze, sculpted c. 350 BC, on the Mausoleum of Halicarnassus.*

ABOVE RIGHT: *In this detail of the frieze of the battle of the Greeks and Amazons, from the Mausoleum, it is apparent how fierce the Greeks (and Greek-influenced states) believed these mythical Amazonian women to be.*

Halicarnassus was later ruled by Antigonus I (382–301 BC), a famous Macedonian general who was commanded by Alexander the Great. He was a a good ruler who aligned Halicarnassus with Athens. The Ptolemaic Dynasty of Egyptian rulers, who reigned during the period 305–145 BC took control of Halicarnassus c. 281–197 BC, but the city achieved independence for nearly seven decades until it fell under Roman rule in 129 BC and eventually became a bishopric, in the early Christian era.

Crusaders – Knights of Saint John of Malta – who had occupied the ancient city in the thirteenth century, used the stone of the damaged Mausoleum to fortify their castle – the Crusaders were Christians and felt justified in plundering the Mausoleum as it was a pagan memorial. The Crusaders needed to fortify the castle from attack, as by c. 1500 the native Turks had developed a cannon that could destroy walls.

In c. 1522, after several hundred years of plundering the stone of the Mausoleum, the knights finally broke the seal of the tomb, entering the great double doors and stepping down into the burial chamber itself. They began to loot it of its precious objects, statuary and possibly even gems. However, lack of time on the day of the discovery forced them to leave the chamber largely intact – the retreat had already been sounded, and the Knights, who were under curfew, were called back to the castle for the night. When they returned the next day, only some fine fabric and decorative jewels were left – robbers had finished the crusaders' work overnight. This was a sad end to a fabulous memorial.

Little remains of the Mausoleum today. The statues that the crusader's had taken from the tomb to their new castle at the renamed Bodrum were acquired by a British ambassador in the early nineteenth century. He gave them to the curators of the British Museum in London. Shortly thereafter, in 1846, Sir Charles

WITHOUT WONDER

ONE OF TURKEY'S WONDERS of the ancient world, the Mausoleum of Mausolus, was destroyed by the actions of nature, thieves, acquisitive archaeologists and occupying forces seeking workable masonry. We have been deprived of an opportunity to experience a true marvel and, perhaps more importantly, a chance to understand the mind of Artemisia. She was clearly a remarkable woman, one who so loved her husband that she created a new art form, often copied but never matched, to celebrate his life.

"HALICARNASSUS is quite impressive as the site of an ancient city, with many layers of settlement revealed. As for the fabled Mausoleum, today it is but a hole in the ground, a very large hole with a quite substantial model of the structure, to give some idea as to what it looked like. It is nonetheless a hole in the ground. It is a terrible shame that it was robbed of its bricks and masonry centuries ago to build the Crusader castle, which is close by. There is not much to see when you remember the structure was considered to be one of the Seven Wonders of the World and made such a lasting impression in ancient times on the writers who described the tomb. It's a tragedy that it's been lost."

DR ROGER MATTHEWS, INSTITUTE OF ARCHAEOLOGY, UNIVERSITY COLLEGE, LONDON

Thomas Newton (1816–1894) was despatched by the museum to recover more relics. Newton had been a member of the museum staff for six years before he was entrusted with the mission to find Mausolus' wonder.

With only the works of ancient writers as a guide, Newton bought a small section of land in Halicarnassus that he thought was likely to harbour buried remains. He put in test pits and discovered foundations and evidence of steps. He knew that he had found the Mausoleum. He purchased more of the land on the museum's behalf, and found extensive fragments of the frieze depicting the battle between the Greeks and the Amazons. In addition, he found one of the wheels of the chariot statue from the top of the structure and fragments of the pyramid roof. The most exciting finds, however, were the statues of Mausolus and Artemisia from the colonnade.

These finds were shipped back to Britain, to a great fanfare. Upon their arrival in London, in October 1859, one journal reported that the Mausoleum, "for architectural design, the excellence of its sculptures, and the interest of its associations, is not surpassed by any of the existing remains of antiquity" (London Illustrated News).

Excavations have continued since the 1860s. In the twentieth century, the entire plan of the Mausoleum was established and the method of its construction was ascertained. Little of the Mausoleum has been found intact, apart from the materials recovered by Newton. The ruins of the city of Halicarnassus are still visible above ground, as are the walls of Mausolus' palace. The Crusader fort is intact and great white marble blocks, looted from the tomb, can be seen in its structure.

HELIKE
POSEIDON'S DOMAIN

I

N 373 BC, DISASTER STRUCK HELIKE (PRONOUNCED "hell-eek-ie"), the principal city in a confederation of twelve cities in the region of Achaia (or Achaea), on the southwestern shore of the Gulf of Corinth. An earthquake of magnitude seven shook the city, which was then swamped by a massive tsunami (tidal wave).

At the time of the catastrophe, Helike was part of the Hegemony of Sparta, a period from 404 to 371 BC when Sparta – a militaristic city-state of ancient Greece, founded in c. 1000 BC – exercised influence over military and governmental decisions in the region. For that reason, there were ten Spartan warships in the harbour on the night of the earthquake. The ships were swamped and cast to the seabed, and it is possible that their wrecks survive (see box, page 81).

Helike dates back to the Bronze Age (c. 2500–1000 BC). By the time of its destruction, its fame had spread far and wide, being reported in many classical sources including Homer's *Iliad*. Homer recorded that Helike provided warships for the Greek commander Agamemnon's battle against Troy (see Troy, pages 100–109.

Perhaps ironically, the city had been the site of a temple and sanctuary dedicated to Poseidon, the god of the sea and earthquakes. The Greek writer Pausanias (AD 143–176) described the site. He wrote in his *Guide to Greece*, "You come to ... a place on the sea called Helike. Here used to be situated a city ... where the Ionians had a very holy sanctuary of Elikonian Poseidon ... [it] is this sort of shock alone that leaves no trace on the ground that men ever dwelt there. This was the type of earthquake, they say,

OPPOSITE: These early Bronze Age walls of prehistoric Helike were excavated in 2001. The discovery of Helike is a story that will unfold for many decades to come.

ABOVE: This bronze sculpture of Poseidon, god of the sea and earthquakes, dates from c. 460 BC and was sculpted by the Greek artist Calamis. It was recovered off the coast of Cape Artemision, and stands approximately 2 m (6½ ft) high.

77

that ... levelled Helike to the ground, and that it was accompanied by another disaster in the season of winter. The sea flooded a great part of the land, and covered up the whole of Helike all round. Moreover, the tide was so deep in the grove of Poseidon that only the tops of the trees remained visible ... the tidal wave swallowed up Helike and every man in it ... the ruins ... are visible, but not plainly now as they were once, because they are corroded by the salt water."

A warning of sorts preceded the disaster. The Roman author Aelian (AD 170–235) wrote in his study *On the Characteristics of Animals*, "For five days before Helike disappeared all the mice and martens and snakes and centipedes and beetles and every other creature of that kind in the town left in a body by the road that leads to Keryneia. And the people of Helike seeing this happening

BELOW: Dr Steven Soter of the American Museum of Natural History in New York, and Dr Dora Katsonopoulou, director of the Helike Project, discoverers of Helike, standing on early Bronze Age walls excavated in 2000.

OPPOSITE: This coin clearly shows the head of Poseidon and inscription "ELIK". The obverse shows a trident flanked by dolphins, confirming it as a coin from the civilization that built ancient Helike.

were filled with amazement.". Sadly, the people of Helike could not interpret this warning and perished.

The destruction of Helike must have come as a great blow. It was the most important city in Achaia and a major centre of Greek culture. The temple of Poseidon was a well-known place of asylum for fugitives and transients, fleeing injustice or seeking protection from wrongdoers. A definitive description of the city still eludes us, but current excavation and research work at the site may eventually reveal the extent and structure of this ancient city.

Although the city was about two kilometres (one and a quarter miles) from the sea, both the city outskirts and the city centre were submerged. The news travelled quickly. People from miles around heard that Poseidon had raised the sea by an earthquake against his own house. The Achaians sent 2,000 men to help, but they were too late to rescue anyone – nor could they recover the bodies. Sailors reported ghosts from the disaster for ages after: some said that there was a submerged bronze statue of Poseidon in the strait, standing erect, holding a seahorse in his hand, which was dangerous for those who fished with nets.

Many archaeologists have sought the ruins of Helike, but the severity of the earthquake and the nature of the inundation put the city out of reach of the traditional techniques of archaeology. A trial magnetometer survey (a sensor that detects the magnetic fields of iron and steel objects) of the seabed and in fields near the shore, carried out in 1966 by the University of Pennsylvania at the request of the Director of Greek Antiquities, Spyridon Marinatos (see page 66), who was particularly keen to find Helike, failed to discover traces of the city.

In 1988, the Helike Project, directed by Greek archaeologist Dora Katsonopoulou and Steven Soter, a scientist from the American Museum of Natural History in New York, renewed the search for the lost city. They began with a sonar survey of eight square kilometres (three square miles) of sea floor in the Gulf of Corinth. In such surveys, the sonar is towed behind a boat and transmits sound waves in a triangular pattern towards the sea floor. The reflected sound waves are monitored by the sonar's sensors to produce a computer-image of the surface of the seabed. The results of the survey revealed evidence of seismic disturbances, but no obvious signs of the city on, or beneath, the sea floor.

Paul Kronfield, a geophysicist who ran the survey, found ten shallow anomalies (irregularities) under the seabed, and their appearance suggested that they might be man-made rather than natural phenomena. Soter, remembering the story of the ten Spartan warships at harbour in Helike, speculated that the anomalies might be the lost ships. The ships might produce strong sonar signatures because they would have been filled with stone ballast and may have had bronze battering rams fitted to their prows for use during battle. These items would stand out from the sea bed in the survey results as being man-made objects.

After their sonar survey showed that the remains of Helike were not under the sea, Katsonopoulou and Soter transferred their search to the coastal plain. They reasoned that the site of the once-submerged city might have become dry land due to the shifting of the coastline in the last 2,400 years.

Between 1991 and 2001, the team drilled ninety-five boreholes, to the depth of around 20 metres (65 feet), along the coastal plain, stretching over an area of about 10 square kilometres (4 square miles). They found ceramic material in many of the sediment cores removed from the boreholes. Radiocarbon dating indicated that the layers containing pottery spanned the eras from the Bronze Age, beginning c. 2500 BC, to the Byzantine era (c. AD 330–1453), suggesting habitation of the area long before and long after the time of Helike's destruction. These were tantalizing hints of long-term ancient occupation in the plain.

Katsonopoulou shared Marinatos' frustration and desire to find Helike – one of the last great mysteries of ancient Greece. Soter believed that understanding the local geology could help them to isolate the location. Lacking a permit to excavate, they decided to employ remote-sensing technologies, including magnetometry and ground-penetrating radar – a technique in which radio pulses are sent through soil to detect buried shapes and changes in the soil itself. They hoped that these methods would penetrate the silt and sediment of centuries and locate the lost city, and these techniques did in fact reveal the presence of some large man-made structures.

RIGHT: Roman walls at the Klonis site of Helike, excavated in 1995.

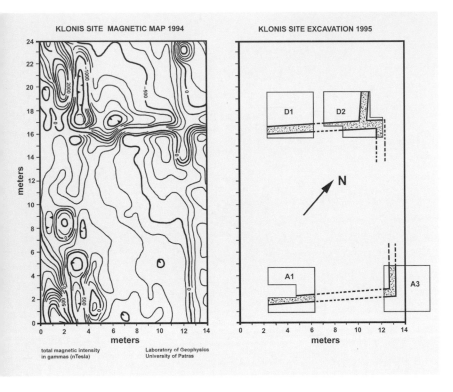

KLONIS SITE MAGNETIC MAP 1994

KLONIS SITE EXCAVATION 1995

D1   D2

N

A1   A3

meters

meters

total magnetic intensity
in gammas (nTesla)

Laboratory of Geophysics
University of Patras

ABOVE: The Helike project used remote-sensing techniques, including ground-penetrating radar and magnetometry at various sites. This magnetic map revealed the presence of a large man-made structure at the Klonis site. Excavation in 1995 showed that these contours were produced by Roman walls.

In the summer of 2000, the team finally obtained a permit to excavate. Based on nearly a decade of borehole and remote-sensing results, they knew where to dig, and they unearthed the remains of ancient buildings. They found ruined walls and foundations buried beneath sedimentary layers clearly deposited in the sea. These dated from the early Bronze Age, c. 2400 BC. This was by far the oldest site ever found in that part of Greece, and was perhaps the prehistoric predecessor of the Classical-era Helike destroyed in 373 BC.

On the last day of excavation in 2000, the team found a deposit full of black-glazed Classical pottery fragments, and a silver coin bearing the image of a dove – the symbol of the city of Sikyon, a neighbouring settlement to Helike. Coins would have been exchanged in regions with common borders and the people of Helike would have used the coinage as freely as they used their own currency. The coin belongs to the period immediately before the inundation.

In the summer of 2001, the Helike Project continued excavating and found the ruins of buildings that seemed to date from a time immediately prior to 373 BC; some of the city's inhabitants may have been living in these buildings when the tsunami hit. They also found more coins and pottery fragments. The team discovered the main coastal Roman road and traced it for 800 metres (2,600 feet). In addition, they brought to light more buildings from the early Bronze Age settlement, containing many complete pots and vases, and some small gold and silver ornaments.

The discoveries so far have given us a limited glimpse of times gone by. Sediment samples from the excavations and boreholes have proved that the Bronze Age site was once below sea level, by revealing microscopic marine fauna known as forams. Similar results showed that the Classical-era site was submerged in a lagoon. Later, perhaps in the second century BC, a freshwater lake may have covered the site, as suggested by the discovery of freshwater varieties of tiny crustaceans known as ostracods in a shallow layer of black clay.

The team have brought to light the first ancient building found in the coastal plain southeast of Aigion, and have evidence that the area was occupied from Early Bronze Age to Byzantine times. There can now be little doubt that they have found the lost city of Helike. The Helike Project will continue to explore these discoveries for years to come. In time, we may be able to piece together an understanding of the structure of the city itself and of the way of life of the people of Helike.

BELOW: Geophysical techniques produced this stunning radar image at Helike. The hyperbolic profile reflects a massive tile floor dating from the Roman period.

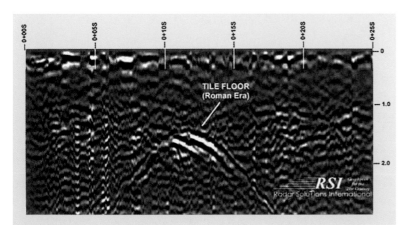

TILE FLOOR
(Roman Era)

SECRETS OF THE SEA

STEVEN SOTER believes that most of what remains of Helike will be found on land. His research suggests that new land has been created over time by sedimentation and uplift of the coastal plain.

"THERE MAY STILL BE antiquities under water. It's quite possible that a lot of debris from the city was washed into the Gulf by the tsunami that followed the earthquake. It will be difficult to get at, but we might be able to do it in time. For example, our sonar survey revealed a large narrow rectangular structure extending out from the shore. It's covered by sandy silt and may be natural but, unlike the normal bottom sediments, here, it's opaque to the penetrating sonar and therefore looks dense, like stone. It might be an ancient harbor mole or breakwater. To expose it would require special equipment to remove the silt. That might be a project for the future. Helike surely had a harbor town, and this submerged structure might belong to it."

STEVEN SOTER, ASTRONOMER AND GEO-ARCHAEOLOGIST, AMERICAN MUSEUM OF NATURAL HISTORY, NEW YORK, USA

SEEING IS NOT BELIEVING

GEOPHYSICIST PAUL KRONFIELD was involved in the original surveys of Helike, working mostly offshore in around 55 m (180 ft) of water.

"YOU HAVE TO BE CAREFUL when you are looking at the sensor records to ensure you don't see things which aren't there. We found ten subsurface anomalies on the sea floor, which could be the remains of the ten Spartan ships reported to have sunk in the harbour at the time of the catastrophe. I think any confirmation of the ancient reports would be very exciting. We also found what appeared to be the remains of the harbour wall. It looked man-made, very regular about 150 m (492 yd) long with the characteristics of a jetty under 15 m (49 ft) of water. I would have liked to drill a bore hole at the landward end of the structure to further investigate what could be part of the city's harbour but we couldn't get the funding. Just to show you how sonar can mislead you, we also found a large circular structure about 10 m (33 ft) deep by 60 m (197 ft) across. One could imagine it to be an amphitheatre but Steven identified the feature as a giant submarine "pockmark", the result of gas bubbles which break the surface during earthquakes, leaving a calcified ring around what is, in effect, a hole in the sea floor."

PAUL KRONFIELD, GEOPHYSICIST, INTEC ENGINEERING PARTNERSHIPS, HOUSTON, TEXAS, USA

KNOSSOS
MINOS' LABYRINTH

THE LARGE AND BEAUTIFUL ISLAND OF CRETE, 833,000 square kilometres (320,000 square miles) in area, lies to the south of mainland Greece. To the northwest lies the Peloponnese region, to the north the Aegean Sea, and to the east Turkey and the island of Rhodes. Crete is renowned for its beautiful landscape, not least the great Knossos valley rising up to a huge mountain. There, on the hill of Kephala, lie the remains of a fabulous Bronze Age town, the home of the Minoan civilization, a place known as Knossos.

Flourishing throughout the second millennium BC, the settlement covered an area of about 500,000 square metres (598,000 square yards), dominated by the grand palace of King Minos. The palace itself stretches over 20,000 square metres (24,000 square yards) and was one of the most elaborate feats of architecture achieved in Bronze Age Europe.

Knossos was the birthplace of the Greek myth of Theseus and the Minotaur. The fable tells how the despotic King Minos demanded a tribute from Athens of seven young men and women every year to sacrifice to the Minotaur – a terrible creature, half-man, half-bull, said to dwell in the labyrinth of Knossos, whose hunger could only be assuaged by human flesh. The Minotaur was the bastard son of Minos' wife Pasiphae, the daughter of Helios, the sun god. She made love to a bull sent from the sea by Poseidon and became mother to the Minotaur (the name means "Minos' bull"). The maze at Knossos is said to have been constructed for Minos by the legendary Greek inventor Daedalus, to hold the Minotaur captive. The terrible tribute was exacted for

OPPOSITE: A vestibule with columns and relief of a bull at Minos' palace hints at the origin of the labyrinth and Minotaur myth. It is easy to imagine the effect the palace would have had on visitors, hence the emergence of the Minotaur legend.

ABOVE: The throne room of King Minos, legendary King of Crete, from the Palace of Knossos destroyed 1375 BC – as restored and seen today – still contains the gypsum throne of the Minoan kings.

many years, but the great Athenian hero, Theseus, was determined to survive the ordeal and end the carnage. Ariadne, Minos' daughter, was disgusted by the sacrifices demanded by her father and helped Theseus to survive by giving him a ball of twine before he entered the labyrinth. He secured this at the entrance to the maze, and, having fought and killed the Minotaur, followed the twine trail back out. He fled to freedom with Ariadne, leaving the peoples of Athens and Knossos free of the Minotaur at last.

This story fascinated scholars for hundreds of years. The idea that Minos' palace and its maze might actually have existed obsessed archaeologists and adventurers, particularly in the nineteenth century. Then, in 1884, a local merchant discovered a number of pottery storage jars, clearly of great antiquity, on a hill known as Kephala in the Knossos valley, triggering further interest.

The discoverer of Troy, Heinrich Schliemann (see page 106), expressed a desire to explore the site in 1889, but he died before launching an expedition. This left the field open for Sir Arthur John Evans (1851–1941), a wealthy Englishman who was the curator of the Ashmolean Museum in Oxford. Evans had a keen interest in ancient coins and was fascinated by a hitherto unknown form of writing on seals recovered from Crete. The discovery of the storage jars in the Knossos valley excited his interest. He purchased a stake in the mound at Kephala – which promised to hold more historical remains – in 1894.

Following the abatement of a war between Muslims and Christians in the region, Evans and a team of diggers, paid for out of his own fortune, began excavations in 1900. He spent the next thirty-five years excavating and renovating the site, and publishing his findings in a four-volume set entitled *The Palace of Minos*, between 1921 and 1935. While Evans is not without his detractors, his discoveries made him world-famous and guaranteed him a place as one of the most renowned discoverers of lost domains.

Evans' team of diggers exposed the ruins of a vast palace complex, dating to the Bronze Age, which must have been home to tens of thousands of people. They found elaborate frescos and artefacts suggesting the existence of a Cretan bull-cult from which the legend of the Minotaur may have derived. These discoveries indicated that the rites of the bull-cult (a fascination with and worship of the bull) included occasions when men and women would take their lives in their hands and try to dance or leap over

LEFT: Sir Arthur Evans (1851–1941), the British archaeologist who discovered the ancient city of Knossos, and gave the name "Minoan" to the sophisticated Bronze Age civilization that built it, worked at the site for twenty-five years. He is pictured here with his colleagues Theodore Fyfe and Duncan Mackenzie and pottery "pithoi" (large painted storage jars) that were discovered at the site.

OPPOSITE: This aerial view of Knossos puts the site in context: it is located about 5 miles (8 km) from Crete's northern coast and stands on a mound between the confluence of two streams.

and around a captive bull. The frescoes might also portray an impression of the dangers involved in rounding up bulls in the wild. In either case, the bull was greatly revered in Knossos.

Evans was able to date the civilization at Knossos using the pottery he found and comparing it with pottery found in Egyptian tombs with good dating records. This, coupled with the discovery of Egyptian wares in Knossos, allowed him to place the building of the original palace at c. 1900 BC. Certain that the title of Minos was hereditary – in tribute to King Minos of legend – Evans named this civilization Minoan, in honour of the kings.

Evans discovered that the huge palace had been built and extended over many centuries. His excavations eventually revealed 1,300 rooms in the palace complex. The palace had a complicated layout, featuring elaborate buildings with halls, corridors and chambers, which seemed maze-like because, unlike the Greeks, Minoans did not care greatly for symmetry in design. The palace also featured ceremonial rooms, and the entire complex was clustered around a main courtyard. The maze-like nature of the place may have been another feature that was embellished in the legend of the Minotaur.

In one of the most astonishing rooms, found on the west side of the mound, Evans discovered shards of crumbled fresco. He realised that the walls must have been elaborately decorated and painted. When he found a high stone seat that was flanked by stone benches, Evans was sure that he had found the ancestral throne of the kings of Knossos.

Further excavations revealed statues and erotic sculptures featuring women grasping sacred snakes. Women apparently fascinated Minoan artists, and they were represented repeatedly in artworks throughout the palace. This fact and the absence of clues regarding the state's form of government and paintings or frescoes of bearded males has led many antiquarians to conclude that the women in the images were priestesses. Although Knossos was not a matriarchy, it is possible that both priests and priestesses played an equal part in decision-making in all aspects of Minoan life, including trade, art and religion. The role of priests and priestesses in the government of Knossos is particularly relevant, as King Minos was characterized as a god-king, the son of Zeus, in Greek myths. In common with many other cultures, the king may have been considered to be a human incarnation of one of their

gods and his priests and priestesses were, therefore, at one with a god in his human form.

Perhaps most exciting of all Evans' finds was the discovery of hundreds of records etched onto clay tablets and other artefacts such as seals. Evans was unable to decipher the writing, although he did distinguish them into three separate groups: Linear A, Linear B, and a form of hieroglyph.

The earliest form of writing, the Cretan hieroglyphic or phonetic script, was discovered on more than 200 objects, including seals and jewellery, especially signet rings. This form of writing was used for approximately 300 years between c. 1900–1600 BC. Little of this script has been deciphered.

Evans named the second form of writing Linear A because it renders its characters in a linear format – it is quite unlike a pictographic script in style. Linear A is a syllabic script: it features characters representing syllables, which serve the purpose of an alphabet. This script too has not yet been completely deciphered. The texts vex cryptologists and linguists as they are very complex and have so far yielded no obvious key to allow total decipherment. The surviving texts are mostly administrative in nature, found on discs, seals and tablets, and were generally written on unbaked clay.

It is notable that no creative works have been found at the site. It is possible that written language was not used for creative and artistic purposes in Knossos at this time – their stories and legends were probably relayed in oral form. The crude and rudimentary way in which documents using Cretan hieroglyphic and Linear A were written – on unbaked clay – suggests that they were not intended to be preserved for a long time. It is possible that literary works were recorded in other ways, perhaps on baked clay, but that they have since been lost or damaged.

The third form of writing found at Knossos, Linear B, was deciphered by British scholar Michael Ventris (1922–1956) in 1952. Linear B was preserved on about 10,000 items at the site. Ventris' work on tablets from the site revolutionized our understanding of

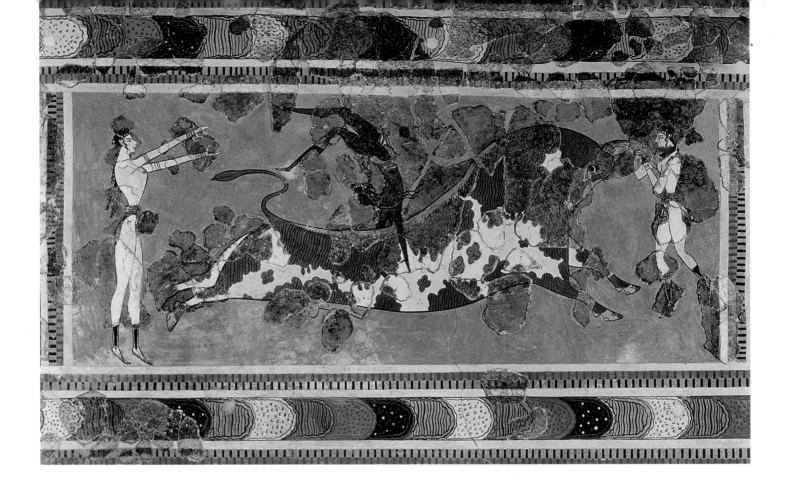

the Greek Bronze Age, as most of the tablets are inventories of property or records of agricultural production. However, these tablets were produced by the Mycenaeans who succeeded the Minoans on Crete, and they do not give an insight into Minoan life. Like Linear A, Linear B script is syllabic, but with the addition of logograms – abstract symbols that denote commonly described items such as people and livestock. Ventris realized that Linear B script was used to write Mycenaean Greek. The script of the Mycenaeans may have been influenced by Minoan Linear A; this may have come about because of contact and trade between the Mycenaeans and the Cretans from c. 1450 BC. The prevalence of Linear B from 1450 BC to c. 1200 BC suggests that the Mycenaeans came to dominate the Cretan domain in that era.

Evans believed that the volcanic eruption at Thera was to blame for the downfall of Knossos, but it is now thought that the Theran eruption occurred too early, in c. 1628 BC, to account for the end of Knossos (see pages 62–67). It is possible that the end of the Minoan civilization had more complex causes, perhaps being triggered by civil war, trading or economic problems. Or it may have been a result of the imposition of a more dynamic, youthful culture upon one set in its ways.

Pottery and other finds indicate that the Minoans were great traders, having good commercial links with Egypt. They imported large quantities of produce from neighbouring areas. It is conceivable that trade disputes precipitated the civilization's collapse, perhaps with the Minoans being invaded by mainland Mycenaean forces. No definitive answer has been produced, and the mystery is likely to intrigue archaeologists for years to come.

Evans sparked off controversy in the archaeological world with his attempts to reconstruct the palace complex. He hired Éduard Gilliéron, a Swiss fresco artist, to restore the damaged areas of some of the Minoan paintings and used builders to reconstruct the palace walls with concrete. Many antiquarians argued that he was defiling the discovery with his reconstructive "guess work". Others felt that it offered the world a chance to see Knossos as it might have been.

Excavations, conservation and study have continued apace since Evans' death in 1941. It has become clear, for example, that

EARTHQUAKES AND ARCHAEOLOGY IN THE EASTERN MEDITERRANEAN AND CRETE

OLD CONCEPTS about the destruction of Knossos and its neighbours may need to be reassessed in the light of modern research.

"WHY ARE THERE SO MANY archaeological ruins in the eastern Mediterranean? Assumed by many to be the result of time and wars, many of these ruins are due to historic and prehistoric earthquakes. Modern science reveals that some of these earthquakes must have been so destructive, or happened at times of such political and military stress, that they changed history (for example, the fall of Jericho before Joshua, the catastrophic collapse at the end of the Bronze Age). Crete, the site of the largest earthquakes in the Mediterranean region, suffered repeatedly from destruction by earthquakes and most of the levels of collapse of Knossos can be ascribed to this agent."

PROFESSOR AMOS NUR, DEPARTMENT OF GEOPHYSICS, ACADEMIC DIRECTOR OVERSEAS STUDIES PROGRAM DIRECTOR, SRB PROJECT, WAYNE LOEL PROFESSOR OF EARTH SCIENCES, STANFORD UNIVERSITY, STANFORD, CALIFORNIA, USA

the Minoans were master sailors. The sea provided the island with a natural defensive barrier, with mastery of the sea being the Minoans' primary weapon. There is a noticeable lack of war imagery in the artworks that have been found at the site; depictions of religious imagery and leisure pursuits prevail. The people seemed to have been more concerned with pleasurable pursuits than with war. The fact that the Minoan civilization thrived for a millennium indicates that the people could afford the luxury of pleasure, which is generally only available in times of peace. The palace was first built at the beginning of the second millennium BC and was added to by successive generations. Sadly, their civilization proved ephemeral, and fell in c. 1450 BC.

Today, the work of archaeologists and historians at Knossos focuses largely on the repair and conservation of the site. There is a constant battle to preserve the frescoes and delicate plasterwork and to maintain the buildings at Knossos. The large numbers of visitors who come to the site accelerate the decay. To make matters worse, there is a lively black market trade in pottery and artefacts looted from Knossos. Nonetheless, Knossos has survived for four millennia and the legends of its Minotaur will last just as long.

ABOVE: The importance of women in Minoan society is seen in this sculpture of the snake goddess, made c. 1500 BC, from the Palace of Knossos. Women may have played an equal role with men in religious, political and societal decisions and functions.

POMPEII
ETERNAL CITY

POMPEII, A ROMAN CITY ON THE BAY OF NAPLES in southern Italy, was buried under a thick layer of lava and ash by the eruption of Mount Vesuvius in AD 79. The eruption swamped the territory, thereby preserving under its volcanic debris a moment in the life of a provincial Roman town in astonishing detail. These remains allow us a remarkable insight into Roman life at the time.

Pompeii was a small town near the coast, close to the river Sarno and lying in the shadow of the 1,800-metre (6,000-feet) high Mount Vesuvius. It was probably founded by tribal farmers, known as the Oscans, in the first millennium BC. By the seventh century BC, the acquisitive Greeks had penetrated the area and taken control. The settlement expanded considerably under their rule. The Samnites, a fierce group of peoples from the mountains organized in clans, snatched control from the invaders in c. 425 BC. The Samnites had migrated into the area, first absorbing and then replacing the Oscans.

Under the Samnites' rule, between c. 425 and 375 BC, Pompeii's size grew significantly and it became a thriving trading town. The rule of the Samnites was not to be permanent, however. The whole of what is now Italy was consumed by conflicting factions. The Samnites engaged in a series of terrible wars, from c. 343 to 290 BC, with rival tribes, and gained Rome as an ally. In time, however, the Romans and the Samnites came to loathe one another. At this time Rome, the great city-state, was set on building a nation and then an empire. The people of Pompeii saw no reason to fall in behind the Roman banner. They

ABOVE: "The Great Eruption of Vesuvius" was vividly captured in this watercolour by Louis Jean Desprez (1743–1804). It was painted at a time when Pompeii leapt into the public consciousness thanks to major discoveries at the site.

OPPOSITE: The Lararium (family altar) for the Lares, or tutelary deities, was an important area in many homes in Pompeii.

ABOVE: The House of Venus in the Shell was excavated in 1952 and revealed this beautiful peristyle area with a real garden which merged with an imaginary garden, frescoed on the wall behind.

and the peoples of the peninsular region rebelled in 91 BC. The rebellion was crushed, ruthlessly and efficiently, and the Samnite aristocracy – still in power until that point – was butchered. In defeat, Pompeii had to accept Roman rule. The city was made a *municipium*, a satellite of Rome, and the Pompeians were granted citizenship, in *c.* 88 BC. Local governors were set in place in this region, as was the norm in areas under Roman control.

Under Roman protection, Pompeii prospered further. At the time of its destruction, Pompeii was a thriving community filled with shops, administrative and religious buildings, houses and workshops. Its 10,000 inhabitants worshipped their gods, created great art and manufactured goods. This civilization was ancient Rome in microcosm.

Pompeii's city walls stretched for three kilometres (two miles) and were entered through any one of eight gates, positioned at

RIGHT: *The tepidarium, or tepid bath, was one of three kinds of baths used by the Roman citizens of Pompeii to purify their skin, socialise and relax. The other baths were the frigidarium (cold room) and the caldarium (hot room). Citizens also exercised in swimming pools.*

intervals around the city. The city was arranged into four blocks, and the houses were divided by narrow streets. The homes of the wealthy classes were very fine. Land was at a premium within the city walls, and so space had to be used sparingly. Consequently, many houses had two floors. Wealthier homes on the main street often had stores and shops built into the walls. Shops have been discovered belonging to sculptors, surgeons, fishermen and bakers.

Houses were often complete with fully equipped kitchens, fitted with charcoal-burning hearths and round-bottomed bronze cooking pots. A modern-day chef would have little difficulty adjusting to a Pompeian kitchen. The living quarters were rather small by modern standards, but sumptuously appointed. The stucco walls were often decorated with *tesserae* (small fragmented tiles) made into mosaics depicting mythological or erotic scenes, or were decorated with painted murals, accomplished works of art in their own right. Mosaics also ornamented the floors. Latrines, storage areas and, in some cases, private baths were included in the design. Entrance to the houses was often through a vestibule, so as to offer security. Grander homes might feature courtyards with roofs open in the centre to the elements, with large water-gathering pools beneath. These houses were imposing and comfortable and reflected their owners' personality and status.

Pompeii also had impressive public buildings. There were no fewer than seven temples, including those dedicated to Apollo, Jupiter, Isis and Venus. These grand edifices remind us that the deities played a huge part in the daily life of Roman Pompeians. The Roman pantheon of gods, including Jupiter, their chief god, and Neptune, god of the sea, were worshipped publicly in the temples in ceremonies led by priests, but were also honoured privately in people's homes. Maintaining household shrines was a part of everyday life. Roman religion was a positive one, associated with success: the gods were seen as a means of helping people control their environment and lives. Consequently, prayer was a very common activity. In temples, public prayers were led by priests; the *paterfamilias* (head of a household) performed the same function, on a daily basis, within the home.

Apart from temples, Pompeii contained a number of important public buildings. At its height, Pompeii boasted a large open-air amphitheatre and a smaller, roofed theatre alongside it, called the Odeon. The amphitheatre could hold approximately 20,000 spectators who came to be entertained by gladiatorial combat. The theatre saw performance of plays by such tragic poets as Seneca and comedy writers such as Menander.

RIGHT: *From the air Pompeii could be mistaken for a modern city. Set out in clearly defined blocks and areas, with its great amphitheatre, it seems in every way a city of the living, rather than a city of the dead.*

LEFT: *This fresco from the House of the Centenary portrays the god of wine, Bacchus, before Vesuvius. It serves to remind us how Pompeians valued the gods' intervention in their daily lives and how they linked their spiritual lives with pleasure and nature (wine and Vesuvius).*

Outside the city walls, nestling on the green and fertile slopes of Mount Vesuvius, stood palatial residences, some of them boasting forty-five rooms or more. These were the holiday homes and countryside retreats of wealthy Romans.

In AD 62, the Pompeians suffered a terrible shock – an earthquake, which destroyed their forum and many shops and homes. Few people realized that Mount Vesuvius was volcanic, and even fewer connected the volcano with the tremors. Nero, the Roman Emperor, hesitated over whether to restore Pompeii or to abandon it. However, the local people – who had fled the settlement – were determined to return to their homes despite any future risk from earth tremors or earthquakes, and Nero chose to rebuild the damaged areas of the site.

Between AD 62 and AD 79, the Pompeians spent a large amount of money and energy on rebuilding their city. They had even decided to build an additional public bath, to further embellish their public amenities. Yet, before their reconstruction efforts were completed, the terror of Vesuvius struck again.

In August AD 79, people began to report that wells had dried up and that spring waters were no longer flowing as normal. Herd animals began behaving strangely, with sheep and horses becoming unnaturally still and quiescent. Then an earth tremor, very mild in comparison to the one in AD 62, shook the land. A few people, fearing another earthquake, packed their belongings and left the city, but most stayed. No municipal order was given, and no preparations were made in case there was another disaster.

The volcano erupted on 24 August. At first, a release of ash spewed harmlessly from the cap of Vesuvius. Then, a little after midday, the great volcanic plug, restraining the molten energy of

The Forum, a large and ornate central compound, was the administrative, social, religious and commercial centre of Pompeii – as it was in all Roman towns and cities. Today you can still see the remains of the Temples of Apollo, Jupiter, and Vespasian; the public buildings that housed the principal magistrates; the Sanctuary of the Lares Publici (the gods who protected the town); the Macellum (food market); and warehouses.

There were at least three public baths in Pompeii. These bath complexes included enclosed gardens, promenades, gymnasiums, lounges, libraries and even museums. A bath complex has been unearthed in Pompeii that measures nearly one mile in circumference. It is clear that to a Roman citizen, the public bath was far more than a place dedicated to hygiene or sport. It also had an important social function, and going to the baths was an essential part of being a citizen of Pompeii.

the planet, gave way in a tremendous screeching roar. A vast explosion shot fragments of earth and dust into the atmosphere. They were "superheated" and drifted into a huge tree-shaped cloud above the mountain.

Edward Bulwer-Lytton, Lord Lytton of Knebworth, wrote a novel entitled *The Last Days of Pompeii* in 1834 (during the excavation of the city) which brings the shocking destruction of Pompeii vividly to life: "Suddenly … the Palace became lighted with an intense and lurid glow. Bright and gigantic through the darkness, which closed around it like the walls of hell, the mountain shone – a pile of fire! … The slaves shrieked aloud, and cowering, hid their faces … A simultaneous crash resounded through the city, as down toppled many a roof and pillar!" The most famous account of the events is that of Pliny the Younger, who was in Pompeii at the time: "The sight that met our still terrified eyes was a changed world buried in ash like snow."

ABOVE: Pompeian ladies enjoyed beautifying themselves, with new hairstyles, make-up, jewellery and clothes, much as wealthy ladies do today. The only major difference between modern Western ladies and their Pompeian ancestors is that in Pompeii hairdressers and other functionaries were often slaves, as in this image.

LEFT: *This is a cast of a sleeping Pompeian boy, captured at the moment of his death, as the cloud of gas and ash from Vesuvius smothered his city. When his body decayed it left a hollow in the ash, which was later discovered and filled with cement to produce this cast — a technique introduced by Guiseppe Fiorelli in the mid-nineteenth century. It is small wonder that Pompeii has captured our imaginations when such emotive discoveries are made.*

RIGHT: *Giuseppe Fiorelli (director of excavations from 1860) did introduce archaeological method to the work at Pompeii but his late nineteenth-century excavations and restorations remain controversial, as many believe he did untold damage to the site and the remains would have been better preserved than restored.*

There were many stages to the eruption. At first, the town was covered in a light layer of relatively harmless pumice stone. Most of the people fled at this stage. A few, perhaps one-fifth of the population, stayed behind. Over the next eighteen hours, the volcano spewed ash, rock and volcanic lava onto the surrounding land. Herculaneum, Pompeii's neighbouring town, was destroyed. Many of the people in Pompeii had survived thus far, taking refuge in cellars or under the canopies of sturdy buildings, but they were never to escape. As the power of the eruption waned, the great column of ejecta began to collapse. At last the huge debris and gas cloud fell over the earth, bringing with it toxic gases such as hydrogen sulphide and carbon dioxide. The gas sheet smothered Pompeii, suffocating the residents who had survived the burning ejecta and superheated air. They and their animals died. Death for many of them came so speedily that they were rooted to the spot, preserved for all time, their bodies smothered by the falling debris. Pompeii was dead.

Antiquarians had long been aware of Pompeii's existence by the nineteenth century: Herculaneum was rediscovered in 1736 and Pompeii in 1748. These discoveries brought the Classical world into vogue, and influenced popular culture — art, architecture, design and literature. Despite this passion for antiquity, it took nearly forty years until excavations, organized by Charles of Bourbon, began in earnest.

It was well known that valuable antique objects could be dug up at the site. However, most believed that the site was too difficult to excavate because of the scale of the task — millions of tons of ash and debris covered the site. Then, in 1860, Giuseppe Fiorelli was appointed Director of Excavations at Pompeii. He began the mammoth job of clearing the volcanic debris. A meticulous planner and logician, Fiorelli took the process stage by stage. Unlike other great diggers of his time, like Schliemann (see pages 100–109) or Evans (see pages 82–89), Fiorelli demonstrated restraint in his excavations and

ensured that finds were documented before moving on to excavate another area. Fiorelli was a pioneer of the scientific method in archaeology.

As the first murals and sculptures were revealed, it became apparent that Pompeii offered the modern world a unique window on the past. Many Pompeians have achieved a macabre form of immortality. The cavities left behind in the ashes of the volcano, after the victims' bodies had decomposed, have been used as a form of mould. Even today, archaeologists seek out and then carefully fill the fragile cavities with plaster. Once set, the plaster forms are excavated to reveal the statue-like forms of the dead, preserved in their final death throes.

The excavations have produced an astonishing array of finds, such as food left on tabletops, and idols in their place of worship in the home shrine. Dogs, fastened by their chains, had been smothered and preserved, as had the frescos and artworks of the city. Here was the long-dead civilization of Rome, preserved untouched as it was in its heyday.

Much of the city has now been revealed, although there are still treasures to be excavated and analyzed. For example, archaeologists knew from literary references that temple gardens existed in Pompeii. However, none had been excavated until a project, initiated in 1998, discovered that the precincts of the Temples of Apollo and Venus (located just west of the Forum on the road to Porta Marina, the sea gate) were planted, and the patterns and types of vegetation for the gardens revealed. These sorts of initiatives continue to reveal new areas of the town. It is also possible that remote-sensing technologies will assist in our understanding of the development of the site and in locating any further ruins.

PRICELESS POMPEII

POMPEII IS ONE OF THE most important sites in the Classical world for addressing numerous aspects of ancient life. But this site and its treasures may not be with us forever.

"THE VAST AREAS OF Pompeii that have been excavated in more than 250 years constitute a city-sized treasure trove of information that has not been fully exploited. This priceless cultural resource is decaying through natural processes of degradation that affect exposed ruins. Through these processes we are losing evidence on which to base new studies.

With these conditions in mind, the Pompeii Forum Project of the University of Virginia belongs to a new trend in Pompeii research that avoids excavations in the undug areas and concentrates instead on the already cleared, but understudied parts of the city. We are not primarily a digging project, although we do excavate when research questions cannot be addressed through other means of investigation. Our project goal is to understand the dynamics of urban evolution in the forum zone of Pompeii and the urbanistic relationships between the forum and the surrounding areas of the city. Our collaborative team is interdisciplinary, including specialists in classical archaeology, architecture, urban design, urban history, computer technology, structural engineering, and videoing. Drawing upon the knowledge and skills of all project members, we have been studying and recording the standing remains of the forum. A major feature of the project is our use of CAD technology to record the buildings of the forum. Taking into consideration the three serious conditions listed above, we realize that only a massive and a systematic study and recording of the data can preserve for future generations the important physical evidence from Pompeii that might be damaged or destroyed at any moment.

In order to preserve sub-soil data for investigation by later generations, we avoid invasive and inherently destructive excavation whenever possible. When we determine that excavation is required to address one or more important research questions we place relatively small trenches in critical areas to extract data by means of a kind of precise surgical intervention. To date, our analysis of buildings and our excavations have been extremely successful in shedding new light on the development of the Pompeian forum. Most recently, we have employed remote sensing both to test magnetometer technology in the forum and to search for the buried remains of structures that predate the buildings now standing at the site."

JOHN J. DOBBINS, PROFESSOR OF CLASSICAL ART & ARCHAEOLOGY, MCINTIRE DEPARTMENT OF ART, UNIVERSITY OF VIRGINIA, USA

TROY
SCHLIEMANN'S OBSESSION

"I HAVE TRAVELLED MUCH, and have had much to do with heroes, but I have never seen such another man as Ulysses ... What courage he displayed within the wooden horse ... lying in wait to bring death and destruction upon the Trojans."

THE ODYSSEY, HOMER, TRANSLATED BY SAMUEL BUTLER

ABOVE: A well in the hill of Hisarlik has been excavated by the Troy Project — an international project to excavate, document and understand Troy.

OPPOSITE: Ancient Troy was long thought to be a myth, despite references in works by ancient Greek and Latin authors. The precise location of the city remained unidentified until 1822 when Charles McLaren suggested a mound called Hisarlik as the location and in 1872 Heinrich Schliemann proved him correct. Today the city of legend is laid bare.

T HE REMAINS OF THE MANY INCARNATIONS OF ancient Troy are located on a hill, named Hisarlik, a limestone plateau 49 metres (160 feet) high, near the Dardanelles Straits (known in ancient times as Hellespont) between Europe and Asia, in northeast Asia Minor. The site was chosen for its strategic importance: the winds were strong and reliable for trade ships, and the site gave access to the Aegean, Bosphorus and Black Seas. The city was once known as Ilion (or Ilium in Latin), as reflected in the name of Homer's epic poem the *Iliad* (believed to have been composed in the eighth century BC), a work that tells the legend of Troy's fall. Lost beneath more recent Greek and Roman settlements, Homer's Troy was rediscovered by German explorer Heinrich Schliemann during his excavations in 1870–1890.

The Trojans were part of the Aegean civilization, which flourished in the Bronze Age (c. 2500–1000 BC), on the shores of the Aegean Sea. We know from pottery finds that they traded freely with the Minoans (see page 88), a highly civilized race of people who lived on the island of Crete, to the south of Troy, and other cultures. Indeed the city's location, at the centre of Middle-Eastern Europe and the borders of Asia, allowed the Trojans access to traders from right across the northern and central Mediterranean. Their lifestyle was prosperous and cosmopolitan, with people from many different cultures coming to the city. The Trojans had an open economy that thrived on international trade, and they exported and imported both finished goods and raw materials.

According to Homer in the *Iliad* and the *Odyssey,* mainland Greece was ruled by a great king, Agamemnon, at the time of the Trojan War. Troy was a separate principality with its own king, Priam. It is true historically, as well as in legend, that Troy was ruled by a monarchy following the pattern of the ancient Greeks. In addition, the Trojans worshipped the pantheon of Greek gods, including Apollo, god of the sun; Artemis, goddess of the moon; Athena, the goddess of wisdom; and Poseidon, the god of the sea. Homer's portrayal of the fortified city and the Trojan army are also based in fact. The city was prosperous and would have needed a force to protect its wealth.

The landscape then was subtly different from that seen today. The water extended farther inland from the Dardanelles, forming a large bay – a natural marina that reached close to the bottom of the hill, making it a near-perfect site on which to build a fortified city. Indeed, not one, but nine, cities were built on this site over a

TROIA - ILION
Magnetic Prospection of the Lower City

◄◄ Troia VI - Defense Ditch
◄◄ Hellenistic City Wall

Status: October 2001
HGJ / Troia-Projekt

ABOVE: The result of twelve years' geophysical prospection in the area south and southeast of the citadel, undertaken by the present Troy Project. The results – mainly from Bronze Age Troy VI and Hellenistic/Roman Troy VIII and IX) phases – put the building remains of the citadel into the proper perspective. The visualized measurements are overlaid for reference over a high-resolution satellite image obtained in 2000 by the Ikonos satellite from a distance of 680 km (422 miles).

period of 3,500 years. Archaeologists have named these Troy I through to Troy IX in the course of attempts to classify and date each incarnation of the city.

Homer portrayed Troy as a massive and impenetrable fortified city. Troy VI, now believed by many scholars to be the Troy of Homer's era, was a walled town with a massive pillar house that dates back to the thirteenth century BC. The pillar house, located near the northern gate, is the best surviving example of a house within the walls. Its remains are the most complete of any excavated, yet its function remains a mystery. The walls of the city were constructed of great limestone blocks, punctuated by five gateways. The northeastern tower functioned as the city's watchtower. Its heavily fortified walls contained a large well, guaranteeing both soldiers and ordinary people a constant supply of water in times of siege. The southern gate, protected by a 7-metre (23-foot) high tower, was the main entrance to the fortified city. After entering through the gate, visitors would travel along an avenue towards the inner citadel. It is difficult to be certain of the nature of the citadel, but it most definitely would have been grandiose.

Within the walls, people lived in individual houses. These were laid out meticulously, suggesting a degree of careful city planning. The houses were large, with relatively simple ground plans. They were two-storey structures, most likely with storage areas on the ground floor and living compartments above.

No palatial residences survive from Troy VI. The structures were probably destroyed in later periods to make way for new developments. It is difficult to ascertain how large the population of the city was, because there may have been many dwellings outside the main walls of the structure, and because the city would have had a large transient population of visiting merchants and sailors.

Archaeological evidence suggests that Troy VI was destroyed by an earthquake in c. 1250 BC. The entire region – the Aegean islands, Greece and Turkey – is on a tectonic fault line, and was (and still is) geologically unstable – the catastrophic eruption of Thera in c. 1628 BC (see pages 66 and 88) being evidence of this. The destruction of Troy VI would have been a blow, but was not without precedent in the region. The building of Troy VII, a reconstruction of the collapsed city, began soon afterwards. As an illustration of the contention regarding this site, Troy VIIa, built in the mid-thirteenth century BC, is also argued to be the city attacked by the Greeks in the Trojan War. More study is needed before agreement is reached. The site was of enormous strategic and economic importance, and the local inhabitants had little reason to abandon it, especially if they were being threatened by the Greeks, so reconstruction would have been their first thought. Troy VII was larger than its predecessors, but still a small settlement by today's standards. Inside the citadel, which was approximately 200 metres (650 feet) long and 140 metres (450 feet) wide, grand houses were built in concentric terraces, one above another. Many more houses and buildings were constructed without the citadel's walls and by rights should be considered part of the settlement, although the true extent of these additional buildings is still unclear (see pages 104–105.

By the mid-nineteenth century, antiquarians had long believed Homer's *Iliad* to be a work of fiction, with no basis in fact. Homer's story is one of passion. It recounts the tale of a Trojan prince, Paris, and his infatuation with the beautiful Greek queen, Helen, wife of Menelaus, the king of Sparta. Paris seduced Helen and together they fled to Troy. Mounting a huge expeditionary force, King

ABOVE: Many discoveries have been made at Troy. This ~~*te*~~ *acotta vessel and cup – from the Bronze Age Troy* ~~*II*~~ *period – have survived between* ~~*~*~~ *and 4,000 years buried in the earth. Despite the passage of millenia, our concept of design and the production of pleasing but functional ceramics has changed little.*

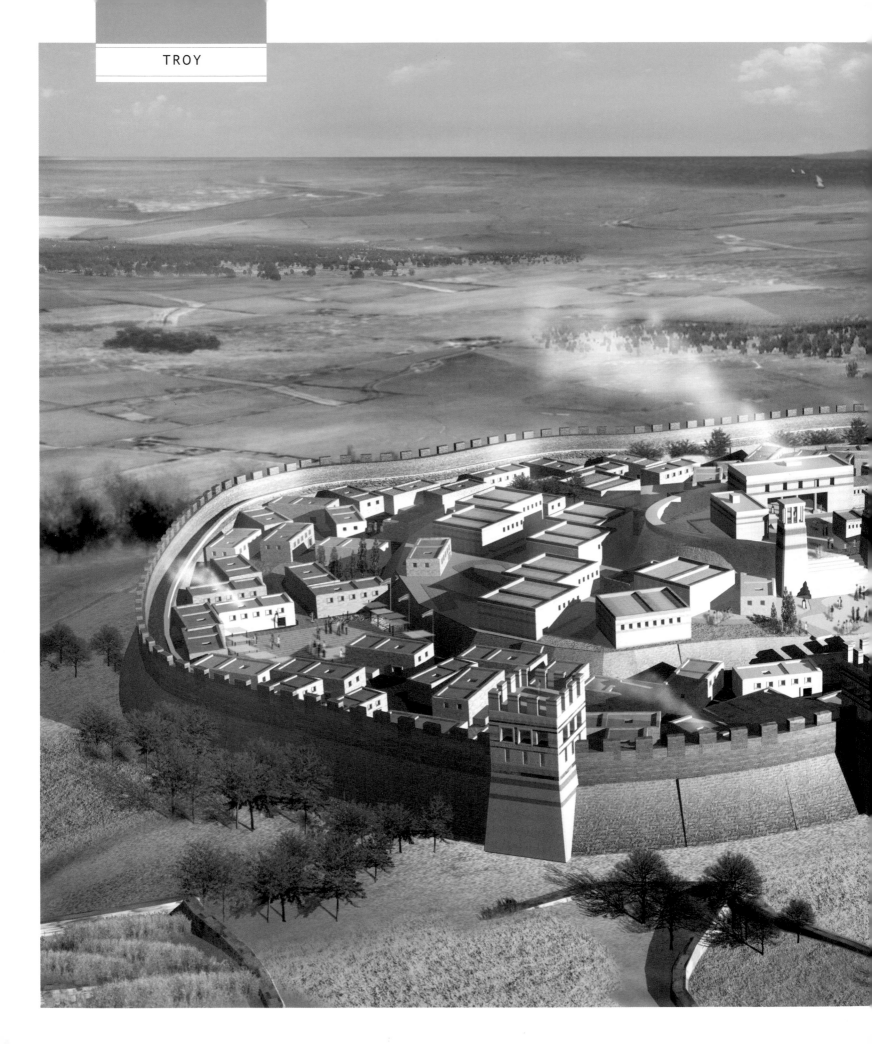

A computer-generated reconstruction of Troy VII, showing its location in the landscape with the sea in the background and visiting sailing boats making their way toward the site. Troy VII was larger than its predecessors but still a small settlement by today's standards. The heavily fortified walls protected the citadel for many years.

Trésor de Priam découvert à 8½ mètres de profondeur

ABOVE: Schliemann's first photograph of some of the objects he discovered at Troy. The great man could barely conceal his deserved excitement. The artefacts became objects of great fascination because of their possible links with figures described in Homer's much-loved telling of the Trojan War.

Agamemnon, Menelaus' brother, built a fleet of ships from Greece and Crete and attacked Troy. The Greeks laid siege to Troy for ten years. The legendary Achilles, fighting with Odysseus, Agamemnon and their Grecian comrades, slew all who approached him on the battlefield, but still the city did not fall. Only by feigning retreat did the Greeks triumph. They constructed a vast, hollow wooden statue of a horse, within which some of the Greek army hid. They left it outside the walls for the Trojans, insinuating that it was a gift of defeat. When the Trojans, fooled into accepting the gift, moved it within the walls of Troy, the Greek soldiers leapt from their hiding place and finally sacked Troy.

Heinrich Schliemann (1822–1890) was obsessed with the tales of these ancient heroes. He was determined to prove that Troy had existed and that the great war of the Bronze Age had taken place, much as Homer had written. Schliemann was considered something of an eccentric. He was, as far as the academic community was concerned, unschooled, and his activities were driven by insatiable curiosity. He had read copiously, educating himself in the scholarly works of the time.

Schliemann favoured the hill of Hisarlik as a location for Troy, following clues in Homer's text. It was on a hill; set by two springs, one hot, one cold; and in the middle of a plain that was prone to strong winds, all as described by Homer. Archaeologists at the time considered the nearby hill of Ballidagh to be a more likely site, and Schliemann's peers ridiculed him for his choice of location.

The Turkish government forbade excavation without a permit, but flouting rules, Schliemann began to dig at the site, for two weeks without ceasing, in 1870. In that time, he discovered the ruins of enormous walls, constructed on a huge scale. They were 2 metres (6 feet) thick and part of a building 20 metres (65 feet) long. Schliemann was elated. Although Turkish officials brought his work to an abrupt end at that time, he returned to the site, legitimately, in 1872.

Upon his return, this time with an army of recruits to help him excavate, Schliemann found not one but several cities, one on top of another. His methodology was crude but effective. His entire focus was to reveal Homeric Troy, and he therefore took a cavalier approach, in the process damaging the other historical layers. He felt sure that the Troy he sought was that located at the bottom of the layers. He was wrong. Troy II, as it has become known, was built in c. 3000 BC, about 2,000 years before the time of Homer's Troy. Schliemann destroyed the other layers on his mission to reach the deepest level. Ironically, he paid Troy VI and VIIa no heed – indeed, he missed many of the layers entirely.

LEFT: *Sophia Schliemann, Heinrich Schliemann's wife, modelled for the world's press adorned with part of Priam's treasure. Schliemann and his wife became major celebrities of their time as a result of this showboating.*

His critics attacked him in print and at discussions at the Royal Society, in London, but Schliemann did not care. He would not be turned away from his course of action and he continued to exploit the work of ancient writers such as Homer and the Greek historian Thucydides (c. 460–400 BC) to help him locate finds. He was skilled at interpreting these works, with an innate ability that allowed him to see things in the texts that others missed, although his single-minded approach to excavation may not have worked in history's favour. In his later excavations Schliemann employed a talented German archaeologist, Wilhelm Dörpfeld (1853–1940), who ensured that the work was conducted more professionally.

Schliemann's efforts at Hisarlik guaranteed him international fame and fabulous wealth, as well as many detractors. In June 1873, he unearthed almost 9,000 pieces of highly worked gold. Goblets, jewellery and other beautiful objects comprised the hoard that came to be known as the Treasure of Priam. Schliemann felt sure that this was the treasure of Homer's Troy. He even believed that he had found "Helen's crown": a diadem headdress that was actually made in c. 2300 BC – a millennium before Helen would have been born.

By law, Schliemann should have surrendered a portion of his finds to the Turkish authorities, but much that he discovered was spirited out of the country. He awarded the treasure trove to the German nation and for many years, until the Second World War, it was on display in Berlin. The hoard vanished during the Second World War. It is most likely that Soviet troops seized the gold upon their entry into Berlin in 1945. The location of the treasures remained a mystery until the mid-1990s, when they were rediscovered in the Pushkin Museum in Moscow. In 1996, 259 of the thousands of objects unearthed by Schliemann went on public display for the first time in fifty years.

Although modern scholars now consider the Homeric epics, the *Iliad* and the *Odyssey*, to be metaphorical records of a past era, modern research suggests that there may have been a great Trojan war, taking place between 1193 and 1184 BC, but that it was fought for different motives – financial ones.

Manfred Korfmann of Tübingen University, Germany, and his American colleague, Brian Rose of the University of Cincinnati, have been working together for many years at Troy. In the 1980s they excavated the bay area and found many human remains. The methods of burial differed greatly, and include both interment and cremation, suggesting that different religious rites from different cultures were being observed. Other finds, such as pots and metal artefacts such as tools, indicate that this site was used by merchants. Many may have died waiting for the prevailing winds, generally blowing from the north, to change so that they might sail through the Dardanelles.

Korfmann believes that the Trojans may have demanded a percentage of takings, or a tariff, from merchants, in exchange for

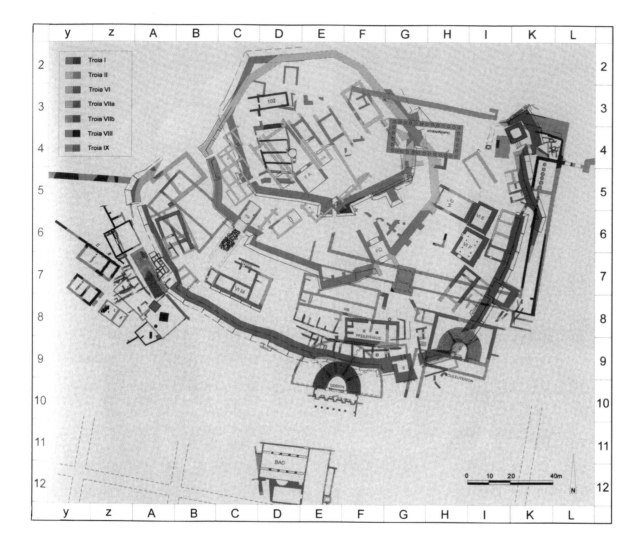

Troia I
Troia II
Troia VI
Troia VIIa
Troia VIIb
Troia VIII
Troia IX

LEFT: Plan showing the major settlement layers of the mound, the main points of which are included on a routed tour open to the public. The coordinate symbols along the edge of the plan correspond to the original scheme designed by the excavator W. Dörpfeld in the 1890s, still used by the Troy Project today for orientation.

OPPOSITE: The treasures of Priam – the King of Troy referred to in Homer's Illiad *whose capital (Troy) was destroyed by the Greek armies of Agamemnon – caused a worldwide sensation. The jewellery, such as this earring, was beautiful, finely crafted and, in historical terms, priceless. OPPOSITE BELOW: A view of the southeastern part of the plain of Troy from the hill of Hisarlik from Schliemann's original work* Troy and its Remains, *first published in English in 1875.*

mooring rights as they waited for good winds to take them through the Dardanelles and the ability to travel unhindered through an area that was notoriously difficult to navigate. This may, in time, have added considerably to Troy's wealth, while causing resentment against the Trojans themselves. In time, raiders and aggrieved merchants may have tried to sack Troy, and such events may have been distorted and recorded as the ten-year siege.

Archaeological work continued at Troy in the 1990s. In 1992, Korfmann and Rose worked with seventy-five scholars, from many disciplines, at the site. Their combined knowledge and skills allowed them to reverse some of the damage done by Schliemann to the city on the mound. Their excavations covered more than 1,200 square metres (1,440 square yards). The team discovered well-preserved stone and wooden houses from the time of Homer's epic, Troy VI (and Troy VIIa), built in front of the primary

entrance to the fortress – the south gate – as well as near the east tower and about 160 metres (525 feet) from the citadel itself.

Using geomagnetic sensing (see Glossary), they revealed the existence of a large mud-brick wall, probably built as a fortification for Troy VI, 400 metres (1,300 feet) south of the citadel wall. Despite fears that Schliemann's activities had obliterated much of the overlying deposits on the citadel, Korfmann and his colleagues revealed archaeological layers from the periods of Troy III and Troy IV, including houses built on the slope below the outer limit of the main settlement.

Work continues apace and each year, we learn more about this settlement. The site remains one of the greatest finds in archaeological history, proving Homer's work to be far more than mere fiction. Schliemann's obsession led him to unearth one of the world's most famous lost civilizations, but his inexpert enthusiasm nearly destroyed the remains he sought.

HIGH-TECH EXPLORATION OF TROY

Tʜᴇ ᴜsᴇ ᴏꜰ ʀᴇᴍᴏᴛᴇ-sᴇɴsɪɴɢ ᴛᴇᴄʜɴᴏʟᴏɢɪᴇs has enabled a new generation of explorers to peel back the layers of time at Troy without having to rely on the sort of invasive techniques employed by Schliemann.

"Rᴇᴍᴏᴛᴇ-sᴇɴsɪɴɢ ʜᴀs ᴇɴᴀʙʟᴇᴅ us to reconstruct relatively quickly the city plan of Hellenistic and Roman Troy, including streets, kilns and waterways. If we had tried to assemble the same information by conventional digging, it would have required several decades and millions of dollars. Although we excavate in order to reconstruct and thus protect the past, digging nevertheless involves destruction, since structures have to be dismantled in order for the lower levels to be investigated. Remote sensing provides a wealth of information and allows us to avoid, in most cases, the destruction that often accompanies traditional excavation. In cases where excavation is still necessary, remote sensing allows us to identify quickly the areas that will be most productive for investigation, thereby enabling us to focus directly on the topographical or stratigraphic problems that require elucidation."

Pʀᴏꜰ. Dʀ. Cʜᴀʀʟᴇs B. Rᴏsᴇ, Pᴏsᴛ-Bʀᴏɴᴢᴇ Aɢᴇ Gʀᴏᴜᴘ, Dᴇᴘᴀʀᴛᴍᴇɴᴛ ᴏꜰ Cʟᴀssɪᴄs, Tʀᴏʏ Pʀᴏᴊᴇᴄᴛ, Uɴɪᴠᴇʀsɪᴛʏ ᴏꜰ Cɪɴᴄɪɴɴᴀᴛɪ, Cɪɴᴄɪɴɴᴀᴛɪ, USA

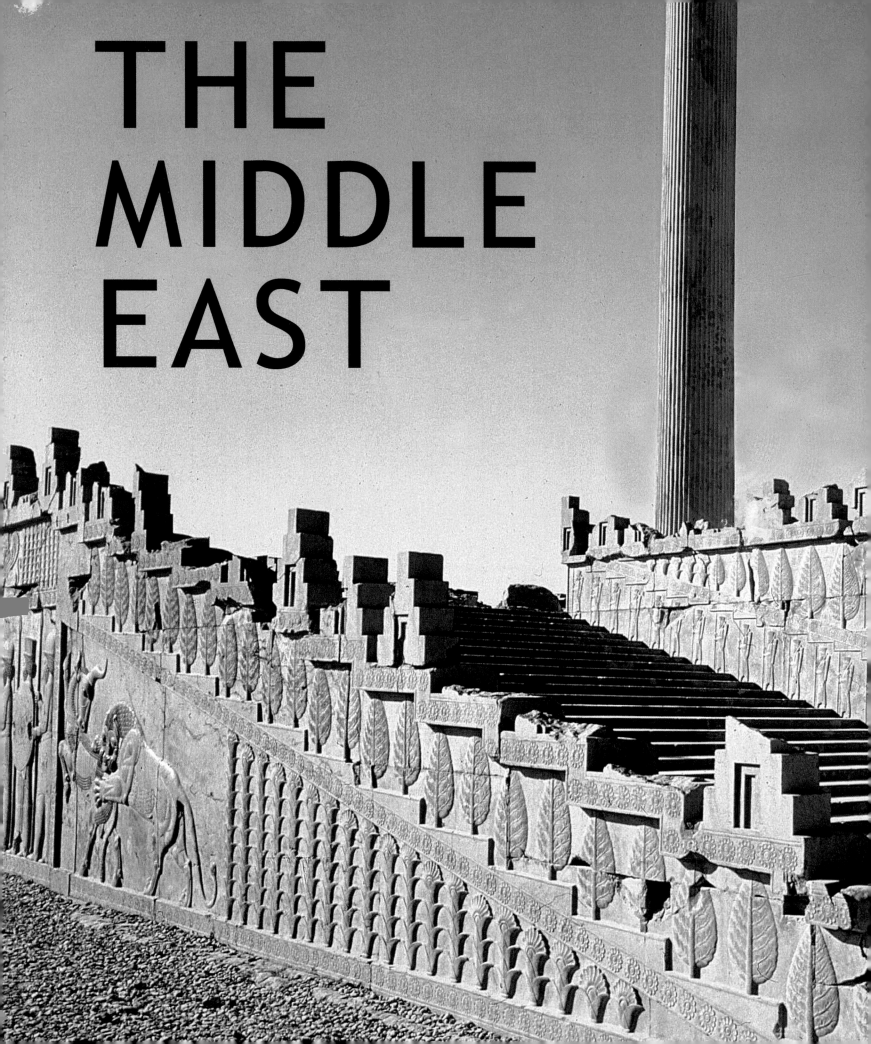

THE
MIDDLE
EAST

BABYLON

NIMRUD

MAHRAM BILQIS

PERSEPOLIS

UBAR

UR

BABYLON
NEBUCHADNEZZAR'S WONDER

... And it came to pass, as they journeyed from the east, that they found a plain in the land of Shin-nar ... And they said ... let us make brick, and burn them thoroughly. And they had brick for stone, and slime had they for mortar. And they said, Go to, let us build us a city and a tower, whose top may reach unto heaven ... And the Lord came down to see the city and the tower, which the children of men builded. And the Lord said, Behold, the people is as one, and they have all one language ... and now nothing will be restrained from them ... Therefore is the name ofit called Babel; because the Lord did confound the language of all ... and from thence did the Lord scatter them abroad upon the face of all the earth.

GENESIS, 11: 1–9 – THE GENERATIONS OF NOAH, KING JAMES VERSION OF THE BIBLE

THE CITY OF BABYLON WAS FOUNDED 5,000 YEARS ago on a site between the rivers Euphrates and Tigris, 88 kilometres (55 miles) south of modern Baghdad, in an area known as Mesopotamia. This area took in the land encompassed by the Tigris and Euphrates – modern-day Iraq, parts of Syria and other adjacent lands. Southern Mesopotamia became known as Babylonia, and northern Mesopotamia was known as Assyria (see page 129).

Babylon came to dominate the culture of ancient southern Mesopotamia. This civilization had some similarities with modern-day Iraq – it was driven by war and religion, and led by men gripped with fervour to acquire new lands. However, the Babylonians were also capable of great aesthetic achievements.

There had been settlements on the plain of the two rivers long before the founding of Babylon. Farming communities, with a form of organized polytheistic worship, were established in the area about 8,000 years ago. The ancient city of Ur, which flourished between 3000 and 2000 BC (see pages 154–161) was also sited on this plain. Important though Ur was in the region, it was Babylon that has really left its mark in history. It came to dominate the region to such an extent that it was eventually renamed Babylonia.

The land of the Babylonians was a flat alluvial plain. It was a harsh environment, with the heat reaching 50 degrees Celsius (122 degrees Fahrenheit) in the shade in summer. The vast tracts of desert were broken by the Euphrates and the Tigris. The waters of these rivers allowed life to flourish on the plain, and their often-violent floods made the land rich and fertile. This was a key factor

OPPOSITE: This stunning aerial view of the "Tower of Babel" and its surrounding lands reveals the scale of the entire complex and the enormity of its architects' vision.

ABOVE: Because of its biblical connotations the Tower of Babel has long fascinated Christian society. It has been represented many times in works of art, most famously in this painting (c. 1563) by the sixteenth century Flemish master, Pieter Brueghel the Elder.

ABOVE: *The Ishtar Gate, a beautiful and powerful totem to the gods of Babylon, has been reconstructed at the Pergamon Museum in Berlin, Germany. It enables us to see how the structure looked in its heyday.*

in Babylon's rise to dominance in the region; the city prospered by trading its surplus grain. Important trade routes, including one running from Sardis (the ancient capital city of Lydia and the political centre of Asia Minor at that time) via the eastern edge of the Tigris, to Susa (in Elam, the country lying just outside the Tigris and the Mesopotamian area, to the southeast) allowed the traders of Babylon access to a massive market. This route traversed Anatolia (modern-day Turkey) and Assyria to southwestern Persia, covering more than 1,000 kilometres (620 miles) in total. In return, Babylon gained access to the vital materials that it lacked. Babylon's location was ideal for cultivating crops, but the terrain offered no stone for building (the city's buildings were made from baked-mud bricks) or trees for wood, and there were scant mineral resources.

Another factor that facilitated Babylon's rise to power was its politically opportune location. It was mid-way between Egypt and Jerusalem to the west and Persia to the east. Babylon could reach out to these neighbouring lands, to form allegiances or to make war against them in the hope to claim them as its own.

After the collapse of Ur in c. 2005–2003 BC (see page 159), Babylon grew to become the political centre of the district. It is likely that the creation of a new dynamic dynasty of kings, the Amorites, led to Babylon's ascendancy. The Amorites dominated what historians have named the Old Babylonian period, between 1800 and 1530 BC. This era was the breakthrough period for the city. In fewer than 100 years, Babylon had given its name to the lands of southern Mesopotamia and established itself as a centre of learning and commerce. The warmongering kings of Mesopotamia came to hold the ancient world in their brutal grip. All the kings of the cities in the area were either at war with each other or in coalitions that were constantly shifting in the unstable political atmosphere, yet Babylon dominated from c. 1700 BC.

One of the most dynamic of the Amorite kings, Hammurabi (c. 1792–1750 BC), had a talent for political intrigue. This made him very powerful and popular during what was a politically unstable time, and allowed Babylon to take the advantage over other city-states in the region. Hammurabi was notable for establishing justice in the land, and issued a code of laws (known as the Code of Hammurabi), which greatly influenced the behaviour of future generations. He also centralized the administration of Babylon, laid down new laws of ownership, and organized religion. He adopted aggressive military policies during his reign and consequently became ruler of Babylonia and Assyria. The commercial success and prosperity of Babylon helped to fund the wars, and tight control of trade in the city, which secured wealth for the state, was maintained in order to facilitate this expensive activity.

Babylon was sacked and rebuilt many times throughout its existence. After the Old Babylonian period, aggressors who wrested control of the city between the sixteenth and seventh centuries BC included the Kassites, the Hittites, and the Assyrians. However, the city re-emerged, and, with the leadership of the Chaldean kings, known today as the Neo-Babylonian period, the city entered possibly its greatest era. This period began with King Nabopolasar in c. 625 BC, ended with Nabonidus in c. 555–539 BC, and saw the reign of perhaps the most famous king of Babylon, Nebuchadnezzar II (604–562 BC).

Babylon is described harshly in the Old Testament, as Nebuchadnezzar was responsible for the destruction of Jerusalem. He defeated Jerusalem's leader, Jehoiakim, in 597 BC, but razed parts of Jerusalem after further rebellion in 587 BC. Jehoiakim attempted to realign the city's allegiance with Egypt, prompting Nebuchadnezzar to lay siege to Jerusalem for eighteen months. He ordered the city to be destroyed: the walls were crushed, and the palace and great temple were razed to the ground. Vast numbers of political activists were slaughtered. Many of the surviving Jews were captured and taken to Babylon.

ABOVE: The great ceremonial Ishtar Gate, in Babylon, was covered in beautiful polychromatic tiles, many of them forming images, such as this representation of the god Marduk, which was on the front wall of the gate. The artistry of the tiles is staggering and the overall impression is of a great and powerful culture well able to express itself through religious art.

The "Tower of Babel" (above), realized here using computer graphics, was a place of enormous religious and political significance — representing the King's close links with the gods and his might to all would-be usurpers. Biblically the Tower is one of the most hated symbols of a civilization that dared to build a tower to God's domain: heaven.

The computer-generated image of the "Hanging Gardens of Babylon" (right) is of necessity based on conjecture. It shows the blue-green polychromatic tiles that were used in areas of ceremonial importance in Babylon. These gardens must have been truly remarkable and beautiful to be seen as one of the Seven Wonders of the World.

Jewish prophets promised divine vengeance for the Babylonians' sins of debauchery and avarice. St John the Divine warned (in Revelations 18:10–18) "alas, alas, that great city Babylon, that mighty city …! The merchandise of gold and silver, and of pearls, and fine linen … cinnamon … and wheat, and beasts … chariots … slaves, and souls of men … And they cried when they saw the smoke of her burning saying, What city is like unto this great city!" As far as St John was concerned, the people of Babylon had traded their spiritual lives and morality for greed and avarice, a state of affairs that could not continue indefinitely without prompting God's wrath. Such judgements, were, however, the adverse propaganda of a hostile people – the Israelites – and was not the generally held view.

By Nebuchadnezzar's reign, the city had developed into a rectilinear shape, lying east to west along the banks of the Euphrates. It spanned an area in excess of eight square kilometres (three square miles) and was the largest city on the Mesopotamian plain. The river played a vital role for traders, farmers and other city-dwellers – all depended on it for transport, irrigation and drinking water (to supplement aquifers and wells). The river divided the city into east and west Babylon. One huge bridge, stretching more than 90 metres (300 feet), spanned the river. Two great walls surrounded the city, as well as vast moats that Nebuchadnezzar likened to a sea on land. He also built a massive earth embankment to form another barrier all around the city. However, Babylon was not merely a functional fortress: it was a place of stunning architectural achievement.

The city had three main palaces: the Northern, the Southern and the Summer Palace, the latter of which was situated at the city's northernmost point. The grandest was the Southern Palace. This is thought to have been the home of Nebuchadnezzar. It featured splendid courtrooms, luxurious living apartments, and was built around five courtyards. The most impressive courtyard led to the throne room. The door to this room was 55 metres

OPPOSITE: *A different view of the Ishtar Gate reconstruction at the Pergamon Museum in Berlin, Germany. Great processions passed through the ceremonial gate at new year as the goddess Ishtar prevented evil entering the city.*

(180 feet) tall and 45 metres (150 feet) wide. This edifice was undoubtedly designed to impress visitors with the power of the Babylonian king and to inspire awe in those who had come to beg an alliance or, more intimidatingly, forgiveness.

Another notable architectural achievement was the "House that is the Foundation of Heaven and Earth", better known as the Tower of Babel. The so-called tower was in fact a ziggurat temple (see Glossary), built within the confines of a sacred precinct known as Etemenanki. Various sources suggest that the temple was 88 metres (290 feet) high, constructed of eight or nine tiers, one block above another. The base block was 90 metres by 90 metres (295 by 295 feet) in area. Each successive block above it was a smaller square, creating the stepped effect of the typical ziggurat temple. The tower is thought to date from the Old Babylonian period, though it was rebuilt many times, including by Alexander the Great when he was ruler of Babylonia in 330–323 BC. Nebuchadnezzar II built a temple to Marduk, the city's patron deity, at the tower's summit.

The tower was a magnificent edifice, but one that adherents of other religions found threatening. The Jewish prophets judged it to be an insult to the sanctity of heaven. The audacious structure incurred the Jewish God's wrath, and Babylon was damned in the Old Testament as the most sinful of all great cities because it dared to build a tower, the Tower of Babel, which reached to the heavens – a domain reserved for God alone.

The general populace were not allowed to enter Babylon's magnificent temples, only the king, his courtiers and the priests. Despite this, the state religion was an important part of everyday life for all. Indeed, for the Babylonians, there was no division between daily work and belief, as they felt that their work was done in the service of their gods, who required all the things that a living entity needed, such as food, clothing, water and shelter. The priests, human intermediaries for the gods on earth, administered these godly needs, and they became some of the largest landowners and stakeholders in the Babylonian economy.

Temples were believed to be the gods' earthly residences. Priests, servants of manufacturing, stewards and scribes were the gods' servitors. The temple's workers and priests co-ordinated the collection and distribution of agricultural and manufactured craft items. Religious, social and economic issues were not considered to be separate and were dealt with by the city's hierarchy – in particular the priests, who were some of the most learned members of Babylonian society. Priests were wealthy because they controlled the wealth of the city.

The design of the city was grid-like, based around ten rectilinear "blocks", four on the west side and six on the east. There were eight gateways into the city, the most important of these being the Ishtar gate. Ishtar was the goddess of fertility, sexual love and war. The gate named in her honour, in the north of the city, marked the entrance to a vast roadway, known then as "May the enemy not cross" and today as the Processional Way. At New Year, the height of the Babylonian religious year, the people of the city processed in a carnival, carrying totems and symbols of their gods in a ceremony to ensure that the road and therefore the city was a place where the enemy would never walk; as Nebuchadnezzar II put it, evil would never enter. The road led beyond the city walls to the Akitu temple, where New Year celebrations were held.

The walls of this road, running north to south through the eastern side of the city, were decorated with blue-green tiles and decorated with 120 superb bas-reliefs depicting giant striding lions – an animal associated with Ishtar. The gateway itself was a hugely impressive edifice. It was rebuilt many times, becoming more ornate each time. It eventually reached a height of nearly 20 metres (70 feet). It stood as a symbol of power, and was blue, decorated with reliefs in white and yellow tiles depicting the dragon of Marduk and the bull of Adad, the god of weather. The gate, now reconstructed, was an awe-inspiring site.

The temple of Esagila was another of the city's most splendid buildings. This temple, the largest and most important in Babylon, was dedicated to Marduk. Its walls were lined with sheets of solid gold. Babylonians held ceremonies in honour of Marduk for eleven days, around New Year, in and around the temple, as well as at the Akitu temple outside the city. The Tower of Babel was constructed next to the Esagila, and was another symbol of Marduk's central importance in the Babylonian belief-system.

These structures alone make Babylon an archaeological site of great significance. However, much of the fame of Babylon hangs on the legend of the Hanging Gardens of Babylon. These, together with the walls of Babylon, were one of the Seven Wonders of the ancient world, according to Greek historian Herodotus (c. 484–425 BC). The ancient scribe Berossus – a priest in the temple of Marduk during the reign of Antiochus I (c. 281–261 BC), believed that Nebuchadnezzar II built the gardens for his beloved wife, Amyitis. A native Median, she reputedly pined for the lush vegetation of her mountain homelands amid the flat plains of Babylonia. No evidence survives to indicate that plants were imported, but the irrigation of such a garden would not have posed a problem to the Babylonians, as they were expert hydraulic engineers.

The story of the Hanging Gardens has obsessed many explorers and historians, and the site's possible location is hotly debated. Some scholars have even suggested that the Gardens were actually situated in the Assyrian city of Nineveh. A number of possible sites exist in the fully explored areas of Babylon. One of these is a subterranean well and catacomb discovered in the Southern Palace. The catacomb had more than twelve rooms and its walls were extremely thick, suggesting that they were designed to bear a huge weight. The well was accessed via a complex system of buckets, linked by a chain mechanism in order to create a perpetual supply of water. The catacombs may have been storerooms for a government or military facility, but the system for supplying vast quantities of water might indicate that this was an irrigation system for the gardens.

Another possible location is between the Northern Palace and Western Outwork, which was the outer boundary of the city. An inscription has been found here describing a terraced structure in the likeness of a mountain – a possible description of the gardens.

Babylon's fortunes began to fall into terminal decline when its then ruler, Alexander the Great, died in 323 BC. It lost much of its political importance with the foundation of the Hellenistic capital at Seleucia-on-the-Tigris. Seleucia was founded by Seluceus in c. 312 BC, at a time when Babylon was in turmoil caused by a power struggle between Alexander the Great's generals. Seluceus was the victor in the struggle for the control of Babylon. He

THE EARLIEST SCRIBES

I<small>T IS WELL KNOWN</small> that many ancient peoples used writing in their daily lives, not least the ancient Egyptians, but it was the Babylonians, and their Mesopotamian ancestors, who where arguably the world's first great scribes.

"T<small>HE BABYLONIANS</small> were the first literate civilization, and produced an enormous body of written documents from the earliest periods onwards. All their literature was written on clay tablets, so much more of it has survived than on Egypt's papyrus scrolls, which are more perishable. Because Egypt's civilization is more visible, people have the impression that they were the most advanced of the ancient peoples before Greece and Rome. The place of Babylon and Mesopotamia in human history is not widely appreciated. Many technological advances that most people assume we owe to the ancient Greeks are instead Babylonian. A thousand years before Pythagoras, the Babylonians understood the properties of right-angle triangles. It was they who first divided the circle into 360 degrees, so that today we count seconds and minutes in sixties. The thousands of clay tablets that have been unearthed in Mesopotamia indicate that this country has a prior claim to the development of writing as a day-to-day tool for record-keeping in all branches of commerce, government, religion and domestic correspondence. Perhaps more significantly the Babylonians wrote the first recognizable poetry, including the "Epic of Gilgamesh". This masterpiece of world literature is the product of a high intellectual culture, but at the same time a work that is immediately readable today."

PROFESSOR ANDREW GEORGE, SCHOOL OF ORIENTAL & AFRICAN STUDIES, UNIVERSITY OF LONDON, ENGLAND

moved the military and political power to his new city, Seleucia, shortly thereafter. His successor, Antiochus I, like Seluceus, believed that Babylon had had its day and ordered the civilian population to move to Seleucia. The people of Babylon moved away, much as had the people of Ur before them, eventually abandoning the site.

The first modern excavation of Babylon began in 1899 and was brought to a conclusion by the outbreak of the First World War in 1914. Another expedition took place in the mid-1930s. Much has now been learned of the eastern sector of the city, but excavations remain incomplete in the western sector of the city – the harsh climate and political situation in Iraq have made archaeology in the region difficult. Remote-sensing work has been done by the USA using air- and space-based observation craft, but the information must be deemed by the Western allies to be of no military value before it is released. This process is frustratingly slow. Nevertheless, we must wait for the data and live in hopes that peace will return to the area, so that archaeologists and scientists can once again study the remains of one of the most remarkable sites of the ancient world.

MAHRAM BILQIS
The Temple of Sheba

ABOVE: *The American Foundation for the Study of Man's expeditionary team explored the Peristyle Hall during their 1951–1952 expedition. They revealed the eight monumental pillars – proving to be the largest pre-Islamic temple in Arabia.*

MODERN-DAY YEMEN IS RINGED BY THE GULF OF Aden in the south and the desert lands of the Rub' al-Khali and Saudi Arabia in the north. It is a hot and humid country, with temperatures in July and August reaching in excess of 40 degrees Celsius (104 degrees Fahrenheit). It is a landscape of contrasts, from huge desert wastes to fertile valleys and ocean shores. The Yemeni people make their houses from baked-mud bricks, a method thousands of years old. Farmers work the terraced fields of the highlands using traditional methods – ploughing the land with oxen and tending their crops by hand. Here time seems to have stood still for 3,000 years, since the time of the ancient people of the land, the Sabaeans.

If biblical sources are to be believed, Yemen was one of the first places on earth to be settled by man. The Yemeni people speak of their ancestors arriving in the land after the great flood of the Old Testament. Many believe that Shem, the eldest son of Noah, father of the Semitic peoples, established their capital city, Sana'a.

Another Yemeni figure who plays a significant part in history is the Queen of Saba, better known as the Queen of Sheba, who is thought to have reigned in c. 950–930 BC. She is perhaps best known from the Old Testament account of her meeting with the legendary King Solomon of Israel, who is said to have had 700 wives and 300 concubines, possessed prodigious wealth and a vast army of cavalry and chariots. The Queen of Sheba journeyed to Jerusalem to test Solomon's wisdom, heading a great caravan loaded with gifts for the king, including gold, rare spices and precious gems. The conference was successful and culminated in the two rulers bestowing wealth and good favour on one other.

OPPOSITE: *A cast bronze statue dedicated to the god Almaqah, considered to be the finest South Arabian bronze sculpture ever recovered, was found inside the Peristyle Hall, Mahram Bilqis, in 1952 by the American Foundation for the Study of Man's Arabian expeditionary team.*

LEFT: Sheba's legend lives on in popular Arabian culture. The story of King Solomon exchanging gifts with the Queen of Sheba was captured in a twentieth-century Ethiopian-school painting.

OPPOSITE: Aerial reconnaissance photographs of the temple complex put the eight monumental pillars in context. They form part of a ruined and once elaborate entranceway to the circular structure.

Apart from mentions in the Bible and in the Koran, little is known about the Queen of Sheba. There are disputes about whether she originated from Yemen or from Ethiopia. Not even her name is known for certain. The Arabs call her Bilqis; the Ethiopians named her Makeda ("greatness"). Ethiopian legend suggests that the Queen of Sheba became pregnant by Solomon, and that her son by him, Menelik, established a dynasty of rulers in Ethiopia.

It was not unusual, in this region, for women to achieve positions of power and status, and a number of queens ruled Arabian countries in pre-Islamic times (before AD 700). In Assyrian culture (see Nimrud, pages 128–135), the head of a family was female. These matriarchs were referred to as *shebu*. In other eastern areas, a woman could take several husbands. It is possible that women in Sheba's time experienced at least equal rights with men. Indeed, according to the holy book of Ethiopia, the Kebra Negast, Makeda (Sheba) laid down a law that only women could rule the land. Certainly, according to Arabic traditions, the Queen of Sheba was a powerful woman.

The country of Sheba, whose name means "host of heaven and peace", was located in southwestern Arabia on the eastern point of the Red Sea. Sheba occupied approximately 1,250,000 square kilometres (483,000 square miles) of valley and deserts in the area of present-day Yemen.

The Sabaeans are mentioned in the Bible as famous traders, and they engaged in a lucrative trade exporting gold, precious stones, spices and incense to neighbouring kingdoms. The trade in incense, particularly frankincense and myrrh, was especially significant and lucrative (see page 146), as it was used in religious ceremonies in cultures as diverse as Babylon, Egypt, Greece, Jerusalem and Rome. Indeed, some historians suggest that the Queen's legendary visit to Solomon was a trade mission, with the Queen wishing to ensure that Sheba's trade in frankincense and myrrh would continue unhindered by Solomon's armies.

Marib, the capital city of Sheba, lies 225 kilometres (140 miles) from the Red Sea. It is thought to have been established during the first half of the first millennium BC, although the exact date is not known. Marib was central to Sheba's trade; it was strategically situated on the Arabian Peninsula's main camel caravan trading route, which ran roughly parallel with the Red Sea from southern Arabia north to the Mediterranean region.

Marib was agriculturally as well as commercially prosperous. In c. 500 BC, the Sabaean people built the Marib Dam, a great feat of architecture and engineering. The dam restrained the waters from the Yemeni highlands as it dropped down through the desert. The water collected by the dam gave the Sabaeans bountiful supplies with which to cultivate a garden paradise for the production of food, extending over approximately 100 square kilometres (40 square miles).

This supply of water in such an arid region guaranteed the Sabaeans' agricultural prosperity, which the people of the region enjoyed for about 1,000 years. The dam's collapse, which occurred in c. AD 600 was disastrous: the waters burst out of the dam and flooded the entire area. Despite this calamity, the town of Marib exists to this day. It is now a small Bedouin settlement.

The land of Sheba was also known as a centre of a cult based on astronomical wisdom and the worship of the sun and moon. The sun god, Sham, was the creator god, while the moon goddess, Astarte (also known as Ashtar), was the great womb – the Queen of Heaven and Mother of all Deities. She symbolized the life-giving properties of the moon. Astarte was depicted with horns and

travelling in a fireball, in the company of a lioness. The sun was always shown to be close to her forehead. The Queen was central to religious life, acting as chief astronomer and astrologer.

About three kilometres (two miles) outside the ancient town of Marib stands the temple of Mahram Bilqis (pronounced "Mahram Bill-kees"), which is translated as Temple of the Moon God. The temple was built in the tenth century BC and the sacred site was visited by pilgrims from throughout Arabia until c. AD 550. The temple fell into neglect after this time, as people began to convert to Judaism, Christianity and Islam. The destruction of the Marib Dam in c. AD 600 sealed its demise.

The site has yet to be fully excavated, and archaeologists have much work to do before ascertaining exactly how the temple was associated with the Queen of Sheba. The site was first explored, in the modern age, by the antiquarian Thomas Arnaud in 1843. Arnaud drafted a map of Marib and also visited the Mahram Bilqis. He drew up a plan of the site and recorded a number of inscriptions from the temple. He also visited and charted the Marib Dam and a number of irrigation canals in the area. In 1888, Eduard Glaser described the site in detail. Glaser, an Austrian

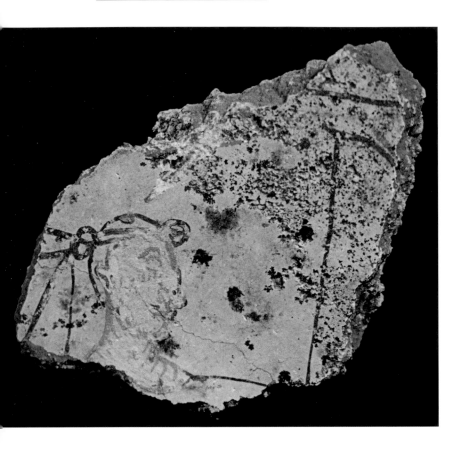

OPPOSITE: *A team from the University of Calgary has modelled the results of the work done by the AFSM using computers, and placed a human figure into the image to give it a sense of scale. The temple complex had a large curved boundary wall, a processional way, eight huge pillars and a Peristyle Hall. The site, ovoid in shape, measures 10,000 square metres (12,000 square yards).*

OPPOSITE BELOW: *Merilyn Phillips Hodgson in front of the limestone altar with sixty-seven Ibis heads, uncovered at Mahram Bilqis in 2001.*

Yemen Arab Republic was formed in 1962 only to be followed by unrest and, later, civil war in 1986 and again in 1994. The situation made archaeological exploration of the area nearly impossible for the best part of five decades, although some teams made progress, including a German expedition in 1988. And it was not until 1998 that the American Foundation for the Study of Man was able to resume excavations at the site for the first time since Phillips' days.

The Yemeni government invited the AFSM to return to excavate Mahram Bilqis, saying that they wanted Wendell Phillips' sister, Merilyn to finish what he had started.

The Mahram Bilqis is a place of great beauty and enormous size – it was easily the largest pre-Islamic temple in Arabia. The total site measures at least 10,000 square metres (12,000 square yards) – in all an awe-inspiring sight, even in its modern, reduced state. We can only conjecture at its magnificence in its heyday.

In 1988 only the top of a large curved boundary wall and monumental structural pillars were visible above the sands. The Peristyle Hall, first excavated in the 1950s by Wendell Phillips, had been reburied by the wind-blown sand. Since the 1988 season of excavation the AFSM team has discovered an impressive Sabaean building. Important inscriptions on the newly exposed walls give new insight to the activities in the temple. Also discovered was the first pre-Islamic fresco of a Sabaean man, a wall inset with an alabaster head of a lovely woman, a series of three rooms with many bronze art objects and the *coup de grâce* of the 2001 season, a large limestone altar adorned with sixty-seven Ibis heads.

It is thought that a great processional way leads into the temple, marked by eight huge rectangular pillars that rise out of the sands.

expert in oriental studies, made several journeys to Yemen between 1883 and 1892. On his third visit, he surveyed and described the Marib Dam and recorded details about the location of the inscriptions at the Mahram Bilqis temple.

Exploration of the site continued sporadically during the twentieth century, notably under the direction of Wendell Phillips, an American archaeologist. Phillips and his team from the American Foundation for the Study of Man (AFSM) began to excavate the temple in 1951. Along with his Bedouin aides he spent four months working at the site concentrating on revealing the monumental Peristyle Entrance Hall – a great court enclosed by elaborate columns.

Phillips was partially able to map the site, giving us a true sense of the site's scale and design for the first time. His efforts were halted in 1952 because of the unstable political situation in Yemen. Indeed, Phillips and his team had to flee to safety to avoid an assassination plot. Phillips died before he could return to the site and fulfil his wish to finish excavating the Mahram Bilqis – the Moon Temple of the Queen of Sheba.

The area suffered from continued political instability following the collapse of British rule during the period 1958–1960. The

NEW TECHNIQUES

WHILE TRADITIONAL excavation methods will never be replaced in the archeological zones, ground-penetrating radar surveys help to identify the most important locations to excavate (see page 9), and mechanical excavation has been utilized to speed the excavation of modern dune sand from the Mahram Bilqis. At a site of this scale and complexity, the multidisciplinary approach taken has radically increased the effectiveness and efficiency of the investigation.

"**A**ERIAL PHOTOGRAPHS taken in the mid- and late-1990s revealed that much of the site was buried by a large longitudinal sand dune. In 2000 we removed part of this dune with a mechanical excavator. Before each lift the sand was probed to a depth of several centimetres (inches) to assure that buried features would not be unwittingly encountered. Approximately 2 metres (2½ yards) below the top of the dune the excavation revealed the top of a masonry wall. Subsequent excavation has revealed this wall is part of a large building unknown to earlier explorers. In just two weeks, several thousand cubic metres (yards) of sand were removed from the site, a task that probably would have required months with shovels and wheelbarrows.

FREDERICK MOOSE, FIELD DIRECTOR,
AMERICAN FOUNDATION FOR THE STUDY OF MAN

The Peristyle Hall, the entrance to the circular temple, will be re-excavated by the AFSM in due course. And even more excavation is needed to be able to map the complete ground plan of this vast site. Further study is also required to ascertain whether the site performed a purely religious function, or if indeed it was the domain of power for the region of Sheba. For example, ancient inscriptions in Sabean script have been found on the walls of the temple, many of them recording female names. One of them might record the life of the Queen of Sheba.

One day we may know more of this queen's story as Mahram Bilqis is fully explored. Even if the biblical stories prove to be exaggerated or fictional, this site is a place of historical importance that is guaranteed to fascinate archaeologists for decades to come.

RECONSTRUCTION OF THE QUEEN'S THRONE

IF THE TECHNIQUES used to construct Mahram Bilqis can be re-learned, the site might be returned to its former glory.

"**T**HE AMERICAN FOUNDATION for the Study of Man has been excavating, surveying and documenting the findings of the temple since 1998. Preliminary results show that there are at least two major stages of construction of the temple, and architectural evidence shows that the Sabaean builders used advanced methods and techniques. Archaeologists and engineers are analyzing and studying these advanced methods and techniques in order to restore and reconstruct it by the end of 2007 to show how it looked during the time of its use.

DR ABDU OTHMAN GHALEB, DEPARTMENT OF ARCHAEOLOGY,
UNIVERSITY OF SANA'A, REPUBLIC OF YEMEN

NIMRUD
PLACE OF THE WAR MAKERS

"And it came to pass ... that Shalmaneser king of Assyria came up against Samaria, and besieged it. And at the end of three years they took it ... And the king of Assyria did carry away Israel unto Assyria ... Now in the fourteenth year of king Hezekiah did Sennacherib king of Assyria come up against all the fenced cities of Judah, and took them."

2 KINGS 18: 9–13, KING JAMES VERSION OF THE BIBLE

THE ASSYRIAN CIVILIZATION AND ITS EMPIRE originated in c. 1170 BC in Assur, in modern-day northern Iraq, on the west bank of the river Tigris. The great plain of the two rivers – the Tigris and the Euphrates – gave rise to a great and powerful civilization, as it had for the Babylonians and the city-state of Ur before. The people of Assyria began building small villages alongside the Tigris river in c. 5000 BC, and pottery and stone tools have been uncovered from this period. The first major settlements developed in the area c. 2800 BC.

As the civilization developed, the Assyrians came to live in cities, although many worked the land or carried on the semi-nomadic traditions of their forebears. The farmers produced milk and other dairy products from their livestock, and built irrigation canals to control flooding and water their crops, which included barley. The Assyrians developed advanced technology for iron smelting, even making steel from iron. They also became sophisticated artisans, working in gold, silver, bronze, ivory and wood and creating pottery. Slaves toiled for wealthy Assyrians.

The reign of King Shur-uballit I (c. 1363–1328 BC) marked a turning point for the Assyrians. Shur-uballit I was set upon expansion, and during his reign the Assyrians developed a way of life dominated by the acquisition of lands and wealth by war. Henceforth, Assyrian kings were raised in a society that was technologically innovative and dominated by war and expansion. The Assyrians succeeded in their aims, and their empire spread from Anatolia (modern-day Turkey) to Egypt, from Cyprus to the Caspian Sea. They ruthlessly conquered all resistance with their

OPPOSITE: A detail of the four-sided "black obelisk of Shalmaneser III", showing Shalmaneser, King of Assyria receiving tributes to mark his first thirty-two years in power.

ABOVE: Sir Austen Henry Layard (1817–1894) found remains of two palaces and mud-brick remains of a giant Assyrian ziggurat temple at the palace of Nimrud, during his excavations. Layard's vision of Nimrud in its heyday was presented to the world in this lithograph by James Ferguson.

disciplined and well-trained army. However, the Assyrians also brought learning and civilization to the societies under their rule.

Toward the end of the second millennium BC, Assyria's growth faltered at the hands of the Aramaeans, a warring nomadic race. However, the Assyrians had re-established their hold on the region by c. 935 BC. King Ashurnasirpal II (c. 884–859 BC) in c. 880 BC chose Nimrud as his capital city and used it to glorify his nation. The might of the Assyrians was set out in masterworks of art and stone: the embodiment of Ashurnasirpal's vision for a great imperial state. His army was drilled in the art of effective war. We can learn much of the Assyrians' military might from bas-reliefs found at Nimrud.

LEFT: The winged monsters of Nimrud captured the imagination of the West in the nineteenth century, as illustrated in this watercolour (c. 1850) by Frederick Cooper.

OPPOSITE: This human-headed and eagle-winged bull is 3 m (9¾ ft) high, and originally one of a pair that guarded the king's residential suite in the palace of Ashurnasirpal II. Made of black alabaster c. 865 BC, this sculpture now resides in the British Museum, London.

They employed chariots in battle and controlled horses by bit and bridle. They had also developed a siege engine fitted with a battering ram. Foot soldiers were equipped with bows and arrows and carried long spears. This was a fearsome force.

The city walls of Nimrud enclosed an area of approximately two square kilometres (¾ of a square mile). There was a citadel in the southwest corner that housed a number of palaces. The Northwest Palace, built during the reign of Ashurnasirpal II, was bedecked with gigantic stone relief carvings. Its doorways were flanked by winged lions and bulls, which can be seen today in London's British Museum. Nimrud (known in ancient times as Kalhu) also had a number of temples, one of which was dedicated to Nabu, the god of language. Assyrian religion was similar to that of the Babylonian city-states. The state cult, ruled over and maintained by the king, was based around a pantheon of gods, Marduk (the god of writing and vegetation and the father of Nabu) and Ishtar (the goddess of sex and war) in particular. The king was responsible for the upkeep of the temples and he acted as a human interface between the gods and the people. The city also had a ziggurat temple of the sort seen throughout the region.

One of Nimrud's most important buildings was a temple known as the Ezida. Built in 798 BC by order of Queen Sammu-rammat, mother of the Assyrian King Adad-nirari III (who reigned from 810 to 783 BC), the Ezida included the temple of Nabu, the god of writing, and his companion Tashmetum. The temple's library was a rich trove of archaeological treasures particularly because it held many religious and political works, and even included supposedly magical texts.

At its height, in the ninth to the seventh centuries BC, the Assyrian Empire stretched from what is now Iran to the eastern Mediterranean and from the mountains of eastern Turkey to the shores of the Persian Gulf. This was a huge kingdom dominated by an autocratic monarchy that demanded a high level of tribute – be it horses from the foothills of the Zagros mountains (to the east of Assyria), slaves or cattle – and absolute acceptance of Assyrian rule. No dissension was tolerated. One of Nimrud's bas-reliefs depicts the governor of Lachish bowing down before King Sennacherib (who ruled in 704–681 BC) in a gesture of surrender following a period of unrest in Lachish. In the same relief, Sennacherib is shown torturing the governor's men.

The Assyrian passion for war was typified by King Sennacherib's siege of Jerusalem in *c.* 701 BC. Jerusalem was then ruled by King Hezekiah. Sennacherib had defeated a coalition of the Egyptians, Palestinians and Phoenicians, but Hezekiah revolted against Assyrian rule, buying Sennacherib off with 300 talents of silver and thirty of gold. Despite his agreement with Hezekiah, towards the end of his reign, Sennacherib returned to Jerusalem with a vast army to enforce his will. The Old Testament tells of how God sent down an angel and killed Sennacherib's army, which amounted to "an hundred and four score and five thousand" men. The soldiers may in fact have suffered from a plague infection, or were perhaps poisoned or ambushed in their sleep. Sennacherib returned home to Nimrud beaten, but unbowed.

In another notable campaign, the Assyrians conquered Egypt in 671 BC. There were sporadic revolts following the conquest, and Assurbanipal, then ruler of Assyria, sacked the great Egyptian city of Thebes in 664–663 BC as part of the efforts to quell dissent.

It took a military alliance between the Babylonians and the people of Medes, led by King Cyaxares, to tear the Assyrian empire apart, ending the rule of the Assyrian kings with Ashuruballit II in 609 BC. The Babylonians and Medes looted and ravaged the cities of Assyria, Nimrud included, and carved the Assyrian territories up between them. Nimrud fell as the empire collapsed. In the seventh century BC, Nimrud declined in importance because the Sargonid kings (who ruled the region from the twelfth to the seventh century BC) preferred Nineveh as their primary residence. Despite this, Nimrud, like Nineveh, then declined in political importance and fell in to decay and disuse.

Although the Assyrians' preoccupation with war and death and their pursuit of expansionism made them famous, it is in the majestic structures of Nimrud that we see a true expression of their civilization. This aspect of Assyrian society was little known until the mid-nineteenth century, when English antiquarian Sir Austen Henry Layard (1817–1894) unearthed the city.

Layard was brought up on the *Tales of the Arabian Nights*. He marvelled at the stories of magic and war, which drove him to pursue the lost cultures of the East. From 1839, he spent many years travelling in the area. In 1843, Layard found a diplomatic post with Britain's ambassador to Turkey, Sir Stratford Canning. In the same year, a Frenchman, Paul Emile Botta, unearthed Nineveh, another great Assyrian city.

Until then, the British government had shown little interest in financing archaeological expeditions in the area, but it then became a matter of national pride to discover something in a similar vein. Layard used his position to influence Canning, and

convinced him to finance a small expedition. Layard struggled with minimal finance, although his expedition was later supplemented by £2,000 from the British Museum.

Layard reached the mound at Nimrud, with his six-strong team of local recruits, in 1846, and began to dig. There was little to see above ground but the mound itself, which covered an area a quarter of a square kilometre. At the end of the first few days' excavation, there was no doubt that this was an ancient and very important site. Digging trenches into the mound, Layard discovered alabaster slabs, covered in cuneiform writing (see Glossary). He and his team then exposed the remains of two palaces and the mud-brick remains of a huge ziggurat temple.

During his excavations at Nimrud, Layard opened twenty-one halls, chambers, and passages, and twenty-seven portals, formed by colossal winged bulls and lion sphinxes. Nearly all of the walls of these halls and chambers were decorated with carved slabs of alabaster. There were about 3,000 metres (9,880 feet) of bas-reliefs, recording the wars, victories and the deeds of Sennacherib.

Layard worked at Nimrud until 1851, during which time he uncovered the Northwest Palace of Ashurnasirpal II, the monarch

NIMRUD

LEFT: Max Mallowan found numerous ivories at Fort Shalmaneser. This ivory panel shows a regal seated lion.

RIGHT: King Ashurnasirpal II chose the new site for his capital city at Nimrud c. 880 BC. He is captured here in this impressive sculpture.

who had built Nimrud. Layard removed the finds, which included cuneiform scripts written on stone, the bas-reliefs and elaborate sculptures, from their resting places and transported them to London, where they were met with astonishment from scholars.

Perhaps the most striking of Layard's finds were enormous black alabaster sculptures, about three metres (ten feet) in height, of human-headed, eagle-winged bulls, known as *lamassu* – mythological guardians that kept evil spirits away from the king and his palace. These creatures were discovered flanking the entranceway to Ashurnasirpal II's palace. The sculptures bore cuneiform writing on a square backing slab, visible between each creature's legs and above its back.

One of Layard's most important finds was the so-called Black Obelisk of King Shalmaneser III, which dates back to c. 827 BC. This beautiful four-sided black alabaster obelisk is more than two metres (six feet) high and bears twenty picture sections, five on each side. These depict vassal (subordinate) kings bringing tributes such as horses, food and gold to Shalmaneser III, and are supported by delicately sculpted cuneiform writing. The structure is a remarkable record of thirty-two years of Shalmaneser III's reign.

Layard went on to do excavation work at Nineveh in 1846. There, he found perhaps the most important cache of ancient writing ever discovered in the region, stored in the city's Royal Record Office and Library. He discovered 26,000 clay tablets in total. The tablets included lists of medicines and illnesses, some personal correspondence, records of wars and meticulously worked-out calendars. They also included the oldest recorded descriptions of the great flood myth that features in the histories and legends of many civilizations, the equivalent to that suffered by Noah in the Old Testament. This was probably the original flood reference from which the Noah version was later adapted. Layard gave us the key to decipher the language, history, customs and medicine of the ancient Assyrians.

Prince Albert's celebration of Victorian England, the Great Exhibition of 1851 in London's Crystal Palace, displayed some of Layard's finds. The exhibition met with great public approval and Layard was greeted as a national hero upon his return to London. Knighted for his work, Layard died in 1894, a successful man who had fulfilled his dreams of adventure in the East.

Many people have worked at the Nimrud site since Layard's time, including Max Mallowan (1904–1978), a British archaeologist working with the British School of Archaeology in Iraq. During his dig in 1951, he found a sandstone stele or plaque that represented King Ashurnasirpal II in full ceremonials. One hundred and fifty-four lines of inscription were carved beneath the king's portrait. These list an inventory of the buildings of Nimrud and the 47,074 people who attended the great banquet, held over ten days, to celebrate the city's completion. This stele, a remarkable piece of documentary history, gives historians a unique insight into Assyrian splendour and public life. It reminds us that Nimrud was custom-built to inspire awe. The throne room, for example, was astonishing. Both sides of the room were decorated with enormous bas-reliefs depicting scenes of war. A pair of giant winged bulls flanked the doorways. Further sculptures include depictions of lion and bull hunts, and two carved sequences that show the king and his attendants by the mystical Sacred Tree of the Assyrians.

Iraq's Department of Antiquities and Heritage made a remarkable breakthrough in 1989, when it was carrying out much-needed maintenance and archaeological work at the Northwest Palace of Nimrud. They stumbled into a hidden tomb, which proved to be the tomb of a queen of Nimrud – Queen Yaba, daughter of Tiglathpileser III, who ruled from 744 to 727 BC. The queen had been at rest for more than 2,700 years. She died at the age of fifty-five – more than a decade beyond the average life expectancy of a woman Nimrud at that time. Her body had been carefully preserved in traditional Assyrian style, similar in some ways to Egyptian methods of preservation. Her body, and the tomb it lay in, were ornamented with nearly 100 items of exquisitely engraved jewellery, and her intestines and internal organs were carefully stored in ornate jars.

The Iraqi team went on to find two other tombs of the Queens of Nimrud: those of Banitu, wife of Shalmanasser V (who reigned between c. 726 and 722 BC) and Atalia, wife of Sargon II (who ruled in 721–705 BC). Their graves were notable for their caches of beautiful jewellery: figures of goddesses were carved into anklets, earrings and bracelets made from gold and embedded with semi-precious stones and crystals. Other items discovered included vessels, seals and ornaments, all displaying Assyrian artwork and iconography. These finds have proven that even

BUILT TO IMPRESS

THE ANCIENT CITY of Nimrud, which has now been exposed to modern scrutiny for over one and a half centuries, still inspires awe in its visitors despite many ornamental and historically important items being placed in museums.

"NIMRUD IS IN NORTH IRAQ covering a huge area of a flat, rather featureless plain and is an impressive site even though it mostly consists of mounds of crumbling mud-bricks, marking the remains of walled structures. As you approach the city, you first catch sight of the ziggurat from a considerable distance away. It dominates the horizon. Although it is also a massive mound of crumbling bricks, with none of the steps visible, it is still a very impressive monument to the people who built the city, and its ziggurat, all those centuries ago. One is left with an impression of power and tremendous wealth, that stays with you over time."

DR ROGER MATTHEWS, INSTITUTE OF ARCHAEOLOGY, UNIVERSITY COLLEGE, LONDON

LEFT: This ivory bas-relief of an Assyrian warrior was discovered at the palace of Shalmaneser III, Nimrud. It illustrates the style of ceremonial dress worn by the King's men.

sites long exposed to the scrutiny of archaeology can still harbour treasures.

The ongoing political instability of the Iraqi region hampers archaeologists and historians' attempts to do further work at the site. Nevertheless, it is believed that the Iraqi government has carefully preserved the site. Meanwhile, treasures from the site, held in institutions such as the British Museum, give us a tantalizing insight into the beauty, splendour and power of ancient Nimrud and its Assyrian inhabitants.

PERSEPOLIS
JEWEL OF THE PERSIAN EMPIRE

THE RUINED CITY OF PERSEPOLIS LIES ON THE PLAIN of Dasht, 640 kilometres (400 miles) south of modern-day Tehran in the shadow of the Kzuh-I-Rahmat, the Mountain of Mercy. This site is dedicated to the great power of one of the ancient world's most magnificent civilizations, that of the Achaemenids. These people were probably descended from a little-known mountain king, Achaemenes. King Cyrus the Great (580–529 BC) established Achaemenid Persian rule with the defeat of Astyages (584–c. 550 BC), a king of the Medes. Cyrus' empire stretched from the eastern Mediterranean to northwestern India. It became a magnificent, wealthy and organized society, famed for its lavish architecture and efficient government administration.

The Persians developed literature and written communication, using a form of cuneiform writing, on wet clay tablets. By the time of King Darius I (548–486 BC), cuneiform was highly developed. His people also used papyrus, and sometimes animal hides, as a medium to carry and transmit information. This helped to enhance communications within the Persian world – something that Darius I thought crucial. Indeed, one of Darius' great achievements was the establishment of an efficient communications network across the empire, by initiating the building of a grand road. This "Royal Road", as it was known, was 2,700 kilometres (1,680 miles) long. It linked the capital with Susa (the administrative centre of the Achaemenid Empire) and with the outlying regions of Lydia, Phrygia, Babylonia (see pages 112–121) and Assyria (see pages 128–135). A series of 111 post stations, along the length of the road, kept horses ready for the relaying of strategic and royal messages. Communications

OPPOSITE: Although today it is a ruin, the Hall of Audience (Meeting Hall) at the Royal Palace in Persepolis is still a magnificent sight. Begun by Darius I it was finished by his son Xerxes I, upon Darius' death in 486 BC. It ws a structure designed to instil a sense of awe in all visitors and the design is effective to this day.

ABOVE: The imagery of animals was used repeatedly across Persepolis. The bull was of particular importance and is seen here atop a column. The skill of the craftsmen of Persopolis is reflected in the city's once great statues.

LEFT: *Sculptures of magical and mythical creatures, such as this double-headed gryphon, were common in Persepolis.*

OPPOSITE: *Darius I, seen in this stele, was a great administrator. He ensured that the empire was governed via a system of satrapies, and set a tariff for tributes to be paid by each of these self-governed districts to the king each year.*

between the satellite regions and the capital were excellent, thereby guaranteeing a flow of information and culture.

The Achaemenids followed the beliefs of Zoroaster (c. 628–551 BC), a prophet and spiritual teacher of old Persia. Zoroaster struggled to establish a holy agricultural state to achieve unity against all aggressors beyond the borders of his country. He believed that his people needed to be united in order to repel invaders. He propounded a belief in a supreme god, known as Ahura Mazda (Persian for "wise lord"), who fought an ongoing battle in his arena (earth) against Ahriman, Lord of Darkness and Death. Zoroaster preached that in time Ahura Mazda would win against evil and become omnipotent. Zoroaster also taught that animals should be treated with respect, because they provided food through their labour. He believed in cultivating a good harvest and in achieving spiritual, social and political harmony through good thoughts, words and deeds. Zoroastrianism featured rites of worship performed by Magi (priests) who taught from the Avesta, scriptures that included hymns attributed to Zoroaster. The religion was central to the Achaemenid way of life and remained so until the coming of Islam, which originated in Arabia in the seventh century AD.

Darius I wanted to demonstrate the power and achievement of his people. He dreamed of a new capital city, Persepolis, which would stand as a testimony to Persian success and wealth. He dreamed of a place worthy of the gods. Construction began in c. 518 BC, and was continued by Darius' son Xerxes (486–465 BC) and completed by his grandson Ataxerxes I (464–425 BC).

Persepolis was a city that was very advanced in its architecture and engineering. Before building work began, the terrain was prepared for the planned structures. The city's engineers created a huge, level platform for the city's base by digging into the rocky mountainside and filling in unlevel ground with rubble. This artificial terrace measured 300 metres (1,080 feet) by 450 metres (1,480 feet). It stood 14 metres (45 feet) above the surrounding plain, and could only be accessed by ascending a monumental double staircase. This was a grand site that needed engineering on an equally grand scale. The city's architects wanted to protect the city from flooding, and installed an elaborate system of drains in the foundations.

Persepolis featured fifteen grand state buildings, including the Apadana (the meeting hall); the Throne Hall; the Gate House of

Xerxes; the Treasury; the Harem and a series of majestic palaces, all built with supreme artistry and designed to impress visitors with a sense of the city's wealth and power. Greek author Diodorus Siculus (c. first century BC) recorded that the completed city was "the richest city under the sun and the private houses had been furnished with every sort of wealth over the years … many of the houses belonged to the common people and were abundantly supplied with furniture and wearing apparel of every kind."

The grandest of Persepolis' palaces were those dedicated to Darius I (known as Darius the Great) and to Xerxes. These were buildings of astonishing complexity, which demonstrated remarkable art in their construction.

The entrance to the palace of Xerxes was through the Gate House of Xerxes, also known as the Gate of All Nations. This features the famous Tribute Reliefs, extraordinary carvings depicting the Armenians, the Assyrians, the Babylonians, the Egyptians and the Medes offering up tribute to the Persians (see page 143). Then there were two vast staircases, each a gallery of impressive art sculpted in stone. They displayed striking scenes, including an allegorical depiction of good destroying evil in the form of a bull succumbing to a savage lion. The staircases led to the Apadana. The palace complex also featured the Treasury and the king's Harem.

Any visitor would have been awe-struck by the complexity of design and the proliferation of columns in the buildings, which was a particular feature of the city's construction. The Throne Hall is often referred to as the Hall of One Hundred Columns – it features row upon row of stone columns with elaborately decorated bases and capitals, all designed to display the king's wealth. Even the doorways of the Throne Hall display elaborate carvings showing the king victorious in combat. The Throne Hall and the Gate House of Xerxes were conceived with ceremony in mind, reaffirming the king's might, year upon year, as noble visitors paid tribute to his greatness.

Persepolis, the testament to the glory of the Achaemenid kings, flourished for two centuries, until its beauty and opulence were destroyed by a man set on vengeance.

The Macedonian king, Alexander the Great (356–323 BC), caused the downfall of Persepolis in c. 330 BC. He was motivated by the intention to avenge the sack of the Greek capital, Athens, by the Persians in 480 BC.

Alexander quelled resistance to his will at home before launching a campaign to free all the Greeks in Asia Minor and to destroy Greece's enemy, Achaemenid Persia. The Persian-Greek Wars had begun when most of the Greek city-states refused to submit to imperial Persia, which had been enraged by some mainland Greek

cities' support of rebellious Greek colony cities in Anatolia (modern-day Turkey). These Anatolian Greek-origin cities had been conquered by Persia under Darius I, but then rose up against him.

Alexander began his expedition with the aim of freeing Greeks who were living, as he saw it, oppressed and unhappy under the hand of despots. However, some historians believe that Alexander faced a turning point in his career as a general and as a king when he reached Persepolis. This was the heart of Persia – the centre of Achaemenid rule. By penetrating so far into enemy territory, Alexander's army had won the opportunity to right what

LEFT: In this bas-relief on the Apadana, the Royal Meeting Hall at Persepolis, a Medean officer is immortalized during a visit to pay homage to the king, Darius I.

he perceived to be the wrongs of the past. Alexander chose not only to liberate his people, but to launch a fierce attack at the heart of his enemy's power base.

The historian Diodorus said that Alexander described the city as the "most hateful of Asia". On taking Persepolis, his soldiers were given free rein to loot the treasures of the city, to murder the men and to defile and enslave the women they encountered. The soldiers' frenzy and lust became so great that they even began to fight among themselves. Persepolis had been designed as a ceremonial and cultural centre, not with defence in mind, and it and its people were soon overwhelmed and destroyed.

Diodorus disagrees with other accounts of the sacking: some claim that the city was set alight in a final act of violence and destruction. Diodorus, however, believed that Alexander took the city with little intention of destroying it. Diodorus suggests that it was a young woman named Thais who proposed that the

conquerors burn down Persepolis. She was from Attica, a region that had suffered at the hands of the Persians. Her people, like the Athenians, had a deep-rooted hatred of the Persian Empire. Diodorus claims that Alexander, drunk from carousing and feasting in celebration, was taken with Thais' idea, and that he tossed the first burning torch to start the fire, with Thais throwing the second.

However the event occurred, the once-magnificent city of Persepolis was destroyed by the fire. Its people were either murdered or taken into slavery. Its riches were looted: the haul of stolen gold and silver was so huge that 20,000 donkeys were required to carry it away. The capital of the Persian Empire was no more, and Alexander had achieved vengeance for his people. Some argue that this event changed the impetus for Alexander's expedition. He was no longer motivated purely from an urge to right injustice, but to claim power for himself. However, Alexander did make efforts to appease the Persians, which gives

LEFT: The enormity and magnificence of Darius' vision is apparent in this aerial view of the site which reveals the city's system of fortifications and its complex of palaces. The image was taken at an altitude of 2,440 metres on 20 April 1936 and offered one of the first overall views, putting the buildings at the site in context.

ABOVE: *Reliefs on the staircase of the palace of Darius I show the presentation of tributes to the king from his satrapies. The reliefs are symbolic of the rich diversity of produce and great wealth within the Persian Empire. They also reach across time to remind us of just how powerful and wealthy the Persian kings were.*

credence to Diodorus' idea that Alexander destroyed the city on a whim rather than as a calculated act. The sacking of Persepolis was a vital symbolic victory for Alexander – he had defeated Persia and in effect had become king of Asia. Equally, the loss of the city was a devastating blow for the Persian Empire.

The ruins of Persepolis attracted the attention of European sightseers as early as the seventeenth century. Dutch travel writer Cornelis de Bruyn (1652–1727) famously travelled to the Levant and to Russia, and in 1701 left the Netherlands for the second time to travel to Persia (via Moscow) to see the ruins of Persepolis. Rudimentary excavations were undertaken in the nineteenth century, but it was not until 1931 that the first modern scientific study of the site began.

MONUMENTAL ART

Persepolis is an astonishing site. Its magnificence, even in its ruined state, captures the imagination of tourists, Iranian patriots and archaeologists alike. It is not difficult to imagine the impact the city would have had on visitors in its heyday, in the sixth to fourth centuries BC.

"Most exciting is the incredible monumental art on the sides of the main palace buildings; scenes of lines of dignitaries from the Babylonian empire carrying tributes, waiting to present them to the King. Apart from their intrinsic value as a visual history of an age and a people long gone, they provide archaeologists and anthropologists with illustrative evidence of subjugated civilizations. This includes their manner of dress, physical characteristics, differing beard and hair styles. We even have a clear idea of the type of weapons worn, and artefacts considered of high enough value to be offered as a tribute to the conquerors of their individual countries or city-states. Many of these artefacts can be compared to items unearthed while excavating the site, giving a clear insight into their actual use and significance which might have been otherwise unknown. There has been some Government-sponsored reconstruction. Consequently there is a fair bit of the impressive statuary and relief art to view, which ensures that visitors understand the past magnificence of the city and the importance of the culture that produced it."

Dr St John Simpson, British Museum, London, England

The Oriental Institute at the University of Chicago hired German archaeologist Ernst E. Herztfeld (1879–1948) to mount an expedition to the site. His brief was to investigate, excavate and restore the complex, if possible. Hertzfeld, accompanied by architect Fritz Kefter, excavated the great terrace. They discovered the elaborate stairway leading to the Apadana meeting hall, and the king's Harem, known as the Harem of Xerxes. Hertzfeld had found a city of astonishing beauty. In March 1933, a British journal ran a headline declaring, "The Magnificent Discovery at Persepolis: stairway sculptures that will rank among the greatest works of art surviving from Antiquity" (*London Illustrated News*). Hertzfeld and his colleagues had given the world its first glimpse of a lost empire's crowning achievement.

Hertzfeld left the project in 1934, but the excavations continued. For the next five years, the team, sometimes comprising 500 people, worked at the site, revealing evermore splendour and signs of opulence. The outbreak of the Second World War in 1939 brought their efforts to an end. Excavation and study at the site has continued since the 1940s, and UNESCO granted the site the status of World Heritage Site in 1979.

Today, the palace is almost completely excavated; all the administration buildings are known and are, in the main, well preserved, helped by the arid climate. There may be structures lying beneath the visible city, but none have yet been unearthed. This is mostly because of the difficulty created by heavy redevelopment throughout the area. The ruined city stands as a testament to the might of the Persians and the imperialist obsessions of its leaders. Their warmongering ways cost them dear and brought about the destruction of the edifice that symbolized their way of life.

ABOVE: Alexander the Great won a decisive victory against the Persians at Issus, a plain on the coast of the Gulf of Iskenderun, in Turkey, and went on to sack Persepolis, raiding and looting the great city in 330 BC. This story was immortalized in one of the greatest mosaics of ancient times — known as the "Battle of Issus" mosaic, it was found in the ruins of Roman Pompeii in 1831.

UBAR
THE ATLANTIS OF THE SANDS

ABOVE: The Rub 'al-Khali — the
Empty Quarter — is a very
unforgiving environment. The vast
expanse of desert sands was a difficult
place to live and work; for merchants
travelling in caravans c. 805 BC to
c. AD 400 — Ubar would have been
a welcome sight and offered a vital
stopping point on their trade route.

I N THE DESERT LANDS OF OMAN, BEYOND THE great fertile range known as the Dhofar mountains, lies the Rub 'al-Khali. Stretching over 648,000 square kilometres (250,000 square miles), it is known in English as the Arabian Empty Quarter. It is appropriately named – this is a land of harsh beauty, barren, arid and inhospitable, with an unforgiving climate.

This land was the site of an important trade centre that flourished from c. 850 BC to c. AD 400. It was founded by the people of 'Ad and was known as Ubar. The city has been identified as one referred to as Iram (or Irlam), the "city of towers" in the Koran. Until the rediscovery of Ubar in the 1990s, many people had believed this city, and the people of 'Ad, to have been only a legend, kept alive in the Koran, in the oral stories of the local Bedouin people (the inhabitants of the area today), and romanticized in the *Tales of the Arabian Nights.*

According to the Koran, the people of 'Ad showed animosity to Hud, a messenger from Mohammad the Prophet, and rebelled against Allah. Consequently, they were dealt a terrible punishment: a severe sandstorm wiped out the 'Ad, as though they had never existed: "[the] 'Ad ... were destroyed by a furious wind, exceedingly violent; He made it rage against them seven nights and eight days in succession: so that thou couldst see the people lying prostrate in its [trail], as they had been roots of hollow palm-trees tumbled down. Then seest thou any of them left surviving?" (Surat al-Haaqqa: 6-8). Archaeological evidence suggests that the city was destroyed, in c. AD 400, but was a victim of geological disaster rather than divine vengeance (see pages 151–153).

ABOVE: The Rub 'al-Khali — the
Empty Quarter — is a very
unforgiving environment. The vast
expanse of desert sands was a difficult
place to live and work; for merchants
travelling in caravans c. 805 BC to
c. AD 400 — Ubar would have been
a welcome sight and offered a vital
stopping point on their trade route.

OPPOSITE: The northeast circular
tower discovered at Shisr told of a
settlement lost to the sands, leading the
expeditionary team to wonder if they
might actually find Ubar.

In general, Iram or Ubar has not been portrayed kindly – it has been damned as a place of debauchery and avarice, and its people depicted as eating from golden plates, indulging in endless merrymaking and pleasure seeking and caring nothing for their immoral acts. Roman writer Pliny (AD 23–79) recorded stories, told by the Bedouin Arabs, of Ubar's legendary finery and that its ruins and lost treasures were guarded by great Djinns (powerful and magical genies). These tales have fired the imaginations of adventurers and archaeologists for centuries.

Some historians believe that the 'Ad were the ancestors of the Hadramites, one of the four peoples who lived in South Yemen – the others being the Sabaeans (see pages 122–127), the Minaeans and the Qatabaeans. The Hadramites emerged in c. 500 BC and then disappeared in AD 240. These people were often called the "Fortunate Arabs". They earned their soubriquet because they lived in an area that was extremely fertile. At the time of the 'Ad, a great part of the region was covered with green areas and springs. Deserts existed, but did not encroach on the land quite as much as today – indeed, forests made the area more habitable. Pliny described the area as being very fertile and mist-covered, with forested mountains, rivers and unbroken tracts of forests.

These people were also considered fortunate because of their wealth. Ubar and its people grew rich on the trade of frankincense – the resin of the Boswellia sacra, a tree that grows principally in Southern Arabia. The people of 'Ad controlled its harvest, sale and transportation, and traded their goods with the great civilizations of the time, including Rome, Egypt, Greece and Mesopotamia.

Pliny commented that "that control of the frankincense trade had made the south Arabians the richest people on earth." Frankincense was a commodity that was as precious as gold – hence the gifts of gold, frankincense and myrrh that the Wise Men brought to the new-born Christ. Frankincense was used as perfume, but more importantly, was burned as incense in the religious ceremonies of many cultures. Egyptians used frankincense in embalming, and the pharaohs believed that burning it allowed them to commune with the gods. Pliny wrote that an entire year's harvest of frankincense was burned at the funeral of the Roman emperor Nero's wife in AD 65. The Egyptians and the Jews both believed frankincense to be holy – the use of it gave one a direct link to the divine.

The people of the region displayed great prowess in the building of their settlements. Pliny and Strabo (c. 64 BC–AD 19) describe their cities as being adorned with beautiful temples and palaces. Satellite imaging (see page 151) has also revealed an extensive system of ancient canals and dams used in irrigation in

OPPOSITE: In 1930 Bertram Thomas led an expedition across the Empty Quarter to map the region for the British Royal Geographical Society. Despite his best efforts Thomas was not destined to discover the Atlantis of the Sands.

the area, which is estimated to have been able to support 200,000 people in the associated cities. Little is known of the religion of these people, but inscriptions found in temples close to Shabwah, the capital city of the Hadramites, indicate that animals were hunted in this region and that some were sacrificed in pagan ceremonies.

Ubar was one of the oldest trading entrepots in the Arabian Empty Quarter. During excavations in the 1990s, archaeologist Professor Juris Zarins dated the settlement to at least 850 BC, although there may have been sporadic occupation of the area as far back as 2800 BC. Ubar would have been one of the first great crossroads for travellers making their way across the desert. This wealthy city would have impressed all who approached it, and it must have been a welcome sight for weary travellers. Many traders wished to avoid the coastal roads, which were rife with crime. The desert was by far the safest route, and traders could travel largely unhindered if they could endure the harsh conditions. As well as dealing in frankincense at Ubar, they came to trade livestock, spices, fine cloth and herbs.

In 1930, British explorer Bertram Thomas, an explorer and cartographer, went on an expedition of the Empty Quarter. He was determined to be one of the first Westerners to traverse the Rub 'al-Khali. The journey was difficult and fraught with danger, not least because of the shortage of water. It took Thomas three months to cross the territory between the towns of Salalah, in the southern part of the region, and Doha, on the Persian Gulf. On a map prepared for the Royal Geographical Society, Thomas recorded his sighting of a road, which his local guides called "a caravan track to Ubar". Thomas never had a chance to return to

pursue his discovery, which is, in a way, a blessing. Had he mounted a return expedition, he would have been disappointed, as his ancient road did not lead to Ubar – it was a much older road, which predated Ubar.

T. E. Lawrence (1888–1935), better known as Lawrence of Arabia, was also obsessed with finding Ubar and its treasures. Before the First World War (1914–1918), Lawrence worked in the Middle East, studying Crusader castles, and participating in the excavation of Carchemish, an ancient trading city in northern Syria. Despite interruptions by the First World War, and a lengthy period as a military intelligence and British liaison officer to the Arab revolt (1916), Lawrence remained obsessed with finding Ubar. Frustrated by lack of equipment and unable to benefit from the advantages that remote-sensing technologies offer us today, Lawrence died without fulfilling his dream.

Despite Lawrence's failure, the "Atlantis of the Sands", as he described it, would eventually be found. It was the obsession of a team of high-technology explorers, keen to exploit space-age data, in the 1980s and 1990s, led by author and adventurer Nicholas Clapp, that would finally allow Ubar to be revealed.

Clapp showed Dr Ronald Blom and Dr Charles Elachi, of the NASA Jet Propulsion Laboratory, documents which included a map (which he had discovered in the Huntingdon Library, California) drawn by the Greek-Egyptian geographer Ptolemy (c. AD 87–150). The map referred to a lost city in Arabia, named Ubar, which had been the centre of the trade in frankincense some 2,000 to 3,000 years ago. This reference secured their attention and their commitment to the mission. Their first challenge was how to collect the relevant data and then how to stage a land exploration.

Given the technological advances, collection of the data should have been relatively easy. Blom and Elachi made sure that the orbital path of the Jet Propulsion Laboratory's SIR-B (space-based radar) mission, to be carried aboard the space shuttle *Challenger*, would capture data about the Empty Quarter region. Once the shuttle mission was over, they hoped to have images and data that would indicate a site for Ubar. But tragedy struck in January 1986, when the *Challenger* exploded seventy-three seconds after lift-off, killing everyone on board. Shuttle missions were put on hold until a thorough investigation had taken place.

*Excavations at Ash Shisr uncovered a
large octagonal fortress with thick walls
approximately three metres (ten feet) high
and great towers at the corners, as
illustrated here in this computer-generated
image. The expeditionary team also found
Greek, Roman, and Syrian pottery, the
oldest of which was c. 4000 years old.
These artefacts suggested that this had
indeed been a major centre for trade
and most probably the Atlantis of the
Sands: Ubar.*

Clapp and Blom realized that they had little chance of obtaining data via a NASA mission, at least in the short term, and decided to try a different approach. They speculated that other satellites might have already covered the region, and set about collecting and analyzing such data. They used images taken from a European satellite (the Systeme probatoire d'observation de la terre (SPOT) satellite) as well as Landsat and military air reconnaissance photographs. Blom and his colleagues combined image data and overlaid elements from one picture on top of another to improve the overall detail and resolution.

Long-abandoned tracks were identified on the images, and these allowed archaeologist Juris Zarins, who had become involved in the project, to determine the location of the trading centre, known as Ubar, at the point of their convergence. This exciting discovery prompted an expedition to Oman and the Empty Quarter in 1990, focusing on the area around Ash Shisr. The expedition team included Clapp, Blom, Zarins, and British explorer Sir Ranulph Fiennes, who had been on previous Ubar searches and had been invited to join the team because of his intimate knowledge of the area.

150

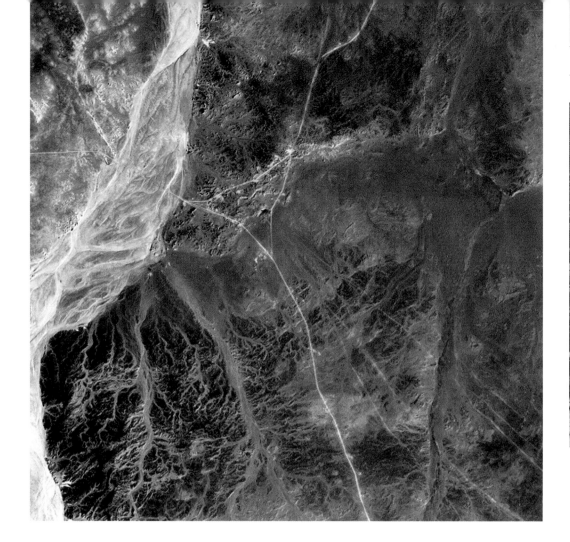

Subsequent excavations directed by Professor Zarins from 1991 to 1996 revealed that Ubar had been a fortified city. Its focal point was a fortress constructed around a great natural well. This fortress was designed to guard the desert's two most valuable commodities: life-giving water and the international trade in frankincense. The city was bounded by irregular, but essentially hexagonal, shaped city walls, with eight or more turrets at the corners.

Excavations revealed abandoned pottery and charcoal pits all around the site, indicating that a large number of the city's inhabitants lived outside the walls, in tented communities. This habit is still practised in the Empty Quarter today by the Arab Bedouin tribes, some of whom are nomadic. The city's walls and its permanent structures were built of stone; other dwellings were temporary tented ones, much like the larger tent city of the migratory population beyond the walls.

More than likely the area was occupied during the winter caravan season, by traders, merchants and travellers, falling back to little more than a caretaker garrison, probably manned by armed guards, during the summer months. It is believed that the site was destroyed in c. AD 400. The city was built over an underground

OPPOSITE: *Andy Dunsire, an experienced caver and Ranulph Fiennes descended into a long-abandoned well described by Ptolemy as the "Oracle of Diana". Zarins wished to excavate the shaft itself and the ruined village around, so a mobile crane was borrowed from BP at Salalah. Unfortunately, in spite of Dunsire and Fiennes' bravery, the well contained more dead foxes, bats, stinging insects, scorpions and poisonous wolf spiders than ancient artefacts.*

ABOVE: The team worked in extreme heat to determine the true extent and nature of Ubar. Here they are pictured at work on the northeast wall.

RIGHT: Finds from Ubar include this soapstone chess set from c. AD 1000. The pieces are a soldier, king, castle, elephant and bishop.

limestone cave. The cave, created by a naturally occurring subterranean well, known as a sinkhole, provided the city with its water supply. As Ubar's population grew, in line with its economic success, so the demand for water increased. It now seems likely that as the water level in the caves dropped, the sinkhole crumbled. When the caves collapsed, the fortress-city fell into the chasm and was destroyed, possibly without warning.

It is also possible that an earthquake caused the disaster and it is likely that the site was never redeveloped or reconstructed after its collapse because it was no longer needed. The price of frankincense in the ancient world dropped dramatically when the Roman empire adopted Christianity, and Ubar's function as a trade centre disappeared.

Excavation of the site is a vast undertaking, as much of it lies buried under metres of sands, and it may be many years before the full extent of Ubar is known. Lawrence's description of Ubar as the "Atlantis of the Sands" may have been more accurate than he could have possibly imagined, for as Atlantis was submerged by the sea, so was Ubar consumed by the desert.

ALL ROADS LEAD TO UBAR

THE INNOVATIVE USE of satellite- and Shuttle-based images from space, analysis of ancient texts, and archaeological fieldwork has finally solved the riddle of Ubar. The final clue to Ubar's location, garnered from the image analysis, was the place where ancient caravan routes crossed.

"OUR WORK DEMONSTRATING the existence of Bertram Thomas' ancient road gave us confidence that we could depend on other road evidence leading us to Ubar. There couldn't have been many roads, ancient or modern, in that region of Oman, that we wouldn't have seen on our space images. The road concentration in the area left little doubt that this site must be Ubar. Additionally, the geography of the site was perfect. It was just north of the frankincense source areas. If you wanted to walk around the sand dunes west, or north, both directions were possible from this location. Fieldwork established that the site had an abundance of water in ancient times, enough to grow dates and supply caravans. So this was a place from where camel caravans could have started their long trek across the desert. There is nowhere else in the area suitable. Excavations revealed a fortress with artifacts from the right time period and from places all over the ancient world. The fortress collapsed into a sinkhole, sparking the legends of the catastrophic demise of Ubar. The fortress surrounded the water well, allowing Ubarites to control the water and protect their frankincense. Although the fortress is a good deal smaller than legendary accounts would have one believe, it is worth noting that the ancient city of Jerusalem was less than about 1 km on a side."

DR RONALD G. BLOM, NASA JET PROPULSION LABORATORY, PASADENA, CALIFORNIA, USA

UR
THE LAND OF GOD'S HAND

ABOVE: *Sir Leonard Woolley's excavation of the great ziggurat at Ur, seen here during excavation, caused great excitement in the Western press.*

THE RUINS OF THE ANCIENT SUMERIAN CITY OF UR (modern-day Tell Muqayyar), lie on the plain of the Euphrates and the Tigris rivers, 300 kilometres (187 miles) southeast of Baghdad in Iraq, near the coast of the Persian Gulf.

The first settlers arrived in the region some time in the fifth millennium BC. These people were capable agriculturalists who also bred livestock. They lived in mud huts and small farmsteads built on islands of river silt that stood above the marshy plains. Tools found from this era, which is known as the Ubaid period, include hoes, threshers and stone querns (stone mills turned by hand). Here, in fertile marshland, the people took control of the environment, cultivating crops in the rich soil. They built irrigation canals to manage the water supply to feed their crops.

These farming settlements prospered and eventually developed into self-contained city-states. Sumerian cities, such as Eridu, Larsa, Uruk, Lagash and Girsu, had a written culture and shared a common language which meant that all aspects of life – legal, religious and mythical – could be communicated from one city to another. They had a shared policy for trade that put them in competition with each other, but allowed free trade between them. The Sumerians also shared a polytheistic religion. They had a tradition of taking a personal god to look after their interests on behalf of the deities. There were more than 2,000 gods, mostly embodying aspects of the natural world, such as wind, water, fire and various animals. Some of the more important deities included Anu, the supreme god of heaven; Enki, the god of wisdom; Nanna, the god of the

OPPOSITE: *This three-quarter on diagonal view of the great ziggurat at Ur reveals the great staircase leading to the first of the three terraces. The ziggurat or stepped pyramid temple was the domain of high priests, incarnation of gods on earth.*

moon; and Inanna, the goddess of love, fertility and the bringer of good harvests.

During the fortieth century BC, the farming community based in the fertile area that would become Ur grew in prosperity and their civilization developed. This culminated in the foundation of the city of Ur. The land around Ur was green and fertile, and this was a key factor in the city's success – the farmers produced crops, such as wheat, in such abundance that the surplus could be traded. The city came to thrive on commerce. The territory was on an important trade route from the Gulf to the northern territories. As well as exporting food, the city traded textiles and fine artefacts, such as small stone statues, copper bowls, musical

155

ABOVE: *Woolley's workforce manned the archaeological staircases to bring the ancient site to life for his readers and colleagues back home in the west. It was important for Woolley, from a funding and status point of view, to maintain a high public profile and this sort of image guaranteed the dig column inches in the press.*

instruments and golden vessels. In return, merchants brought wood, metal ores, stone, gems and spices from areas as far away as the Indus Valley and Anatolia (a region between the Black Sea and the Aegean Sea, in the area of modern-day Turkey).

Ur, like all Sumerian city-states, developed a well-organized economic system. This was originally run (c. 4000–2000 BC) by the priesthood-élite, who, as well as governing religious affairs, were the city's principal administrators. In the third millennium BC, trade in and out of the city-state was closely monitored and controlled by state organs. By the second millennium BC, a highly organized class of merchants had developed who worked in co-operative-like organizations, albeit still under the watchful eye of the ruling priest élite.

The organization of trade was helped by the invention of cuneiform writing (see Glossary), on clay tablets, which was fully developed as early as 2500 BC. Many records from this site still exist. Writing allowed the city-states to keep records of trade movements, goods owed in trade agreements and so on. It was, in essence, a crude form of accounting. The cuneiform records from c. 1900 BC make it clear that Ur's economic system was carefully balanced, with state, religious and merchant elements of the economy contributing to the whole (see page 161).

Ur's heyday was between 3000 and 2000 BC, and in particular between 2112–2004 BC, when it was the capital of the Sumerian Empire. By the third millennium BC the Sumerian empire included at least a dozen distinct city-states, such as Adab, Ereech and Ur. Each of these states was constructed on similar lines: a walled city and its surrounding villages and land, and each worshiped its own deity, whose temple was the central structure of the city. During this era, King Ur-Nammu (who reigned between 2112 and 2095 BC) built the impressive wall surrounding Ur. The city stretched out in a teardrop shape. Its boundary was demarcated by a great wall that was almost 8 metres (26 feet) high on the outside, but 1.5 metres (5 feet) on the inside; the city was built up on the inside and encircled by a moat. A canal from the river to the north filled the moat and there were two harbours in the north and west of the city.

The city contained districts divided by wide boulevards, built around the vast temple complex of the moon god Nanna, which was dominated by a ziggurat pyramid built by Ur-Nammu. Other notable buildings in the city included the shrines of past kings.

The ziggurat was a symbol of the Sumerian civilization and was found throughout the region. As seen at Babylon (see page 119), the tower was a sign of great symbolic and religious importance. Some archaeologists suggest that the ziggurats were constructed

RIGHT: *This intriguing period photograph captures the frenzy of activity, at the site of the ziggurat, during Woolley's excavation there from 1922–1934. Archeology was fashionable in this period, and was a discipline that saw men and women working together in the early twentieth century.*

as a ladder to heaven. The ziggurat had a base 61 metres (200 feet) long and 15 metres (50 feet) wide. There was a temple at its summit that was the domain of the high priests. An important rite that may have taken place in this temple was the symbolic marriage between the ruling king and the goddess Inanna. This "marriage" was done to ensure good harvests, and probably took place once a year.

The residential quarter contained private houses. The middle classes – traders and functionaries of the state – had homes that were rather splendid. Built around a central courtyard, they contained residential rooms, storage areas, lavatories, and a raised terrace that looked out over the courtyard from the second floor. At the centre of the courtyard there was a drain for sanitation. Drains were sunk into the earth (most of the city was built up having been raised for security), and water would be flushed down the drain and allowed to seep into the subsoil. The houses were made from bricks of burnt clay and mud. Mosaics and murals ornamented the walls of the larger, more important, buildings, such as the ziggurat and the royal tombs, but ordinary houses too were often plastered and painted to achieve a decorative finish.

In the city's busy streets were children at play and people going about their trades. Smoke climbed from cooking fires and from artisan workshops. There would have been the smell of copper, tin and gold smelting, as the fine jewellery and sculptures of Ur were prepared and dressed with lapis lazuli and shell, which was used for inlay work. Armourers hammering spears to a point and shields to a hardened surface would have created a near-deafening din. Weavers prepared cloth for kilts, capes and fine dresses. Ceremonial garments and cloths were gaily coloured, and adorned with silver and gold, and silver ribbon was produced as decoration for women's hair.

Ancient texts, including the Old Testament of the Bible, mention Ur as the home of Abram, son of Terah, a tenth-generation descendent of Noah. Abram grew to be a man of great importance. He is thought to have spent his childhood at Ur in the early second millennium BC. He and his family then went to live in Haran. It was here that the God of the Semitic faith spoke to Abram and told him, "get thee out of thy country, and from thy kindred, and from thy fathers house, unto a land that I will show thee. And I will make of thee a great nation, and I will bless thee, and make thy name great" (Genesis 12, 1–2). Abram would, in time, be renamed by God as Abraham (or Ibrahim), meaning "father of many". Abraham is an important figure in the Jewish faith, and is regarded as the founding father of the Hebrew religion, in which he is often referred to as Khalilullah – the "Friend of God".

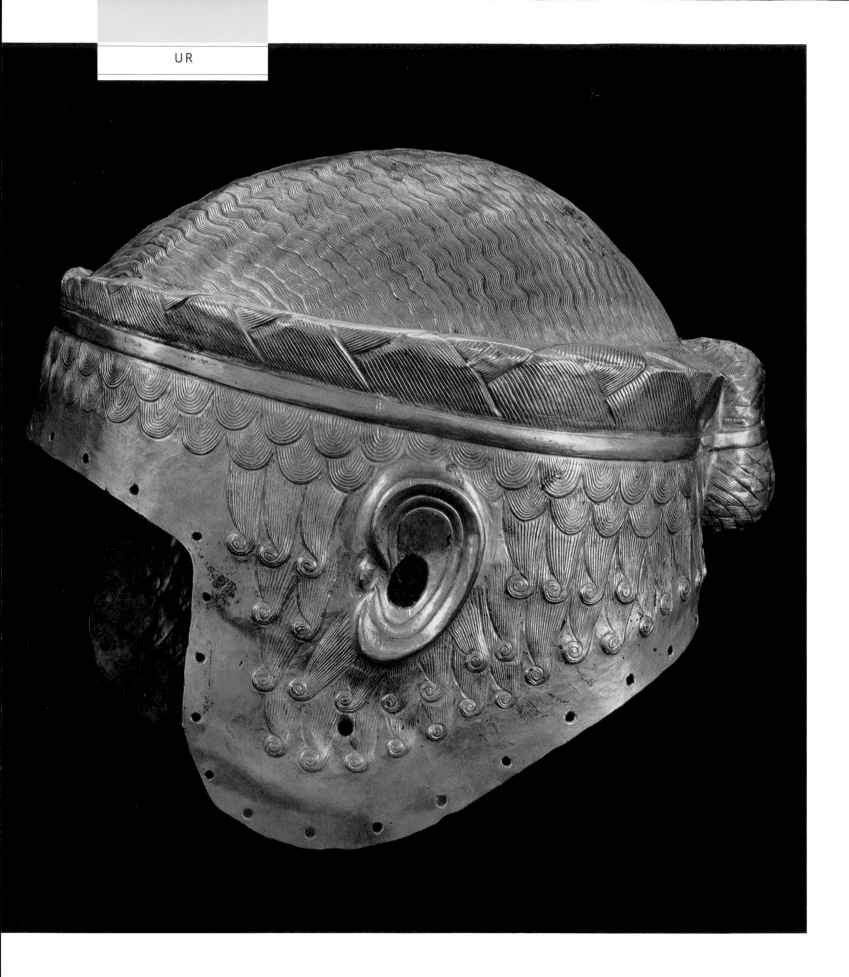

The city-state of Ur survived, in various incarnations, for 5,000 years. In that time it had seen the Sumerian rule obliterated and a series of occupying dynasties take its place, including the Greeks, under Alexander the Great (356–323 BC; see pages 120 and 139–142). Finally, probably in the fourth century BC, Ur faced its final years. No single cataclysm destroyed Ur – its decline was gradual and it was eventually abandoned.

The river Euphrates had always been vital to Ur's success, and during the Neo-Babylonian period (604–562 BC), the river shifted its course. The vital supply of water that had fed the canals and irrigation ditches dwindled, and agriculture was threatened. The era of Ur as a great trading city, based on its proximity to the river, was also drawing to a close. The domestication and use of the camel, in caravans, had reduced the use of water transit in the area, further weakening Ur's status. Since that time, the Euphrates has shifted its course by 16 kilometres (ten miles); the plain is now arid and barren, in contrast to the lush lands of Ur at its peak.

J.E. Taylor, British consul at Basra who explored the southern sites of Mesopotamia, rediscovered Ur in 1852. He unearthed inscriptions at the Mound of Pitch, which revealed that the

OPPOSITE: The helmet of King Meskalamdug reminds us of the extreme artistry of the craftsmen of the Ur city-state. It was designed to honour a god-king on earth – a function it performs admirably even today, reflecting the power and status of this long dead leader of men.

ABOVE: This aerial view of Ur shows the 4,000 year old city's moat, sadly deprived of the life-bringing river, and its great ziggurat temple (foreground) which was used as a place of worship for approximately 1,500 years. The scale of this settlement is staggering, but its current dry state reminds us how ephemeral even the greatest human settlements can be.

nameless ruin in Sumer was the site of Ur. Later excavations by Sir Leonard Woolley (1880–1960) in 1922–1934 gave historians a valuable insight into the ancient culture of the region for the first time. One of his greatest breakthroughs was the discovery of the Royal Cemetery. This is situated just outside the southeast corner of the Temenos, a walled sacred precinct containing major buildings, temples and plazas. The tomb of King Meskalamdug (who ruled Ur some time in the period between *c.* 3000 and 2330 BC), opened in 1927–1928, proved that Ur had been of great importance in the Middle-Eastern economy and society of the third millennium BC. The treasures within the tomb included the king's ornate helmet and exquisite jewellery made from gold, silver, carnelian and lapis lazuli. Interestingly, none of these raw materials originated in the region – proof of Ur's importance as a cosmopolitan city that thrived on trade.

Woolley's discoveries made him something of a celebrity. He was keen to publicize his work and wrote articles about his finds in popular magazines. He tried to reconstruct events, in words and artists' impressions, as they might have happened. One such account was of a wholesale human sacrifice, which accompanied the burial of a king at Ur (the name of the king is not known). Woolley wrote: "Now we have definite proof that in the fourth millennium before Christ the … king went to his tomb in company

ABOVE: The royal standard of Ur was made c. 2500 BC. The craftsmen of Ur were extremely skilled at the inlay of wooden objects, such as this standard, with fragile shells and semi-precious stones. The royal standard depicts scenes of peace and war.

with a whole following of soldiers, courtiers and women, who, like the vases of food and drink, the weapons and the tools set in his grave, should minister to his needs and pleasures in another world." (*Illustrated London News*, 23 June 1928.) In all, fifty-nine men and women, and six oxen, died in honour of their king.

Another area of the Royal Cemetery, known today as the Great Death Pit, contained a retinue of six male servants, four female harpists and sixty-four ladies of court. In all, seventy-four people died to accompany their unnamed leader into the afterlife. News of these extraordinary religious and ceremonial practices, together with the beautiful art of Ur, ensured the city fame.

Few Western archaeologists have been able to visit Ur since the 1990s, because of the political situation in Iraq, but when the region stabilizes new treasures may yet be discovered.

UR'S PRINCELY PRIESTS

THE STATE'S ECONOMY was dominated by the demands of the monarch and the priests. Because the priests were seen as the living embodiment of the gods, they were granted inordinate wealth and privilege.

"RELIGION'S IMPORTANCE was reflected in the size of temples erected within the precincts of the city. The general populace were not allowed to enter these temples, only the king and the priests. These great structures were a drain on the economy for they absorbed in maintenance of structure and personnel a high percentage of the Gross National Product. But in return their large flocks of sheep and goats ensured that they played a major part in the economy."

PROFESSOR ANDREW GEORGE, SCHOOL OF ORIENTAL & AFRICAN STUDIES, LONDON, ENGLAND

ABOVE: A detail from a harp or lyre — one of four found in the Great Death Pit. Lyres were frequently left in the Royal tombs of Ur. This was the most magnificent — the bearded bull's head was wrought in heavy gold.

BELOW: The Sumerian games board found at the Royal Cemetery in UR, dates from c. 2250 BC. It is a beautiful, ornamental game and its counters are still intact, as though it is ready to be played once again 4,200 years later.

ASIA

ANGKOR WAT

ANURADHAPURA

MOHENJODARO

ANGKOR WAT
JUNGLE TREASURE OF THE KHMER

ANGKOR, NORTH OF TONLE SAP IN NORTHWEST Cambodia, was the magnificent capital city of the Khmer Empire from AD 802 until c. AD 1431. Lost to the jungle for centuries, it was rediscovered in the 1860s. Its sprawling temples, which are far larger and more intricate than the ancient Egyptian pyramids, are architectural masterpieces, with beehive-like steeples and elaborately carved friezes. The city is based around approximately one thousand temples, built over an area of ten square kilometres (four square miles). The complex contains the beautiful temple of Angkor Wat, which is the largest religious monument in the world.

The Khmer are one of the oldest cultural groups in southeast Asia. They originally consisted of a large number of tribes with strong linguistic and cultural links; their territory covered areas in Laos, Cambodia, Burma, Thailand and Vietnam. The Khmer developed an empire, via territorial gains in war and the exploitation of rich natural resources, which reached from what is now southern Vietnam to Yunan in China and from Vietnam westward to the Bay of Bengal, including the Mekong Valley.

The Khmer had a prosperous and highly advanced civilization that was typified by elaborate architecture dedicated to their gods. They originally worshipped the Hindu gods such as Shiva (a powerful god associated with the destructive forces of the universe) and Vishnu (the god of happiness, kinship and preservation), but eventually dropped the Hindu gods in favour of Buddhism.

The Khmer monarchy was modelled on Indian lines, and the rulers were considered to be God Kings, or Deva Rajas, on earth. They ruled over the Khmer Empire with absolute authority, and

ABOVE: A view from the summit of Angkor Wat to the courtyard of the second level and beyond.
OPPOSITE: The ornate northeast tower and the east staircase of Angkor Wat's central massif, from the courtyard of the second level. The design and carving, when considered in context, makes this site, arguably, the greatest religious monument in the world.

had a powerful army at their command that could be deployed to defend borders or invade neighbouring regions. Another key element of Khmer society was the priests. The priest families were ancient and acted as a force for stability and cohesivesness. They looked after the temples, ran educational projects and maintained and developed the structure of government. The kings took great heed of their counsel, and they ran an efficient, successful and powerful administration.

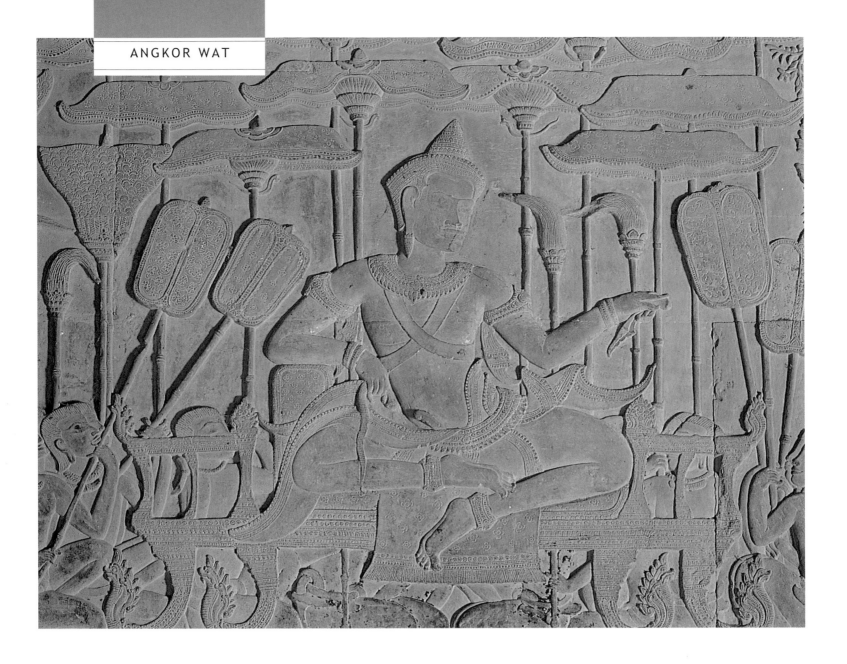

King Jayavarman II founded the Angkor Empire (the Khmer Empire) in the ninth century AD. His successor, Indravarman I, began construction in the Angkor area, at Preah Ko, a little south of the later city. The land of Angkor was particularly valuable as a settlement site because of its strategic military position and its agricultural potential. Khmer labourers, together with foreign slaves captured in battle, constructed and maintained a vast irrigation system that guaranteed a water supply for agriculture in times of drought.

Successive kings founded temples, constructed irrigation reservoirs and built palaces in Angkor city – the focus of the city shifted from place to place within the general area. Suryavarman II, who reigned from c. AD 1113 to 1150, built the splendid temple of Angkor Wat (see opposite). By the time of King Jayavarman VII (who reigned from AD 1181 to 1219), Angkor had become a truly vast settlement. Jayavarman VII built the city of Angkor Thom (within the general area of Angkor city), where the magnificent temple of Bayon can be found. Including the satellite communities outside the core of the city, Angkor had a population in excess of two million people at its height.

The city was ringed by a moat entered via a causeway guarded by 540 stone gargoyles. The royal family lived in very grand apartments, as did their priests, within the main enclosure of the city. The structures which can still be found at the site today – in excess of 100 grand temples – are all that remain of the original metropolis. It is believed that these stone structures would have been surrounded by many public and administrative buildings, palaces and houses, which were built of wood and have since rotted away.

LEFT: The great twelfth-century Cambodian king, temple builder and religious reformer, Suryavarman II seated on his throne from the reliefs in the southern gallery of bas-reliefs at Angkor Wat.

BELOW: The Khmer army in battle as seen from the eastern outer gallery at the Bayon temple complex. Bows and arrows, spears and elephants all reflect the might of the Deva Rajas' army.

The finest temple building within the Angkor site, and the most important sacred building for the Khmer civilization, is that of Angkor Wat. This was built by King Suryavarman II, who intended it to be his mausoleum as well as a temple. But Angkor Wat was not just a place of worship and a seat of royal and religious power; it was also an observatory, an administrative centre, and a centre of education.

Angkor Wat is a testament to the architectural powers of the ancient Khmer. The priest-architects who built Angkor Wat were very learned, and had used several classical languages, including Sanskrit, and astronomical calculations, to work out auspicious days and inauspicious days for building. These architects made mathematical calculations so precise that corridors two metres (six feet) wide and 200 metres (660 feet) long were no more than

a centimetre out end to end. Such a feat was difficult for modern architects prior to the use of laser-sights, and the techniques of the ancient builders have not yet been fathomed.

The temple was constructed of carefully worked sandstone. It rose to a height of 65 metres (215 feet), at its highest point, and covered an area of one square kilometre. It was encircled by a moat 180 metres (590 feet) wide with a great outer wall 1,000 metres (3,280 feet) long. The great corner towers that stand proud of the walls were 32 metres (105 feet) tall. This was a great structure, conceived on a grand scale.

Access to the temple was via a bridge leading into the western side of the temple building. Three central towers formed the entrance from the bridge to the temple. Long corridors ran north and south away from the towers, culminating in huge doorways. The great western walkway linked the entrance and moat to three galleries, the outer of which was adorned with reliefs made in honour of the Khmer kings. The third, innermost, gallery bore wall reliefs dedicated to the great god Vishnu. At the centre of the complex was a vast tower, encircled by the Vishnu gallery.

The building of Angkor Wat is astonishingly accomplished, not only in its design and execution, but also in its artistry. Teams of sculptors worked on the temple's bas-reliefs, with master sculptors creating complex patterns and features, and lesser artists concentrating on smaller details such as flowers or clothing. These sculptures, which included gods, goddesses, animals and mythological beasts, the kings and their loyal followers, cover the temple structure.

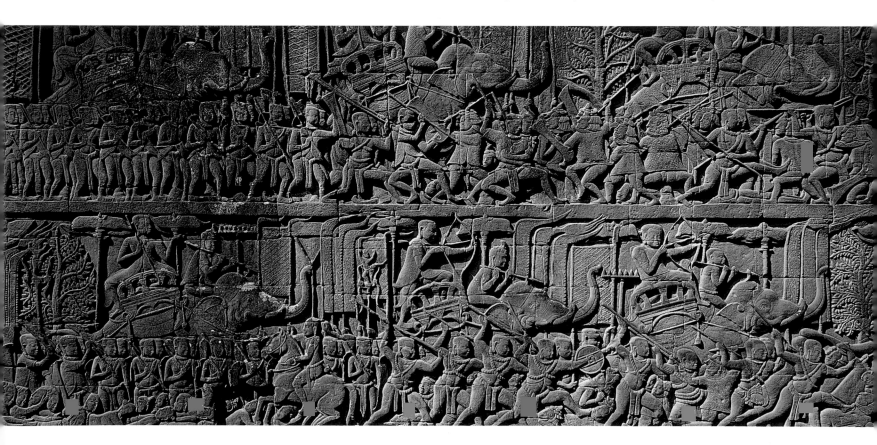

After the death of King Jayavarman VII in AD 1219, the Khmer Empire fell into a rapid decline. The Thai Empire was gaining dominance at this time. The Thais had moved their capital to Ayudhya, close to Angkor, and soon began waging war with the Khmer. Control of Angkor oscillated between the struggling Khmer and the ascendant Thais until about AD 1431, when the Thais finally took Angkor, robbing and attacking the settlement. The Khmer Empire would never recover. By the mid-fifteenth century AD, Cambodia had fallen into decline, and it had become little more than a satellite state of Thailand.

Despite the decline of the Khmer Empire, the temple of Angkor Wat remained in use for worship by Buddhists. However, it was lost to the western world until its rediscovery in the nineteenth century by Frenchman Henri Mouhot (1826–1861). Something of an accidental archaeologist, Mouhot stumbled across the city complex while on a zoological expedition. He had been travelling along the Mekong River, collecting data as he went, and arrived in Battanbang in 1860. There, following the advice of a local missionary, he entered a region of dense forest and stumbled upon a large moat surrounding a jungle-encroached ruin – Angkor Thom. Mouhot was staggered by his discovery. There was a city so vast and so sophisticated that it must have been built by people

with an advanced knowledge of engineering, science, mathematics and art. The young Frenchman soon sent word back to Europe telling of the most beautiful lost city ever to be discovered. However, Mouhot did not enjoy his discovery, or the fame that it brought him, for long. He fell ill to jungle fever and died in 1861.

Many archaeologists visited the site in the twentieth century and it has received the particular attention of architects, who have recorded its magnificence. The advent of modern technology has allowed us a fresh insight into this civilization. The new remote-sensing technology is particularly useful for archaeologists studying Angkor; much of the area is still planted with landmines from the era of the civil war following the establishment of the Khmer Republic in 1970 and is therefore dangerous to excavate.

Data from radar images taken from the Space Shuttle and pictures taken from a DC-8 aircraft fitted with airborne synthetic aperture radar (AIRSAR) has led archaeologists to re-evaluate previous models of the great city and raised doubts about long-accepted ideas of its construction. It is now clear that a much older civilization existed in Angkor, before the construction of the city of Angkor Thom. This data has revealed hitherto unknown mounds and temples, which may predate the construction of the Khmer capital by some 200 years.

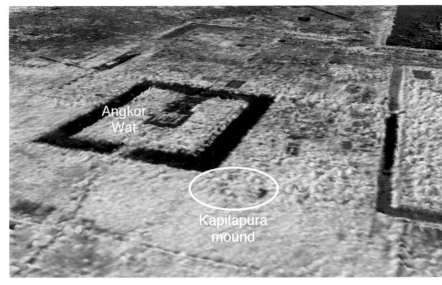

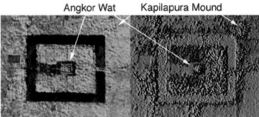

Radar Data   Digital Elevation Model

ABOVE: Three-dimensional mapping of Angkor Wat has been made possible thanks to radar interferometry. By merging data from remote-sensing surveys, archaeologists have produced the first accurate topographical map of the area, revealing new discoveries such as the Kapilapura Mound, located outside the Angkor Wat complex itself.

LEFT: The first panoramic photo of the western facade of Angkor Wat, taken by John Thomson in 1866, caused a stir in the West.

OPPOSITE FAR LEFT: Images captured during overflights by DC-8 aircraft fitted with AIRSAR (airborne synthetic aperture radar) and radar data from space, proved that there were earlier settlements at the site, predating the temple complex by 200 years.

A technique known as radar interferometry, which allows the creation of a three-dimensional map by combining data from a number of sources, has enabled archaeologists to create an accurate topographical map of the area for the first time. The map reveals the true magnificence of the city's grand water management schemes. The management of water was pivotal to the Khmer kings' power. Monsoon season rains were powerful and potentially destructive – to crops and property – and the possibility of drought during the dry season posed an even greater threat. Consequently, the management of water, using reservoirs, tanks and canals, together with the construction of moats around the great temples (see pages 166–167), allowed the kings to preserve and control the flow of water. The greatest of these reservoirs yet discovered, which measures eight kilometres (five miles) in length, was constructed in the twelfth century AD.

ABOVE: Angkor Wat in evening light. The temple is beautiful but not just to the eye – its design has a mathematical beauty too. Its designers were extremely learned and created a temple complex laced with secret meaning and religious symbolism (see box opposite).

OPPOSITE: Detail of a relief on the temple at Angkor. The attention to detail in the artistry of this magnificent temple is made all the more apparent when looked at in detail and then considered in context: every inch of this vast temple is just as ornate. The work undertaken by its twelfth-century architects and sculptors is beyond imagination.

A PROCESSION THROUGH TIME IN STONE

Dr ELEANOR MANNIKKA astonished the academic world with her revelations about the spiritual, celestial and sacred nature of the design philosophy behind the temple of Angkor Wat. The concept of time and gods and the interconnectedness of kinship and rule were physically expressed in stone at Angkor.

"MY RESEARCH revealed to me something that had remained hidden to my colleagues during many decades of scholarship. I was no less astounded than my fellow academics, though I did not expect the controversy or success that followed. I began to take measurements: the builders' unit of measure was a cubit, called a *hat*; in Khmer, equivalent to the length between the elbow and the tip of the central digit. I moved into the structure applying this measurement unit. I started to find lunar months both sidereal and synodic, solar and lunar years, and in the historical gallery, dates related to the reign of the king. I soon realized that these many different time cycles were set up within an orchestrated progression. They moved from the largest cycles on the outer perimeter of the temple to specific historical dates and then into the time of the gods on the upper elevation. The architects were both priests and astronomers and by this brilliant temple design, they expressed their belief in the unity of the gods, the calendar, and sacred cosmology.

One important thing to keep in mind is that time to these architect-priests was not a neutral entity. Long before the Khmers built the monuments at Angkor, the planet had moved into the worst of four successive eras, a period lasting 432,000 years. The negative effects of this degenerate age had to be countered by the temple's design. And so our own dark age is left behind in the measurements of the western entrance bridge, outside the temple's walled compound. We then proceed through the other three, successively better time periods until we have reached the nexus of all creation in the central sanctuary where both time and space pale in the presence of a Supreme Divinity.

The priests who constructed the monuments of Angkor left hundreds of stone inscriptions both in Sanskrit and Khmer. The underlying philosophy of the nature of time at Angkor Wat is implicit in many of these inscriptions. But this philosophy was only made explicit more than eight centuries later when a determined graduate student wanted to find out why two parallel corridors at Angkor Wat measured exactly 202.14 meters."

DR ELEANOR MANNIKKA, CURATOR AND ASSISTANT PROFESSOR, INDIANA UNIVERSITY OF PENNSYLVANIA, INDIANA, PA, USA

A breakthrough in our understanding of the temple of Angkor Wat occurred in the 1990s. Dr Eleanor Mannikka, an American art historian, had spent many years studying the temple via books and journals, but had never been able to study them at first hand until the mid-1990s. She came to a remarkable theory regarding the construction and function of the temple.

Mannikka realized that Angkor Wat had been built using a unique unit of measurement, and that the dimensions of the buildings built according to this measurement held a secret code. When she converted the metric measurements taken during other academic studies of the complex into the cubit measurements originally used by its architects, lunar and solar cycles were revealed in its design pattern (see box). The building was designed so that on certain days of the year, according to the position of the sun or the moon, shafts of light would enter the building and pick out significant details on the bas-reliefs found throughout the temple complex. One such alignment is found in the great tower. On the spring equinox, the path of the sun lit up a bas-relief portraying the king and Vishnu, thereby emphasizing the spiritual connection between the god and the king. This demonstrated that the king was one with Vishnu, the Supreme Being from whom the whole universe emanated. The sacred sculptures of Angkor Wat symbolized the integral part of the monarchy and religion in Khmer civilization.

Archaeologists are continuing their studies of Angkor. High-altitude remote sensing, land-based archaeology and study will continue to produce new insights into this astonishing complex.

ANURADHAPURA
SINHALESE NIRVANA

NURADHAPURA, THE CAPITAL OF THE NORTH
Central province of Sri Lanka, was the seat of the
Sinhalese kings from the fourth century BC to AD
1017. When Buddhism took root in Sri Lanka in
the third century BC, Anuradhapura became one
of Asia's major religious centres. It is the site of a
sacred Bo tree, thought to be descended from the
tree under which Buddha received enlightenment.
Sri Lanka has long been regarded as an island paradise. The famous
Venetian traveller Marco Polo (c. AD 1254–1324) thought the island
one of the finest he had ever visited. It is a beautiful country with a
lush, mountainous interior and a coastline that is alternately craggy
and sandy. According to the Buddhist doctrine to which many Sri
Lankans adhere, Nirvana is the transcendental state in which there
is no suffering, desire, or sense of self. If ever there were a place
where one could achieve such a state, it would be Sri Lanka.

Hunter-gatherers first settled on the island in Palaeolithic times.
It is likely that the surviving tribes of people known as the Vedda
are descendants of these original inhabitants. Today, the Vedda
face extinction, having suffered the crowding-out of their culture,
much like the Aboriginal peoples of Australia.

According to legend, in c. 483 BC, Prince Vijaya arrived on the
island from a North Indian district – most likely Bengal – with 700
followers. Vijaya wanted to establish a new civilization for his
followers, the people of Sinhala. This translates as the "Race of
Lions". The name reputedly came from Vijaya's grandfather, who
was either associated with big cats, or who resembled a lion.

Vijaya did not react well to the presence of the Vedda, believing
them to be demons. Despite his fears however, he successfully

*OPPOSITE: The "gold dust" or
Ruvaneli dagoba, built by King
Dutthaganimi, is an architectural
sculpture dedicated to Buddha and is
still breathtaking today.*

*ABOVE: The Thuparama, the oldest
shrine at Anuradhapura, was built by
Devanampiya Tissa to house the relics
of the Buddha, which were taken there
by Asoka's son Mahinda. The shrine
forms part of the Mahavihara, the
original monastic complex.*

established the settlement and founded Anuradhapura, the capital
of the new kingdom. According to early Sinhalese tradition,
recorded in the written history of Sri Lanka, a work known as the
Mahavamsa (meaning the "Great Chronicle"), when Prince
Vijaya's party landed on Sri Lanka, it was inhabited by demons
known as *yaksas*, whom they fought and defeated. This is a myth
that likely embodies the presence of native Vedda tribes who
objected to the colonists' presence on the island and probably
offered physical resistance. The Sinhalese were probably Hindu,
and so their faith remained until 247 BC, when Emperor Asoka of

ABOVE: *The Jetawanarama dagoba at Anuradhapura, Sri Lanka attracts much attention from modern visitors because of its beauty.*

OPPOSITE: *Beautiful and grand in its vision, the Ruvaneli dagoba (also called the Great Stupa), is surrounded by an amazing wall decorated with elephants.*

India despatched his missionary son Mahinda to Sri Lanka to convert the people to Buddhism. According to the *Mahavamsa*, Mahinda encountered the Sinhalese king, Devanampiya Tissa (who reigned between c. 250–210 BC), while he was hunting deer in the northern territory of Mihintale. Mahinda interceded in the

kill of an animal, warning the king that he was only a guardian of the land and its animals, not their owner. Devanampiya Tissa was quickly won over by Mahinda and accepted the doctrines of Buddhism. Indeed, he was so taken by this new philosophy that he ordered the domain of Mihintale to be a natural park, sacred and protected for all time.

The following year, 246 BC, Emperor Asoka despatched his daughter, Mahinda's sister Sanghamitta, who was a nun, to the island. It was probably she who brought the near-legendary Sri Maha Bodhi (the Bo tree thought to be descended from the original tree at Buddha Gaya (Bodhgaya) where Buddha received enlightenment), to Sri Lanka, although local myth maintained that the tree had sprung up magically. The sapling soon took root in the fertile land, and grew rapidly. The tree, which survives today, is highly distinctive. It is more than 2,000 years old and of great height. Its leaves hang from long, flexible vein-like branches and rustle with a percussive hiss in even the slightest of breezes. This sound is said to have influenced many pilgrims emulating Buddha by seeking enlightenment while seated underneath the tree.

The Sinhalese of Anuradhapura developed a culture capable of great architectural and scientific achievements. In the third century BC, Sinhalese engineers created vast irrigation systems to provide the city with water. From the end of the fifth century BC the people of Anuradhapura built earthen dams to fill great reservoirs. The Kalabalala Tank, for example, created from just such a dam, was used to store monsoon rainfall. These water and irrigation systems not only fed the city but also its surrounding farmlands, creating a controlled environment for arable farming and food production. They are thought to be the most sophisticated of the early world. The systems fed by the large tanks still exist today. One reservoir with a circumference of 80 kilometres (50 miles), built to store the city's water supply, was known as the "black lake" because of its size. Huge rice fields were cultivated to feed the burgeoning population of the island.

The city featured palaces, temples, monasteries, lakes, gardens, hospitals, cemeteries and working-class suburbs that covered an expanse of approximately 780 square kilometres (300 square miles). One of Anuradhapura's main streets ran for 14 kilometres (9 miles). Two broad roads, built with religious processions in mind, ran from east to west and north to south. Anuradhapura was a city of Buddhist laymen, elders and merchants of all trades, whose houses were sizeable and beautiful. The roads were important to the community and at certain times of the month monks would set forth large carpets and preach at major intersections, for the good of the whole population. The most

impressive architectural feats achieved at Anuradhapura are the *stupas*, the largest of which is the ruined Jetavana. The *stupas* were built to a set design, each with a circular base topped by a hemispherical dome. Beautiful statues were placed on elaborate platforms at north, south, east and west.

Following the conversion of King Devanampiya Tissa, the Sinhalese quickly embraced Buddhism and its style of learning, in which each scholar follows a master and learns from his wisdom. Anuradhapura became an important religious site, and its monastery was a notable centre of learning. The *Mahavamsa* chronicles city scholars' achievements in medicine, architecture, mathematics and astronomy.

At the death of every king and during times of change, there was always competition among the royal descendants to ascend the throne. It had therefore become common practice to hire mercenaries from India and other neighbouring countries to protect the reigning monarch and his kingdom. However, in one

instance, the mercenaries proved traitorous, murdering the king and seizing the throne. The rightful royal family recovered the throne twenty years later. Dutthagamani, the king of Sri Lanka from 101–77 BC, is to this day remembered as a national hero because he led his troops to Anuradhapura, where he defeated and killed the Tamil leader Elara and went on to crush Indian-recruited soldiers led by Elara's nephew Bhalluka. But by then the people of southern India, known as the Tamils, had had a taste of ruling the island paradise. They wanted the kingdom and were prepared to take it at all costs. Nearly 400 years later, another Tamil, Elara, won the throne and reigned for nearly fifty years.

Ultimately, the Sinhalese resisted any effort to pervert their line of monarchy and, despite many attempts by the Tamils to overthrow the royal family, always managed to reinstate and maintain the true royal line. By the seventh century AD, Anuradhapura was beleaguered and its population was dwindling, because of repeated invasions from mainland India. Its fabulous monasteries, shrines, and *stupas*, were still in use by Buddhist masters and their students, although no longer in their heyday.

Perhaps the most damaging incursion in Anuradhapura's history occurred in AD 993. The island of Sri Lanka was invaded by the armies of the south Indian Chola dynasty, led by Rajaraja Chola. The Tamils put the great symbolic city to the torch and the by now greatly reduced population of Sinhalese citizens were forced to flee. The Sinhalese, determined not to be usurped, moved their capital to Polonnaruwa and their king, Vijayabahu I, managed to repel the invaders. Anuradhapura fell into disrepair in c. AD 1017 and was finally lost to the jungle.

After the fall of Anuradhapura, the Sinhalese seemed unwilling to settle on a new capital. By the fifteenth century, they had established three distinct administrative areas, each with its own main city: Kandy, in the central mountains; Kotte, in the west; and Jaffna, in the northern territories. All three territories were answerable to the incumbent ruler. However, having survived the Tamil incursions, this long-established, prosperous and sophisticated civilization was soon to buckle under the onslaught of the European invaders.

The Portuguese came in 1505. Initially keen to find and trade exotic spices, such as cinnamon, they soon became more aggressively acquisitive, murdering local kings and establishing outposts on the island. The Dutch were the next invaders. Also keen to take control of the local trade, they took over the island in 1656, after a protracted war with the king of Kandy.

However, it was the British, in 1815, who finally ended the Sinhalese monarchy. Eyeing the fertile island as an ideal plantation for their tea, coconut and other tropical cultivars, they disposed of the Dutch with their superior military might. The Sinhalese of the Kandy region fought valiantly, but to no avail. King Rajasinha was taken prisoner and the British gained control of the island.

It was the British occupiers of the island who rediscovered the ruins of Anuradhapura. They soon realized that this was no barbarian encampment, but the remains of a city of astonishing sophistication. As the Europeans cut their way through the jungle, they came upon ever more buildings, sculptures and shrines. The treasures they found included Thuparama, the oldest *stupa* in Sri Lanka, which had been built in the third century BC. The building is a very important shrine, which is thought to house Buddha's collarbone.

LEFT: This enormous Buddha statue is 14 m (45 ft long) and was constructed by Parakrama Bahu I, in the twelfth century at Polonnaruwa.

ABOVE: Entrances to buildings in Anuradhapura were flanked by guardstones, carved slabs representing supernaural being known as Nagas.

Another extraordinary discovery was the Jetavanaramaya, a *stupa* constructed on a massive scale in the third century AD. The *stupa*'s base is 130 square metres (155 square yards) and its summit is 120 metres (390 feet) high. This enormous shrine is only 24 metres (80 feet) shorter than the great pyramid at Giza. The cultural importance of Buddhism on the island became clear with the rediscovery of the Brazen Palace, known locally as the Lohapasada. Now a ruin, with only its 1,600 supporting columns remaining, the palace was built in the first century BC to house 1,000 monks, 100 on each floor.

The British governor of the island, Sir William Henry Gregory, in 1878 declared that Anuradhapura should once again be inhabited, and made it the capital of the North Central Province. Gregory set about restoring the city, and even after his retirement he petitioned for the official restoration and preservation of the site.

The restoration continued under the British until 1948, when the island obtained its independence. Sri Lanka's first prime minister, D. S. Senanayake, established a new town in Anuradhapura and unveiled a carving – the "Lion Pillar" – at the entrance to New Anuradhapura. Research has carried on at the site and in 1982 UNESCO granted Anuradhapura the status of World Heritage Site.

ANURADHAPURA'S FIRST SETTLERS

MANY BREAKTHROUGHS in our understanding of Anuradhapura's true antiquity have been made since the 1990s. In 1994–1999, a team of archaeologists comprising representatives from Bradford University (led by Dr Robin Coningham), the University of Peradeniya and the Government Department of Archaeology set about determining how and when the first recognizable form of urban settlement emerged in Sri Lanka. Using old maps, surviving archaeological land features, remote-sensing resistivity meters and excavation techniques, the team built up a picture of a previously unexcavated area. In 1994, the team discovered an ancient silted rock-cut moat in a paddy field. The moat, 5 metres (16 feet) deep and 40 metres (130 feet) wide, used to ring the entire city. The team returned over a five-year period and pursued their aim to prove that Anuradhapura had been an urban settlement much earlier than had previously been believed.

"**W**E WERE WORKING IN a beautiful area – parkland scrub all around us, astonishing buildings to the side and people on pilgrimage. It was an unusual experience. We focused on the citadel mound, as we felt a lot had been done on the religious history and significance of the site. We cut in a trench, 30 feet deep and found exactly what we were looking for: a sequence of habitation right through from circular Iron Age houses, dating from c. 900 BC, through 2,000 years of history to AD 1100."

DR ROBIN CONINGHAM, DEPARTMENT OF ARCHAEOLOGICAL SCIENCES, UNIVERSITY OF BRADFORD, ENGLAND

MOHENJODARO
ENIGMA OF THE INDUS VALLEY

I N A REGION OF THE INDUS VALLEY, EXTENDING from the shores of the Arabian Sea to the foothills of the Himalayan mountains, there arose a remarkable culture – the Indus civilization. Along with the Egyptian and Mesopotamian cultures, this civilization was one of the early societies to attain exceptional achievements in economic and social activity.

Human settlements developed in this area in c. 4000 BC. Small farming communities grew up and, over the course of 1,400 years, developed into urban centres. By the middle of the third millennium BC, some 1,500 settlements in this region had blossomed into an elaborate civilization spanning 680,000 square kilometres (260,000 square miles).

Mohenjodaro was located in a vast fertile valley, carved by the 3,000-kilometre (1,860-mile) long Indus River in Pakistan. It was one of the most magnificent cities ever built and was the largest city of the Indus civilization. It covered more than 250 hectares and, at its peak, was home to around 100,000 people. It was surrounded by vast tracts of cultivated lands. Constructed and inhabited between 2600 and 1600 BC, its growth from a farming community was gradual.

The city was carefully planned by its architects and laid out in a grid-like design. Its main thoroughfares were about 15 metres (50 feet) wide, and linked to smaller subsidiary roads along which were ranged the mud-brick houses of ordinary people. The outer walls of the houses were windowless and were constructed without doors leading onto the major roads, to avoid dust getting into people's homes. These houses were built around an inner courtyard.

OPPOSITE: The mysterious ruins of Mohenjodaro. This sophisticated settlement, founded in c. 2600 BC, replete with ritual waterways, a religious public bath, and citadel (seen here with a Buddhist stupa from the second century AD) traded with states as far afield as Ur and Egypt.

ABOVE: Mohenjodaro's Great Bath was the earliest public water tank in the ancient world, measuring approximately 12 m (39 ft) long and 7 m (23 ft) wide, with a maximum depth of 2.4 m (8 ft). Most scholars agree this would have been used for special religious functions, using the water to purify and renew the well-being of the bathers.

The city had a sophisticated sanitation system. Drainage was provided by stone-built, under-street drains and waste chutes, which were connected to all but the humblest of houses. These drains carried away human and other wastes from the homes. This was, in many ways, similar to our modern sewerage systems. Although the city had no treatment works, in the way a modern Western city would, river water from the Indus was probably used to flush the drains.

Japanese archaeologists Ryujiro Kondo, Arata Ichikawa and Tohru Morioka in 1995 put forward a theory that city planning at Mohenjodaro laid great importance on managing the flow of water from the Indus River and its tributaries. They speculate that water had a spiritual importance as well as being necessary for the city's sanitation. There was a connection between water, ablution and ritual cleanliness, and seeing water run through the city would have generated a feeling of religious purity in the city's inhabitants. Following that argument, the drains and public water facilities, such as the bath-house, (see below) were as much a part of the religious "health" of the city as they were an environmental and hygienic necessity.

The belief-system of Mohenjodaro is unknown, although there has been much speculation on the subject. It is thought that the Indus civilization had a pantheon of gods. A number of figurines have been unearthed at Mohenjodaro. One is of a woman in a headdress composed of two baskets, who may be a figure of a mother goddess. Other figurines discovered in the city depict people at work and beautiful dancers. It is difficult to know whether these are representations of deities or are simply humble toys.

Equally, there is a dearth of information regarding the city's social organization (and that of the Indus Valley civilization as a whole). The archaeological record is scant at best. We know that there were no palaces in Mohenjodaro, nor were there any works of art that venerate a king or ruler. Archaeologists suggest that Mohenjodaro may have been ruled by a priest-élite.

Mohenjodaro was centred around a high citadel, built on a 15-metre (50-feet) high artificial mound in the west, which overlooked the domestic dwellings in the east. This mound was close to the right bank of the Indus River, 400 kilometres (250 miles) upstream from the Arabian Sea. The citadel was surrounded by many tall brick watchtowers built to warn of floods and, possibly, of attack. The citadel complex contained a number of important public buildings. These included a large colonnaded hall that may have been an assembly court; a series of rooms believed to be priests' quarters; and, perhaps the most impressive structure at Mohenjodaro, the great bath-house.

The bath-house was rectangular in shape. Made of small blocks of stone, it had what appears to be a ceremonial set of steps that led into the water at one end, and a walkway around its edge. This may have been the first public bath-house ever built. The location of the bath-house within the citadel and the importance of water within the city suggest that it was a ceremonial centre used for ritual cleansing, and not a site for public bathing, as the Roman bath-houses were (see page 96).

Another structure, built on the western side of the citadel complex, has been the subject of argument in archaeological circles. The structure takes the form of a great brick plinth, with inward-leaning walls. Renowned archaeologist Sir Mortimer Wheeler (1890–1976), inspired by thoughts of similar structures found in Minoan Crete and Rome, suggested in 1950 that the building was a vast granary. He posited that carts pulled by oxen would have backed into niches along a loading platform in the base of the granary to unload their grain. The brick plinth, complete with air holes along its length, was thought to give way to a wooden structure above – perhaps wooden silos, topped with a flat roof. However, no grain or storage jars have been found at the site, nor was there any evidence of seals – invariably made of soapstone – which might have identified a trader or the type of item stored in the building.

Modern archaeologists, including Jonathan Mark Kenoyer (Professor of Anthropology at the University of Wisconsin, USA and Co-Director of the Harappa Archaeological Research Project), believe that the building was a grand state hall. Its shape and notable position within the city would imply that the structure was important to the function of the settlement. If it was not the

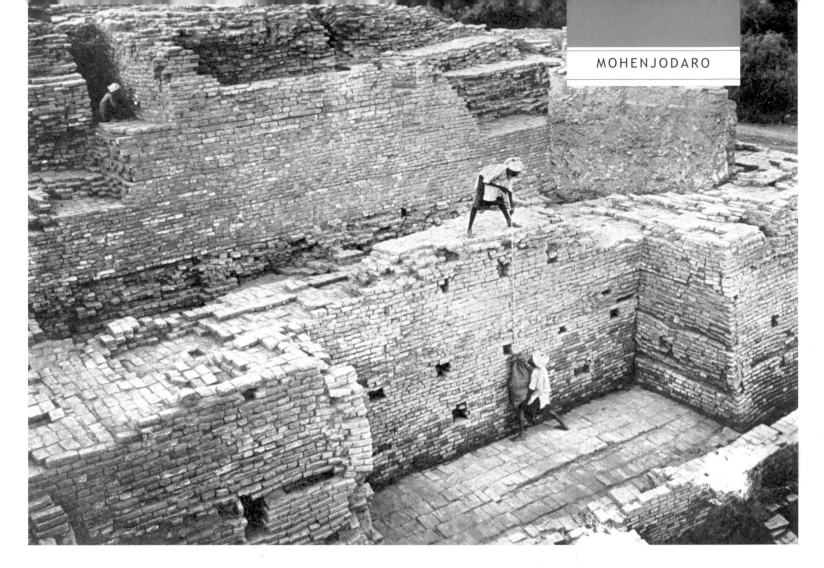

LEFT AND RIGHT: This bearded steatite figure is a statue of a "Priest King" — one of few surviving pieces of sculpture from the ancient Indus civilization. He wears a garment decorated with trefoils, a pattern widely found in the Ancient East, occurring also on Indus beads. The fillet or ribbon headband has a circular inlay ornament worn on the forehead. A similar smaller ornament is on the right upper arm. The flat back of the head may have held a separate carved bun, as traditionally shown on other seated figures, or could have held a more elaborate horn and plume headdress.

This computer-generated reconstruction has brought a small area of Mohenjodaro back to life. It was one of the first planned cities ever built — its streets were constructed in a grid pattern, probably designed to carry wheeled carriages, drawn by bulls or donkeys. This was a well-appointed settlement with an elaborate system of covered drains, beneath the city streets, which ensured the settlement was healthy and complied with the peoples' belief in the purity of water.

ABOVE: This necklace of agate, chalcedony and jasper beads was made in Mohenjodaro approximately 4,500 years ago. It serves as a link across time as such objects are still worn today. Although divided by thousands of years we are not so dissimilar from the ancient people of Mohenjodaro.

OPPOSITE: This steatite seal depicts zebu and monograms from Mohenjodaro and dates from c. 2500–2000 BC. The craftsmen who made the seals knew many animals: elephant, tiger, rhinoceros, antelope, crocodile or gharial. The seals may have represented specific traders or craftsmen.

city's main granary, it is conceivable that the building had a ceremonial or administrative purpose.

Many large storage jars have been unearthed at the site. They were used to store and distribute grain and other foods that were grown at Mohenjodaro. The fact that the city's inhabitants were able to store such great quantities of food suggests the bounty of the region's harvests and the fact that the settlement was highly organized. A terracotta figurine of a cart and rider, being pulled by two animals, offers us some insight into the society: it tells us that the people used wheeled carts and had animals in the yoke, but also that they had time and ability to make toys or sculptures for their amusement.

Indus Valley objects have been found as far away as Egypt and Mesopotamia (see page 156), making it clear that this was an open and successful trading community. Indeed, Mohenjodaro thrived on trade. Lapis lazuli, gold and ivory were loaded onto ships bound for journeys along the Indus, headed for Mesopotamia. Such precious materials were often used in jewellery worn by Mesopotamian nobles. Goods bound for export were marked with the seals of the Mohenjodaro district. These square, sometimes circular, seals may have born a promise of quality and integrity from the élite traders of Mohenjodaro to their customers – although we do not for sure what the seals represented. The seals would also have been a means of controlling and recording the movement of valuable merchandise. Examples of the seals have been found in Ur – evidence of strong trade links between these two civilizations.

Little of the Indus writing system remains, surviving only on objects such as seals, amulets and pottery. These few clues have

made deciphering the language almost impossible – the greater the quantity of written material, the easier it is for linguists to detect patterns and to decipher a language. The Indus language remains a mystery, although some historians speculate that the Indus people may have spoken in the Dravidian tongue, which is still in use in southern India.

There is little evidence for a theocracy at Mohenjodaro. In fact, no temples have been discovered at any of the Indus Valley sites. Religious activity may have been limited to facilities such as the great bath-house. Statues from the era, found at Mohenjodaro and in the Indus Valley, have been identified by some academics as priest-kings. These suggest that Indus nobles wore neatly trimmed beards with a shaven upper lip, and wore headbands over back-combed collar-length hair or hair worn in a bun. They also wore fine cloaks covered in a three-leaf clover pattern. This design was common throughout the region and even seen in Egypt, suggesting a commonality that may have occurred because of well-established trade links between these communities. The cloak with trefoils may have been a special garment for a high-ranking individual, such as a priest.

In 1921, British archaeologist Sir John Marshall (1876–1958) excavated Harappa, another city in the Indus civilization 640 kilometres (400 miles) northeast of Mohenjodaro, along the Indus

River, leading to the rediscovery of Mohenjodaro the following year, in 1922. With these finds came the realization that a fabulous civilization had once flourished in India, extending farther back in time than had been previously supposed. Settlements had emerged around the Indus in c. 4000 BC, with a fully fledged civilization developing in c. 2700–2600 BC.

Initially the site was covered in topsoil, but excavations soon began to reveal a lower city and a high citadel – a feature common in Indus Valley settlements. A raised *stupa* – a monument said to contain relics of the Buddha – was also found at the site, but it had been erected long after the city had declined. Excavations continued, revealing the Great Bath and the "granary".

Further excavations, led by Sir Mortimer Wheeler, took place in the 1950s, and major breakthroughs were made in understanding the Indus Valley civilization. Wheeler, with tremendous energy and zeal, popularized news of the finds and the fact that the Indian subcontinent had millennia of hitherto unknown history. He published images of the many splendid jewels and antiquities discovered; staged reconstructions of oxen-pulled carts; and photographed local people pretending to use what he believed to be the granary. The purported granary had been fully excavated by earlier teams, so Wheeler concentrated on other areas of the city. He discovered many buildings, including fortifications, southeast of the city.

Mohenjodaro and the Indus Valley civilization to which it belonged were highly advanced. Urbanization symbolized this society. Yet, despite the industry and invention of these ancient people, their civilization eventually came to an end. Wheeler postulated that the civilization at Mohenjodaro became a victim of its own success. He believed that as the wealthy and comfortable population had grown, so demands for water, sanitation, food, mud-bricks and wood for construction increased. The demand for raw materials and for extra supplies of food led to the over-exploitation of the land. The likelihood of flooding increased because of the effects of soil erosion caused by deforestation. A shortage of land within the city meant that ever-smaller and poorer houses were built in the dwindling space available. The careful planning of the city eventually failed because the size of the population outstripped the city's ability to support it. To make the situation worse, floods may have swamped the sewers, causing them to crack and distort, creating the ideal environment for potentially fatal water-borne diseases such as cholera. There may have been a final calamity that ended the Indus Valley civilization, but it was dying long before the end came.

Since the 1950s, many rival theories have been put forward to explain the downfall of Mohenjodaro. In the 1990s, J.G. Negi, (Emeritus Professor at India's National Geophysical Research Institute) suggested that environmental flux was to blame. Changing river courses, earthquakes and floods triggered damage and rebuilding at Mohenjodaro many times over a 6,000-year period up to 1700 BC. Negi has estimated rainfall, monsoon fluctuations and flood patterns, and believes that the flow of the Indus River was affected, in c. 2000–1700 BC, by a great earthquake. The geological instability may have created a lake, now known as Sehwan, in the vicinity of Mohenjodaro. The build-up of lake waters triggered severe flooding in the city at least five times. The city's planners and builders could not keep pace with the damage done. Negi states that by c. 1600 BC the site had became unviable for Mohenjodaro and its neighbours.

Another factor in the downfall of the Indus civilization as a whole may have been the disappearance of the Saraswati River. Since the 1950s, many new sites have been discovered that are clearly part of the same civilization as Mohenjodaro and related sites – they possess similar architecture and city design as settlements in the Indus Valley itself. However, these are not located along the Indus River, but in the region of the long-dead Saraswati River. Images taken by Landsat satellites have revealed the course of the dead

RIGHT: This terracotta mother goddess, was made in Mohenjodaro between 2300–1750 BC. Common to the Indus civilization as a whole, the figurine's design was crude: a wide girdle, loincloth, necklace and monstrous headdress. The features are limited to protuberances of barely-modelled clay.

river, as far as the Rann of Kutch on the Arabian Sea. The ancient course of the river has been charted through the Siwalik ranges and down to the Indus tributaries. A change in the flow of river waters may have been caused by the movement of tectonic plates and the build-up of alluvial deposits over time. Water that would have fed the Saraswati may have been captured by the Yamuna and Sutlej rivers – part of the Indus river system – strengthening and influencing the path of the Indus itself. The flooding experienced by many Indus sites, including Mohenjodaro, may have been caused by this change in water flow and would have severely hampered agricultural and economic activity in the region. The people of the Saraswati were eventually forced to abandon their settlements.

It seems likely, therefore, that water was the reason for the success and eventual downfall of the Indus-Saraswati civilization. When water was bountiful, but manageable, it brought agricultural and economic success. But droughts or floods eventually spelled disaster for the civilization.

SITE IN DANGER

THE DISCOVERY OF MOHENJODARO, Harappa and the Indus Valley civilization was an exceptional breakthrough in terms of our understanding of ancient peoples. The area's history is traceable over 5,000 years and how it explains how our development is vital if we are to understand our own culture and those of our neighbours. In 1979 the United Nations Educational, Scientific and Cultural Organization (UNESCO) deemed the site to be of such importance that it was granted the status of a World Heritage Site. This bestowed the protection of the United Nations upon Mohenjodaro and encouraged the mother nation, and other nation states, to make resources available for the preservation and study of the site. Initially these efforts met with great success, but today the site faces threats from the rising water table in the area and increasing salinity. Although government funds have been allocated, many people are asking if it will be enough to prevent disaster.

"MOHENJODARO WAS PUT FORWARD as one of UNESCO's great success stories in the 1980s. It gave UNESCO a lot of visibility, allowing the organization to be seen as working to save world heritage. Since then, considering the economic and political situation in Pakistan, the site seems to have become a lesser priority. The national economy and the site itself might benefit from additional income generated by increased tourist trade, if it could be presented in a positive way. It is an important site and needs preserving, but the economic situation and the differences between the regions can not be helping the situation."

IAN ANDERSON, VISITING FELLOW, UNESCO CENTRE, AUSTRALIAN
NATIONAL UNIVERSITY, CANBERRA, AUSTRALIA

GLOSSARY

ADAD – the weather god and destroyer and bringer of life, in the Assyrian and Babylonian pantheon of gods. The bull and the lion were sacred to him.

AMAZON – in Greek mythology, member of a race of women warriors. Greek mythical hero Heracles was set a task of taking the Amazon Queen's girdle.

ANIMISM – belief in countless spiritual beings which are concerned with influencing human affairs; by helping or harming human interests.

ARAMAENS – one of a group of tribes (the Chaldeans) that spoke Aramaic, a North Semitic language. They occupied Aram, northern Syria, from the 11th to the 8th century BC. In this period some of these tribes took over some areas of Mesopotamia. By the 9th century the whole area from Babylon to the Mediterranean coast was in the hands of the Aramaeans.

ASSYRIA – one of the great empires of ancient Middle East, located in what is now northern Iraq and southeastern Turkey. Assyria emerged as an independent state in the 14th century BC and became a major power in the region.

ASTARTE – goddess of the ancient Middle East and the Queen of Heaven to whom the Canaanites had burned incense and poured libations (Jeremiah 44). Astarte, also known as Ashtaroth, became a word in Hebrew that denoted paganism.

ATLATL – a device for throwing and giving increased power to a spear. It took the form of a rod or board, made of wood or bone, with a groove on the upper surface and a hook at the rear to hold the spear in place until it was thrown.

AYMARA – large South American Indian group living on the Titicaca plateau of the central Andes, in modern Peru and Bolivia.

BO TREE – according to Buddhist tradition, the tree under which the Buddha sat when he attained enlightenment at Bodh Gaya (near Gaya, India). An example of such a tree at Anuradhapura, Sri Lanka, is said to have grown from a cutting from the Bo tree sent to that city by King Ashoka in the 3rd century BC and may be the oldest tree in existence with a recorded history.

CARACOL – known more correctly as El Caracol ("The Snail") is a ruined dome-shaped structure resembling a modern optical observatory located at Chichén Itzá, (see pp. 32–41) Mayan astronomers tracked the positions of the sun, moon, and other celestial bodies for timekeeping and calendrical purposes.

CEIBA – also called java cotton, kapok, or java kapok, is a large tropical tree of the Bombacaceae family. The ceiba had a part to play in mythology and religion for the Maya as they believed that each compass point was associated with a Bacab (any of four gods, thought to be brothers, who, with upraised arms, supported the sky from their positions at the four cardinal points of the compass), a sacred ceiba, a bird, and a colour: north-white, south-yellow, east-red and west-black.

CENOTE – natural well formed when a limestone surface collapses, revealing a reservoir of water beneath. In antiquity, precious objects, such as jade, gold and incense and also human beings (children) were thrown into the cenotes as offerings.

CENTAUR – originally depicted in Greek mythology, centaurs were a race of creatures, part horse and part man, dwelling in the mountains of Thessaly and Arcadia. They ran wild, had no laws and were slaves to their animal passions.

CHAAC – (also Chac) Mayan god of rain, very important in the Yucatán region of Mexico where he was depicted in Classic times with a proboscis-nose, great round eyes and fangs. Chaac was one of four gods associated with the compass points.

CHALDEAN KINGS – a line of rulers with origins traceable to land bordering the head of the Persian Gulf between the Arabian desert and the Euphrates delta. Nabopolassar, king of Babylon in 625 BC, initiated a Chaldean dynasty that lasted until the Persians invaded in 539 BC. Nebuchadrezzar II (605–562 BC) became arguably the most famous Chaldean King.

CHARGE-COUPLED DEVICE – (also CCD), the charge-coupled device uses a light-sensitive material on a silicon microchip to electronically detect light so as to produce an electronic image/picture.

CHERT – very fine-grained quartz. Many varieties are included under the general term chert: jasper, chalcedony, agate, novaculite and the best known – flint.

CODICES – a manuscript/book, containing early religious literature, mythology or historical records. Codices were made by the pre-Columbian peoples of Mesoamerica after about AD 1000. These books contained pictographs and ideograms rather than written script. They dealt with the ritual calendar, divination, ceremonies, and speculations on the gods and the universe.

CONQUISTADORS – a Spanish word meaning conqueror and often used to describe the leaders of the Spanish conquest of America, especially of Mexico and Peru, in the 16th century.

CRUSADERS – soldiers who went on military expeditions organized by western Christians against Muslims so as to capture or maintain control over the Holy City of Jerusalem and the Holy Sepulchre, believed to have been used by Jesus Christ.

CUNEIFORM – meaning wedge-shaped, was the most widespread and historically significant writing system in the ancient Middle East and was used throughout the last three millennia BC.

DENDROCHRONOLOGY – the scientific discipline concerned with dating and interpreting past events, particularly climatic trends, based on the analysis of tree rings. The width of the ring (i.e., the amount of growth) for each year tends to vary due to environmental fluctuations, especially rainfall and temperature changes. Samples are obtained by means of a metal tube with a narrow bore which is forced into a tree to get a core extending from bark to center, giving a cross section of tree rings/tree growth over time. The tree rings are counted and measured, and the sequence of rings is correlated with sequences from other tree cores.

DEVA RAJAS – the Khmer Kings built a mystique around themselves which ensured that they were seen as Deva Rajas (God Kings). Angkor was blessed with good water supplies but the levels fluctuated seasonally and the intervention of the God King's on earth, via religious ceremonies, were believed to ensure water supplies **DJINNS** – mythological figures believed by Bedouin tribes to be powerful and magical genies.

ELECTROMAGNETIC SPECTRUM – (more properly the spectrum of frequencies of electromagnetic radiation). Light is the visible part of the electromagnetic spectrum, heat another. There are parts of the spectrum which are not detectable by our human senses, from radio and television waves, infra-red and microwaves to ultraviolet light, X rays, and gamma rays. Modern devices (known as spectrophotometers) can monitor all areas of the electromagnetic spectrum and the data can be analysed and used to find and understand structures (archaeological remains for example).

EXTENSOMETER – a device for measuring small increases in the length of metals/materials.

FORAMS – part of the foraminifera family of marine protozoa, with shells of calcium carbonate. Some form part of the plankton in the sea, others live on the sea bed.

GEOMAGNETIC SENSING – a branch of geophysics concerned with all aspects of the Earth's magnetic field, including its origin, variation through time, and manifestations in the form of magnetic poles, the magnetization of rocks, and local or regional magnetic anomalies. Measurements taken with a device – known as a magnetometer – capable of sampling a magnetic field in a given area, can reveal anomalies in the magnetic field. When plotted on a map, to produce a "magnetic map" of a given area, the anomalies provide the basis for inferences about the presence and form of archaeological remains in the area studied.

GILGAMESH – the best known of all ancient Mesopotamian heroes. The fullest extant text of the Gilgamesh epic is on 12 incomplete Akkadian-language tablets found at Nineveh in the library of the Assyrian king Ashurbanipal (668–627 BC). The Gilgamesh referred to in the tablets was probably the Gilgamesh who ruled at Uruk in southern Mesopotamia during the first half of the 3rd millennium BC, but there is no evidence that the exploits recorded in the tablets actually occurred.

GLYPH – most scholars believe that the Mayan writing system was logographic. In other words, each sign, known as a glyph, acted as a whole word.

GROUND PENETRATING RADAR – a means of detecting buried structures, buildings and artefacts, by sending short bursts of radio signals through the ground and monitoring the reflected radio signal.

HACHAS – the thin-bladed hacha, or "axe," is thought to have had a ceremonial function of some sort for the Maya. It is possible that some hachas were used in connection with the ceremonial ball game, tlachtli.

HIEROGLYPHIC WRITING – a system that employs characters in the form of pictures. These individual signs, called hieroglyphs, may be read either as pictures, as symbols for pictures, or as symbols for sounds.

HITTITES – members of an ancient Indo-European people who appeared in Anatolia at the beginning of the 2nd millennium BC.

HOPI – the westernmost group of Pueblo Indians, situated in northeastern Arizona, USA. In the late-20th century there were about 6,000 Hopi, living in pueblo structures of stone and adobe in a number of independent towns in Arizona.

HYDROLOGY – a science concerned with the waters of the Earth and the hydrologic cycle (the process by which the waters of the Earth undergo cyclical motions, changing from seawater to vapour to rain and then flowing back to the ocean) and interactions with living things.

ILIAD – an epic poem about the Trojan War attributed to the ancient Greek poet Homer, who lived c. 9th or 8th century BC in the region of Ionia, part of modern day Turkey.

INFRARED – the infrared region of the electromagnetic spectrum, beyond the red end of the visible range, but at frequencies higher than those of radar and microwaves.

INTI – in Inca religion, Inti is the sun god and is believed to be the ancestor of the Incas. Generally represented in human form, his face is portrayed as a gold disk from which rays and flames extended.

IRON AGE – the date of the full Iron Age, whereby iron for the most part replaced bronze in implements and weapons, varied geographically, beginning in the Middle East and southeastern Europe about 1200 BC but in China not until about 600 BC.

ISHTAR – in Mesopotamian religion, the goddess of war and sexual love. Ishtar is the Akkadian counterpart of the west Semitic goddess Astarte. Ishtar was originally seen as a symbol of fertility but evolved into a more complex character, surrounded in myth by death and disaster, a goddess of contradictory powers.

ITZAMA – the main pre-Columbian Mayan deity. The ruler of heaven, day, and night, he frequently appeared as four gods called Itzamnás, who encased the world.

KACHINAS – in Pueblo Indian (Anasazi) religious practice, any of more than 500 divine ancestral spirits who act as intermediaries between man and god. Each tribe has its distinct forms and variations. Kachinas are believed to reside with the tribe for half of each year. Kachinas are also depicted in small, ornamented carved-wood dolls, which are made by the men of the tribe.

KASSITES – member of an ancient people known primarily for establishing the second Babylonian dynasty; they were believed (contentiously) to have originated in the Zagros Mountains of Iran.

KEBRA NEGAST – (meaning "Glory of the Kings") an Ethiopian literary work written in the 14h century. It is a combination of mythical history, allegory, and apocalypse, the central theme of which is the visit of the Queen of Sheba (Makeda) to Solomon and the birth of a son who became the founder of the Ethiopian dynasty.

KIVA – a subterranean ceremonial and social chamber found in the Pueblo American Indian villages of the southwestern United States and common to the Anasazi. Because the kiva is related to the family origins of the tribe and because two or more tribal clans always inhabit a Pueblo community (see pueblo), there are always at least two kivas per village. A small hole in the floor of the kiva (sometimes carved through a plank of wood), called the sípapu, served as the symbolic place of origin of the tribe.

KUKULCAN – the Feathered Serpent, one of the major deities of the ancient Mexican pantheon. Depictions of a feathered snake occur as early as the Teotihuacán civilization (3rd to 8th century AD) on the central plateau. At that time, Kukulcan, also known as Quetzalcóatl, seems to have been seen as an earth and water deity. By the 12th century AD the Feathered Serpent became the god of the morning and evening star and was the symbol of death and resurrection.

LACHISH – a Canaanite city (like Jericho and Jerusalem). Archaeologists have found a form of script at Lachish, dating to the late Bronze Age, that is recognized by most scholars as the parent of Phoenician and thence of the Greek and Latin alphabets.

LARES PUBLICI – in Roman religion, any of numerous tutelary deities. They were originally gods of the fields, worshipped by each family at the crossroads where their allotments joined those of their neighbours. Later the "Lares" were worshipped in the houses. The public Lares (Lares Publici) belonged to the state religion and included the Lares compitales, who presided over the crossroads (compita) and the whole local area.

LINEAR A AND LINEAR B – linear forms of writing used by certain Aegean civilizations during the 2nd millennium BC. Linear A was used in Crete and on some of the Aegean islands from approximately 1850 BC to 1400 BC. It is a syllabic script written from left to right but the language written in the Linear A text remains a mystery. It may be that the language is the pre-Hellenic tongue of Minoan Crete.Linear B is an outgrowth of Linear A and its language is the Mycenaean Greek dialect. Linear B script was discovered on pottery and clay tablets dating to the period 1400 BC to c.1200 BC.

LONG COUNT – to describe accurately a given date, the Maya instituted the Long Count, a continuous marking of time from a base date. The base date 3113 BC, was considered by them to be the beginning of the Mayan era.

MARCELLUM – at or near the centre of a Roman town, such as Pompeii, was the forum, the principal focus of Roman life. Close to the forum was the Marcellum which was essentially a market building consisting of shops grouped around a colonnaded court. Commodities were traded in this space.

MAGNETOMETER – an instrument for measuring the strength and sometimes the direction of magnetic fields. Magnetometers are used in archaeology to detect variations/anomalies in magnetic fields within the soil, so as to determine the presence and type of archaeological remains.

MEDE – one of an Indo-European people, related to the Persians, who entered northeastern Iran probably as early as the 17th century BC and settled in the plateau land that came to be known as Media.

MESA – a Spanish word meaning "table". This was a flat-topped tableland with one or more steep sides, common in the Colorado Plateau regions of the United States; they were used as farm land by the Anasazi.

MESOAMERICA – The term Mesoamerica, meaning Middle America, is sometimes used to describe Mexico, Central America, and the West Indies collectively.

MICROWAVE RADAR – conventional radar operates at microwave and ultrahigh frequencies that propagate in straight lines like light rays, bouncing energy off remote objects and analyzing the resultant reflected energy to determine the presence and type of an object – be it on the earth's surface, in the air or in space.

MUNICIPIUM – a community incorporated into the Roman state. Initially, inhabitants were considered Roman citizens without voting rights. As the Italian provinces were incorporated into the Roman state, residents were granted full political rights.

MARDUK – in Mesopotamian religion, Marduk was the chief god of the city of Babylon and the national god of Babylonia. A poem from the reign of Nebuchadrezzar I (1124-03 BC), known as Enuma elish, describes how Marduk became the master of the gods of heaven and earth after vanquishing Taimat, a beast that symbolized chaos. All things in nature owe their existence to him and therefore the fates of the Babylonian kingdoms and subjects was in his hands.

MYCENAENS – is often used in reference to the peoples of the mainland Greece and its islands except Crete, during the Late Bronze Age, c. 1600–1050 BC.

NABU – (also Nebo) an important god in the Assyro-Babylonian pantheon and the son of Marduk, the Lord God of Babylon. Nabu was the diety of the art of writing and a god of vegetation, hence he was symbolized by a clay tablet and the stylus.

NAVAJO – the most populous of all Indian groups in the United States today. In 2002 there were approximately 170,000 Navajo Indians living in New Mexico, Arizona, and southeastern Utah. It is uncertain when the Navajo and Apache migrated to the Southwest from Canada but the migration probably took place between 900 and 1200 AD. The Navajo were influenced by the Anasazi.

ODYSSEY – another great work from ancient Greece attributed to Homer, which charts the misadventures of many of the characters featured in Homer's Iliad.

OLMEC – the first elaborate pre-Columbian culture of Mesoamerica, and one that is thought to have established many of the patterns of behaviour followed by later Indian cultures of Mexico and Central America. The Olmec people lived along the Gulf Coast in southern Mexico. Their style of art first appeared c.1150 BC.

OSCANS – one of the ancient Italic peoples diverse in language, origin and social traditions who inhabited pre-Roman Italy, and who were heavily influenced by neighbouring Greece.

OSTRACODS – a group of crustaceans resembling mussels. There are 2,000 living species of ostracod which live in marine, freshwater, and terrestrial environments.

PALAEOLITHIC TIMES – the archaeological period before c.10000 BC. In this period Humankind first manufactured stone tools and weapons.

PAPYRUS – writing material of ancient times and also the plant from which it was derived, Cyperus papyrus (family Cyperaceae), also called the paper plant.

PATERFAMILIAS – head of the family charged with accepting responsible tasks, usually but not necessarily the husband, also perhaps the eldest son or mother.

PHONETIC SCRIPT – a form of written language designed to transcribe any oral language into a common script.

PICTOGRAPH – a symbol which usually embodies a single word, in the form of primative writing based on images, often used in antiquity.

PITHOUSES – houses of poles and earth built over pits used by early American Indians, prior to the emergence of the puebloan culture.

PERISTYLE HALL – a peristyle structure is usually defined by an outer colonnade of posts supporting extended eaves, creating a covered walkway, and was often used to denote areas of importance or religious significance, such as at the Mahram Bilquis.

PETROGLYPHS – symbols carved into rocks, such as those left by the Anasazi, are refered to as petroglyphs.

PROTO-MAYAN – early American Indians, from the mountain regions of the Pacific, dating to the preclassic Mayan era c. 1000 BC.

PUEBLO – originally a Spanish word for town, the word pueblo has also come to designate a community of town dwelling Indians of the southwestern United States. The construction of multistoried houses, made of adobe blocks (clay and water blocks dried in the sun), was probably inspired by the cliff dwellings built by their ancestors. Pueblos began to be used c. 1300 AD.

QUECHA – (also Quechua) South American Indians living in the Andean highlands from Ecuador to Bolivia. They speak the Quechua language, which was the language of the Inca Empire.

QUETZALCOATL – see Kukulkan.

RADAR INTERFEROMETRY – a process that is used to search for archaeological remains by receiving and analyzing electromagnetic radiation.

RADIOACTIVE ISOTOPE – also called Radioisotope, any of several species of the same chemical element (such as carbon) with different masses whose nuclei are unstable and dissipate excess energy by spontaneously emitting radiation in the form of alpha, beta, and gamma rays.

RADIOCARBON DATING – this method of dating was first developed by the American physicist Willard F. Libby c. 1946. It has proved to be a versatile technique of dating fossils and archaeological specimens from 500 to 50000 years old. The technique depends upon the decay of an atomic material known as radiocarbon (carbon-14). Carbon-14 is continually formed in nature by the interaction of neutrons with nitrogen-14 in the Earth's atmosphere; the neutrons required for this reaction are produced by cosmic rays interacting with the atmosphere. Because carbon-14 decays in a known way, archaeologists can ascertain the approximate age of remains by their state of decay.

REMOTE SENSING – the many instruments employed produce images that can be interpreted by highly trained experts to find hidden structures on the earth, a process which is of value archaeological investigators. This comprises measurements of electromagnetic radiation from the ground, usually of reflected energy such as x-rays or visible light, measured by instruments aboard aircraft or satellites. Remote sensing encompasses aerial photography and other kinds of measurements – such as thermal infrared scanners, which monitor the infrared area of the electromagnetic spectrum, and multispectral scanners, such as those used aboard the Landsat satellites which observe the green and red areas of the visible spectrum of light as well as two infra red bands of the spectrum.

RESISTIVITY METERS – in archaeology, resistivity is useful in comparing various materials, in the earth, on the basis of their ability to conduct electrical currents. High resistivity designates poor conductors – such as stone. Areas of low resistivity may indicate the presence of man-made objects (such as metal weapons). Resistivity meters measure these abilities to conduct allowing archaeologists to produce maps of resistance over an area, suggesting possible areas to excavate.

SAMNITES – one of the ancient warlike tribes from the mountains of southern Italy. Although allied with Rome against the Gauls in 354 BC, the Samnites participated in three wars c. 343–341, 316–304, and 298–290 BC against the Romans.

SATRAP – provincial governor in the Achaemenian Empire. The division of the empire into provinces (satrapies) was completed by Darius I (reigned 522-486 BC), who established 20 satrapies. The satraps, appointed by the king, normally were members of the royal family or of Persian nobility, and they held office indefinitely.

SEMITES – peoples of the ancient Middle East that included Canaanites, Hebrews, Aramaeans and Sabaeans.

SHAM – the Sabaean creator god

SHEBU – Assyrian matriarchal culture led to women becoming the head of the family, a position that was referred to as the "Shebu".

SHIVA – Shiva is Sanskrit for the phrase Auspicious One. Shiva is one of the most complex gods of India, embodying seemingly contradictory qualities. He is both the the friendly shepherd of human souls and the vengeful punisher, destroyer and the restorer as well as the great abstainer and the symbol of all that is sensual.

SIAPAPU – a small hole in the floor of the *kiva* which served as the symbolic place of origin of the tribe for puebloan/Anasazi peoples.

SONAR SURVEY – short for sound navigation ranging,. Akin to radar, sound waves reflected from an object are detected by sonar apparatus and analyzed. In this way archaeologists can produce a survey of an area of the sea bed, when searching for submerged archaeological remains, such as Helike.

STELA – a standing stone slab used in the ancient world primarily as a grave marker – often bearing renderings of the dead as they were in life. Stelea were also used to for purposes of demarcation.

STRATIGRAPHY – the study of stratification which is the analysis of a series of horizontal layers of earth, sediment, waste, or successive human settlements deposited one on top of another over time. This is a means of ascertaining relative dating of a site and layers within the site.

STUPA – a Buddhist commemorative monument usually housing sacred relics associated with the Buddha or other saintly persons; it is an architectural symbol of the Buddha's parinirvana, or death.

SUMERIANS – the Sumerians probably came from the region of Anatolia, arriving in Sumer c. 3300 BC. By the 3rd millennium BC the country was the site of at least a dozen distinct city-states which included Adab, Erech and Ur. Sumerian culture was submerged and lost, post-1900 BC, when the Amorites conquered the Mesopotamian lands. Nevertheless, humankind inherited the concept of the city-state, cuneiform (the first system of writing) and the first written laws, wheeled vehicles and potter's wheels from the Sumerians.

SYNTHETIC APERTURE RADAR – a device which mathematically combines a series of radar echoes to generate an image that would normally require a much larger single antenna, which would be impracticable in space. This device was carried aboard the Space Radar Laboratory (SRL), a special mapping radar flown aboard NASA space shuttles. The synthetic aperture radar used on the shuttle missions penetrated the ground and revealed hidden structures like ancient dry riverbeds.

TESSERAE – small pieces of ceramic tile, glass or stone, cut to be used in elaborate mosaics. Tesserae became popular in the Hellenistic world c. 200 BC, replacing pebbles and stones at that time, and have been used in mosaics ever since.

FURTHER READING

INTRODUCTION AND GENERAL
E. Bacon, *The Great Archaeologists*, (London), 1976
C. Renfrew, P. Bahn, *Archaeology theories, Methodology and Practice*, (London) Thames and Hudson, 2000

ANASAZI
J. Brody, *The Anasazi: Ancient Indian People of the American Southwest*, (NY), 1990
S. Plog, *Ancient Peoples of the American Southwest*, (London), 1997

ANGKOR
Eleanor Mannikka, *Angkor Wat: Time Space and Kingship*, (Hawaii) University of Hawaii Press, 2000
C. Scarre, *The Seventy Wonders of the Ancient World*, Thames and Hudson, (London) 1999

ANURADHAPURA
R. Coningham, "Anuradhapura Citadel Archaeological Project: Preliminary Results of the Excavation of the Southern Rampart", *Journal of the Society for South Asian Studies*, (London), 1993

ATLANTIS
H. D. P. Lee (Translator), *Plato: Timaeus and Critias*, Penguin, (London) 1977
A. Roy, "The Origin of the Constellations", *Vistas in Astronomy*, Vol.27, pp.171-197, Pergamon Press Ltd., 1984

BABYLON
J. Oates, *Babylon*, (London), Thames and Hudson, 1996
H. W. F. Saggs, *Babylonians* (London) 1995

CANCUÉN
A. M. Schlesinger and F. L. Israel (Editors), "Ancient Civilizations of the Aztecs and Maya: Chronicles from National Geographic" (Cultural and Geographic Exploration), March 1999

CHICHÉN ITZÁ
I. Clendinnen, *Ambivalent Conquests: Maya and Spaniard in Yucatán 1517–1570*, (Cambridge), Cambridge University Press, 1987
M. D. Coe, *Breaking the Maya Code*, (London), Thames and Hudson, 1992
J. S. Henderson, *The World of the Ancient Maya*, (New York) Cornell University Press, 1997
M. Mosely, *The Incas and their Ancestors*, (London), Thames and Hudson, 1992

HALICARNASSUS
E. Cary (translator), 'Dionysius of Halicarnassus: the Roman Antiquities', (Cambridge MA), Harvard University Press, 1939
C. Scarre, *Seventy Wonders of the Ancient World*, (London), Thames and Hudson, 1999
G. B. Waywell, *The Free Standing Sculpture of the Mausoleum at Halicarnassus*, (London), British Museum Publications, 1978

KNOSSOS
A Evans, *The Palace of Minos at Knossos*, 3 volumes, (London), 1921 to 1930

MACHU PICCHU
C.Bernard, *The Incas*, (London), 1994
H.Bingham, *Lost City of the Incas: the story of Machu Picchu and Its Builders*, (New York), 1971

MAHRAM BILQIS
A. Jamme, *Sabean Inscriptions from Mahram Bilqis*, (Baltimore), Johns Hopkins University, 1962

MOHENJODARO
J. Marshall, *Mohenjodaro and the Indus Civilization*, South Asia Books, 1996
M.Wheeler, *The Indus Valley and Beyond*, (London), 1966

NIMRUD
H.V.Hilprecht, *Explorations in Bible Lands*, (Edinburgh), 1903

PERSEPOLIS
D.N. Wilber, 'Persepolis: the Archaeology of Parsa, Seat of the Persian Kings', Darwin Press, 1989

POMPEII
R. Etiene, *Pompei: the Day the City Died*, (London), 1992
H. Flaherty (Editor), *Lost Civilizations- Pompeii: the Vanished City*, (Virginia), Time Life Books, 1992

TIWANAKU
A. Kolata, *Valley of the Spirits: a journey into the Lost Realm of the Aymara*, (New York), John Wiley and Sons, 1996

TROY
C. W. Blegen, *Troy and the Trojans*, (New York), Frederick Praeger, 1963
H. Schleimann, *Troy and its Remains: a Narrative of Researches and Discoveries*, (New York), Amro Press, 1976

UBAR
N. Clapp, *The Road to Ubar - Finding the Atlantis of the Sands*, (London), Souvenir Press, 1998
R. Fiennes, *Atlantis of the Sands - the Search for the Lost City of Ubar*, (London) Bloomsbury Publishing, 1992

UR
L. Woolley and P.R.S. Moorey, "Ur of the Chaldees", (Herbert Press), 1982

INDEX

Page numbers in *italic* refer to the illustrations